E-Commerce and V-Business

E-Commerce and V-Business: Business Models for Global Success

Edited by Stuart Barnes and Brian Hunt

BUTTERWORTH
HEINEMANN

OXFORD AMSTERDAM BOSTON LONDON NEW YORK PARIS
SAN DIEGO SAN FRANCISCO SINGAPORE SYDNEY TOKYO

Butterworth-Heinemann
An imprint of Elsevier Science
Linacre House, Jordan Hill, Oxford OX2 8DP
200 Wheeler Road, Burlington, MA 01803

First published 2001
Reprinted 2003

British Library Cataloguing in Publication Data
A catalogue record for this book is available from the British Library

ISBN   0 7506 4532 6

For information on all Butterworth-Heinemann publications
visit our website at www.bh.com

Printed and bound in Great Britain

Contents

Contributors

Amelia Baldwin Culverhouse School of Accountancy, University of Alabama, Tuscaloosa, USA

Stuart Barnes School of Management, University of Bath, UK

Janice Burn School of Management Information Systems, Edith Cowan University, Joondalup, Australia

Ai-Mei Chang Information Resources Management College, National Defence University, Washington DC, USA

Alina N. Chircu Carlson School of Management, University of Minnesota, Minneapolis, USA

Soumitra Dutta INSEAD, Fontainebleau, France

John Gammack School of Information Technology, Murdoch University, Perth, Australia

Martijn Hoogeweegen Multimedia Skills, Amersfoort, The Netherlands

Brian Hunt School of Management, Imperial College, London University, UK

Lucas Introna London School of Economics and Political Science, London, UK

R. Johnson IBM plc, UK

Robert B. Johnston University of Melbourne, Victoria, Australia

P. K. Kannan The Robert H. Smith School of Business, University of Maryland, College Park, USA

Robert J. Kauffman Carlson School of Management, University of Minnesota, Minneapolis, USA

Sherah Kurnia School of Business Systems, Monash University, Clayton, Australia

Feng Li Department of Management Science, University of Strathclyde, Glasgow, UK

Claudia Loebbecke University of Cologne, Germany

Andrew Lymer School of Business, University of Birmingham, Edgbaston, UK

Horace Cheok Mak School of Business Systems, Monash University, Clayton, Australia

Peter Marshall School of Management Information Systems, Edith Cowan University, Joondalup, Australia

Judy McKay School of Management Information Systems, Edith Cowan University, Joondalup, Australia

Simpson Poon   School of Information Technology, Murdoch University, Perth, Australia

Petra Schubert   Institute of Business Economics, University of Applied Sciences, Basel, Switzerland

Arie Segev   Haas School of Business, University of California at Berkeley, USA

Dorian Selz   Delta Consulting, St Gallen, Switzerland

Pascal Sieber   Institute of Information Systems, Department of Information Management, University of Bern, Switzerland

Craig Standing   School of Management Information Systems, Edith Cowan University, Joondalup, Australia

Thandarayan Vasudavan   School of Marketing and Tourism, Edith Cowan University, Joondalup, Australia

Andrew B. Whinston   Department of Management Information Systems, University of Texas, Austin, USA

Howard Williams   Department of Management Science, University of Strathclyde, Glasgow, UK

Matthijs Wolters   Faculty of Management, Erasmus University Rotterdam, The Netherlands

Preface

Putting the 'e-' in business

It is increasingly becoming an understatement to say that the Internet and related technologies are changing the ways in which we live. Most definitely these technologies will affect our lives in ways we cannot yet even imagine. Indeed, if the Internet pundits are correct, few areas of our lives will remain untouched (e.g., see Negroponte, 1995; Tapscott, 1997).

One of the most significant changes promises to be in the way in which we conduct business. From being primarily a resource for the rapid and secure communications of the scientific and military communities, the Internet and related technologies are developing into the communication systems of choice for a variety of business activities in a diverse range of industries (e.g., see Graphics, Visualization and Usability Centre, 1999; Nua, 2000). For many, if not most, firms these new developments are both fascinating and frightening. Fascinating because they have the power to accelerate the rate of change in companies that adopt them. Frightening because companies who ignore these growth opportunities will fall behind in the competitive race for customers.

Andrew Grove, as founder and chairman of Intel, is quoted as saying: 'In five years' time all companies will be Internet companies, or they won't be companies at all' (Symonds, 1999). This may or may not be an exaggeration but, for many companies, this is old news; they have seen and embraced the future. However, for other companies who may still be debating issues at board meetings, these words may be some of the last clarion calls to act. It is not expected that there will be league tables of 'Internet companies' and 'non-Internet companies'. The facts of the matter are that companies who are adept at doing business electronically will have a distinct advantage. They will seize the greater share of customers, suppliers and profits from companies who are less effective, possibly rendering existing business models obsolete. Some of these successful e-businesses – the real threats to corporate complacency – haven't yet been founded; others may be on the threshold.

One of the major aspects of recent business transformation is in the advance of electronic commerce (e-commerce or EC). In simple terms, electronic commerce refers to transactions taking place over electronic networks, particularly the Internet. Such developments, especially in business-to-consumer markets, have received high coverage in the media. Firms in the online book trade, auction houses and online stockbrokers are memorable examples. In these sectors, trade is more than doubling every year. Moreover, other types of EC are also growing fast: revenues in business-to-business EC will grow from around US$200 billion in 2000 to more than US$800 billion by 2003 (*Financial Times*, 1999).

However, the impact of the Internet goes much deeper. There is no doubt that electronic commerce is changing the way that businesses behave. There is now recognition that becoming 'wired' goes much further than this, and ultimately will change the fundamental nature of what businesses are and business relationships (Symonds, 1999). Whilst most big firms involved in EC have focused on establishing a new and potentially very efficient distribution channel, they have failed to utilize the full capabilities of EC, which go beyond online orders. One of the most important shifts is likely to be away from the traditional idea that any business is more or less a freestanding entity, which requires significant intellectual and cultural changes in order to succeed (Chesbrough and Teece, 1996).

A key concept that has emerged from the synergies between new technological developments and changing paradigms of corporate culture is the virtual organization. Although numerous aspects are considered important in the definition of a virtual organization, it essentially involves virtual business (or v-business) relationships in which partners share complementary resources and technologies to achieve a common goal, such as creating a product or service (e.g., see Siebel and House, 1999). Confronted with a continuously changing competitive environment – owing to issues such as globalization, rapid technological change and shifts towards mass customization and improved customer service – this new and flexible organizational model has provided an attractive proposition to organizations entering the twenty-first century.

Features of the book

This book explores these two important issues, electronic commerce and virtual business, in some depth. Although the literature around electronic commerce and virtual organizations has developed to some extent independently they are, as we shall see, inextricably linked. This text has arisen from extensive investigation into the impacts of such important concepts upon business, each highly dependent upon recent technological developments. It has also arisen from a personal review of the available literature on this and related topics, based on our own experience, and in the context of recent developments in the field.

While the book will hopefully be of interest to executives who are concerned with some of the many complex and interrelated issues associated with managing e-commerce and virtual organizations, its primary audiences are senior undergraduates and Masters students studying for business-related degrees. Students who are about to begin research in this area should also find the book of particular help in providing a rich source of material reflecting leading-edge thinking.

The collected papers in this book illustrate the wide variety of business opportunities afforded by e-commerce and virtual business. They describe and discuss the important issues that follow in the wake of an organization deciding to pursue consumers electronically and organize its operations virtually. The authors in this text have written most recent and emerging research. We have chosen authors whose work sits well within the framework of the book and which brings in a good balance of theory and practical issues.

In the development of this book we solicited articles from authors worldwide. In so doing our purpose was two-fold. First, we wanted the content of this book to have a worldwide appeal. Except for a handful of countries where political considerations are paramount, the Internet is a truly global phenomenon. We wanted our selection of authors to reflect this. Second, we wanted to present the different perspectives brought by writers from different parts of the globe.

It is, of course, impossible to cover all aspects of these emerging topics. Our focus has been on attempting to cover some of the more recent and possibly more important aspects, and from a management perspective. The implications are that whilst technological aspects are covered in some detail, this is always in a mode accessible to the manager.

Structure of the book

The structure for this book reflects the two important topics upon which our discussion is focused. Thus, we have organized the book into two sections.

Section One: Recognizing the potential of e-business

This first section examines the nature and implications of doing business electronically. To some extent, this involves looking at some of the evolving business models that enable firms to take advantage of this phenomenon, particularly in business-to-consumer markets. Indeed, there is strong recognition that electronic commerce changes the 'rules of the game'; being successful in the online environment involves rethinking many aspects of the organization such as strategy, structure, processes, applications and products. The theory in this section is strongly supported by recent case studies and empirical evidence.

Section Two: Shaping the virtual organization

This second section extends some of the thinking from the first section. In particular, it explores new and emergent business models for flexible organizing in business-to-business environments. Such models are almost inevitably facilitated by recent technological developments. In a turbulent business world, alliance, co-operation and sharing between organizations can be a valuable source of competitive advantage. However, creating a dynamic and synergistic organizational form is a very complex undertaking. To provide some direction, this section critically examines in detail the nature, possibilities and limitations of this type of organization. Again, the analysis is interwoven with original case study and other empirical material to consolidate and support the arguments given.

In order to further elaborate on the content of the book and the range of issues covered, each part will now be described in greater detail.

As indicated above, Section One is entitled *Recognizing the potential of e-business* and aims to provide a solid grounding in and understanding of the contemporary e-business environment. The first chapter is entitled 'Business transformation on the Internet'. This chapter reports the results and implications of an ongoing collaborative study of large global organizations conducted by the European Institute of Administrative Affairs (INSEAD) and the Haas School of Business. The research takes a strategic perspective and uses an adapted strategic marketing framework to explore how the Internet is transforming the market space. At the apex, we see a few select exemplary organizations that have radically transformed their business practices to take advantage of e-commerce. However, it is clear that most large corporations have a long way to go in order to exploit the unique transformational potential of the Internet. The results suggest that firms are slow to change their business models; most companies are either simply treating the Internet as a publishing medium or shifting existing business models into the online environment. Customization stands out as one important area of underdevelopment. As such, some large firms may be at risk from agile new entrants such as have been witnessed in some sectors. Interestingly, this global research suggests that corporations in European and Asian markets are not far behind their American counterparts.

The second chapter examines one aspect of business transformation in more detail. In particular, 'Online delivered content: concept and business potential' explores a set of products and services that are likely to become a significant component of online trade. The nature of the Internet medium means that certain materials, including a variety of data, information and knowledge, are likely to be an important aspect of online trade. Observers of recent Internet development and applications will notice, for example, a growing number of providers of news, magazines, music (and other audio), video, educational materials, searchable databases and expertise. This chapter attempts to position electronic trading in online delivered content within the wider field of EC. It identifies its distinctive characteristics compared with other forms of trading content and compared with electronic trading in physical goods. Subsequently, important peculiarities are identified and analysed. Based on two cases of medium-sized specialized publishers the benefits and problems of moving into the business of electronic trading in this area are discussed.

Picking up on the strategic implications of a new industrial order, Chapter 3 looks at 'Digital intermediation in electronic commerce: the eBay model'. Through the Internet, the shape of markets and industries are changing fast. These new markets are very different from traditional, physical markets and so new strategies and business logic is required. This chapter introduces a framework for understanding circumstances under which information technology (IT) innovations for EC change firm-level strategic choices, and the economic forces behind these choices, in Internet market competition. Drawing on a variety of recent examples, it examines a number of important concepts for understanding the role of the digital intermediary and explains the 'IDR cycle': a recurring pattern of 'intermediation', 'disintermediation' and 'reintermediation'. In particular, it describes some of the conditions for reintermediation: where a disenfranchised player is able to compete again by combining tech-nological innovation with leveragable, specialized assets. The chapter also reveals a number of competitive strategies used by firms in the IDR cycle with varying levels of success: partnering for access, tech-nology licensing, partnering for content and partnering for application development.

Chapter 4 is entitled 'E-business and the intermediary role of virtual communities'. Building lasting relationships with customers and between stakeholders is considered an important aspect of electronic business. Therefore, this chapter examines in detail an important business model in which such relationships can be built – virtual communities. Electronic or virtual communities are rapidly evolving on the Internet as marketers have begun viewing them as an online strategic initiative to further consumers' consumption experience. Indeed, marketers see significant selling potential in leveraging virtual communities and, as a result, most virtual communities that are currently evolving on the Internet have been initiated, organized and moderated by for-profit organizations rather than by community members or third-party organizations. Such for-profit communities vary significantly from other types of virtual communities. This chapter examines the various types of virtual commu-nities and explores conditions under which business-oriented virtual communities can evolve successfully. From an economic perspective, it examines the role of virtual communities as intermediaries in exchange relationships among community members and between community members and other interest groups such as marketers and advertisers.

In the complex world of online trade, where community relationships may be important and your nearest competitor may be only a mouse-click away, providing a high quality e-commerce offering is critical. Chapter 5, 'Measuring the effectiveness of e-commerce Web sites', provides some assistance in understanding this important issue. The chapter considers a technique developed for evaluating e-commerce Web offerings – the Web Assessment method. In particular, this approach recognizes the changing nature of sales and marketing activities as supported by the Internet and related technologies. Thus, it sets about identifying, from a consumer perspective, possible success factors that differentiate a Web site from similar offerings. The Web Assessment model is based on three market transaction phases – information, agreement and settlement – and a special 'community component'. This last component – building loyal communities – is considered an important addition to traditional concepts. The model is tested using the classic EC first mover and business-to-consumer Web site, Amazon.com, and this is compared with a traditional EC-enabled bookseller, Barnes and Noble.

Although much attention has been focused on the implications of e-commerce for big business, the impacts go potentially much further. Chapter 6 examines 'Business impacts of the Internet for small and medium-sized enterprises'. As the title implies, this chapter turns our attention away from big business and towards smaller businesses, a sector contributing the lion's share of jobs and export business in many economies. It examines the developing state of Internet use by small and medium-sized enterprises (SMEs), and focuses on the impacts brought about by the introduction of the Internet. Specifically, it provides a model, derived from a long-term research programme, which enables a structured approach to impact analysis. The model is demonstrated using a number of SME case studies from the USA and the UK.

The first section of the book is brought to a close with Chapter 7, 'Industry transformation in e-commerce: Web diffusion in travel agencies'. This looks beyond impacts on the individual firm towards industry-level transformation. It is clear that business-to-consumer applications of the Internet are playing a role in restructuring some traditional industries, shifting the balance of profitability. This chapter describes the impacts of the Internet on the travel industry – predicted to be one of the largest online markets – analysing the changing role of travel agencies in this new environment. Travel agencies are being subjected to increased competition from numerous areas of the travel distribution network. Traditional players in the network, such as airlines and travel wholesalers, are beginning to market products directly to the consumer. New virtual travel agencies, which exist only on the Internet, are also providing new sources of competition. Nevertheless, although the Internet poses a significant threat to travel agencies, it also provides a major source of new opportunities, such as improved accessibility and service. Research findings from Australia suggest that a large proportion of travel agents do in fact use the Internet. However, it is not being exploited to its full potential, as a result, among other things, of a lack of strategic planning and vision. The result is likely to mean varying patterns of success, with failures and industry leaders alike emerging from this new playing field.

Section Two, *Shaping the virtual organization*, takes the discussion a step further to examine the impacts of the Internet and related technologies on the creation of agile business models and the development of strategic business-to-business relationships. As a starting point, Chapter 8 examines the notion of virtual organizations from the perspective of their apologists. It provides a detailed definition of virtual organizations and outlines their main characteristics and functions. This provides a useful, overarching framework within which to consider these new business models in the remainder of the section.

Chapter 9 examines 'Interorganizational systems to support strategic collaboration between firms'. Before launching into a detailed analysis of virtual organizations, it is important to understand some of the foundations of establishing business-to-business relationships using network technologies and applications. This chapter recognizes that interorganizational systems can play an important role in strengthening and stabilizing existing relations between firms but, moreover, can also facilitate new collaborations between firms in strategic areas. Based on intensive case studies and survey work, it examines some examples of strategic collaborations using such systems and, in particular, conceptualizes the barriers to the success of interorganizational systems. The barriers are not only technical but also cultural and political, such as sharing sensitive business information, the integration of business processes across firms, the co-existence of competition and collaboration, and the control of one firm by another. From a strategic perspective, these issues are integrated into a three-layered model that is useful for understanding such a complex phenomenon.

The following chapter, 'Structure, strategy and success factors for the virtual organization', provides a detailed theoretical and practical explication of the virtual organization. It begins by providing a useful discussion of the concept, extending and refining the definition given in Chapter 8. Furthermore, it draws out a number of critical and interrelated success factors for the virtual organization, including shared purpose, risk, trust and mutual benefit. Also key to the discussion are the nature of innovations and the information and knowledge flows involved. Interestingly, the chapter demonstrates, by way of some original case studies, several of the possible types of virtual organization structures/strategies: co-alliance, star-alliance, value-alliance and market-alliance. The empirical material is used as a strong platform upon which to consolidate the theoretical ideas given.

If the virtual organization is to be adopted as a viable business model, it is important to have suitable frameworks to provide management support for this new organizational form. Chapter 11 provides such a framework. The chapter explores how the Internet and related technologies enable the virtual organization to link and co-ordinate activity with a wide variety of business partners. As a precursor, the modular virtual organization is introduced; modularity is proposed as an additional means for the virtual organization to achieve a standardized organizational structure and behaviour to allow for interchangeability and compatibility of the partners and business processes. However, such ideas are fraught with complexity and modular organizations in action are difficult to manage. Therefore, to show how these ideas can be put into practice, a management support tool called Modular Network Design (MND) is introduced. This tool supports managers of a modular virtual organization in four key steps. The applicability of MND is illustrated with a case study at KLM Distribution, a firm at the centre of a globally operating virtual organization; the case study describes how MND supports the management of the modular virtual organization and contributes to better insight in the planning of customized transport orders.

Chapter 12 shifts the focus of attention towards the issue of knowledge networks in virtual teams. In particular, at this unit of analysis, the management considerations relevant to creativity and change are explored. The chapter begins with an examination of trends in organizational drivers – internal and external – that leads to a characterization of virtual teamwork applicable to many organizations in traditional sectors. The requirement for radical change in business practice is set against a backdrop of established work practices, organizational knowledge and human factors. Thus, a human-centred approach is adopted, and illustrative examples of the applications of virtual teams are drawn from several real organizations: distributed marketing in steel manufacture, workflow management in a regional construction services department, and the development of a virtual environment for team-based design activity in a marine engineering organization. Consequently, some factors leading to a successful transition to virtual working, and their general applicability, are considered.

Electronic procurement (or e-procurement) is currently considered a very hot topic in business-to-business EC (e.g., see Kalakota and Robinson, 1999). Using the Internet and related technologies in this area has the potential to create huge returns. Chapter 13, 'The contribution of Internet electronic commerce to advanced supply chain reform: a case study', examines some of the potential benefits of this important area of development. It focuses on the use of business-to-business electronic commerce in the retail and general merchandising industry. In particular, it examines the use of EC by Australia's leading supermarket chain, Coles Myer Limited. Traditional interorganizational systems such as electronic data interchange (EDI) pose a number of problems for large retailers like Coles Myer, e.g., regarding the achievement of 100 per cent EC compliance from small, unsophisticated suppliers. Subsequently, this poses a barrier for large distributors and retailers in achieving supply-chain reform; non-compliance hinders advanced replenishment and distribution techniques, which require strong co-ordination and 100 per cent EC compliance from involved parties. However, new Internet-based EDI products have made a considerable contribution towards a viable solution for the limited capabilities and requirements of small suppliers. In addition, this has provided a powerful platform for the transformation of supply chain relationships.

Chapter 14 takes an industry perspective to the impact of virtual organizations. This chapter illustrates how the principles of virtual organization are being applied through three examples of virtual businesses in the information technology (IT) sector in Germany and Switzerland. The choice of this industrial sector is most pertinent, centring on the use of information systems (IS) for virtual organizing. In sectors with a tradition of collaborative arrangements between companies – such as the automobile industry – proprietary platforms and systems have emerged to meet the need for inter-company information processing. By contrast, similar changes in the IT sector are taking place at a time when, worldwide, open platforms are becoming available for the first time. The Internet is the precursor of these. To advance understanding in this emergent area of virtual organization, the case studies are analysed using a 'virtuality' framework and the role of IS is explicated.

Finally, the book is brought to a close with a theoretically informed critique. 'Recognizing the limitations of virtual organizations' takes a broad view of the virtual organization phenomenon. It examines some of the possible problems of this developing organizational form. Key to the argument is the idea that organizations comprise a set of resources and that knowledge, understanding and communication (which are among the most important resources available to the organization) are tacit, situated and local and cannot simply be located, packaged and made available to virtual partners. Nevertheless, there is a clear role for the virtual organization but its scope is perhaps much smaller than its advocates admit.

As you will now be aware, e-commerce and v-business are diverse and complex subjects. They are not simply concerned with technological issues, but incorporate aspects of strategic management, marketing, operations management and behavioural science, amongst others. Such an interdisciplinary perspective is critical if the subject domains are to be understood fully. Recent examples of e-commerce offerings that overestimate technology and underestimate consumers exemplify this point (e.g., Boo.com, the high-profile online fashion retailer which went into liquidation in May 2000, failing to reap returns from its extensive advertising and expensive high-tech Web site). For this reason, as you have seen, we advocate a broad management viewpoint. The issues debated here are far too important to be left to technologists; although technology is an important enabler, the vision, strategy and management of the transition to bold new business models lies squarely in the hands of managers. To reap the real rewards of e-commerce and v-business, management competence is crucial.

We hope you find this book of interest and that it raises some important issues relevant to consideration in your study, research or organizational context. As you do so, we all take one more step towards the much-anticipated 'digital economy'.

References

Chesbrough, H. W. and Teece, D. J. (1996). When is virtual virtuous? Organizing for innovation. *Harvard Business Review,* January–February, 65–71.

Financial Times (1999). Electronic business survey. 20 October, 1–12.

Graphics, Visualization and Usability Centre (1999). *Tenth World Wide Web User Survey*. Georgia Institute of Technology.
http://www.cc.gatech/gvu/user_surveys/

Kalakota, R. and Robinson, M. (1999). *E-Business: roadmap for success*. Addison-Wesley.

Negroponte, N. (1995). *Being Digital*. Alfred Knopf.

Nua (2000). Internet surveys. *Nua Online*, 4 April.
http://www.nua.ie/surveys/

Siebel, T. M. and House, P. (1999). *Cyber Rules: strategies for excelling at e-business*. Currency-Doubleday.

Symonds, M. (1999). Business and the Internet: survey. *Economist*, 26 June, 1–44.

Tapscott, D. (1997). *Growing Up Digital*. McGraw-Hill.

Section One

Recognizing the potential of e-business

'If you don't see the Internet as an opportunity, it will be a threat' (Tony Blair, UK Prime Minister; *Financial Times*, 1999a). The Internet and related technologies provide tremendous new possibilities for doing business, but this challenging new environment requires a fundamental rethink of traditional strategy and business models (Evans and Wurster, 1999).

In business terms, one of the most important developments to arise from the current swathe of technological advances is electronic commerce. Simply speaking, e-commerce refers to trading electronically: transactions involved with buying and selling products, services and information over a network (Turban *et al.*, 2000). However, the implications are more far-reaching; the interactivity and connectivity of the new electronic medium have huge potential for many other aspects of business operations, including knowledge and information flows, improved quality of service (Seybold, 1998), and distribution of digital products. Thus, perhaps a more appropriate term for this phenomenon is electronic business (or e-business), first coined by IBM. Lou Gerstner, IBM's CEO, refers to e-business as: '. . . all about time cycle, speed, globalization, enhanced productivity, reaching new customers and sharing knowledge across institutions for competitive advantage'. In this text, e-commerce is considered in its broadest sense and the two terms are often used interchangeably.

Electronic commerce is not a new phenomenon by any means, a point that is sometimes conveniently overlooked by media hype. The use of electronic networks for trade began in the early 1970s in the financial sector. Some of the first applications involved electronic funds transfer (EFT) – the movement of money between financial institutions via telecommunications networks. This fast, paperless and secure form of electronic commerce is now the only practical way of handling the massive volumes of transactions generated daily in the banking industry. Even automated teller machines (ATMs), beginning in the 1980s, are a form of electronic commerce; every time the customer uses the ATM, it involves a transaction made over a computer network (an extension of the EFT network).

In the 1980s, the use of electronic commerce expanded considerably, and the prime vehicle for this was electronic data interchange (EDI) – the electronic movement of standard business documents such as purchase orders, bills and confirmations between business partners (e.g., see Stalling, 1990). No longer was EC confined to financial transactions, and this development extended participants to include manufacturers, services, retailers and other businesses. Such systems enable information to travel quickly and efficiently between trading partners (with few errors), reducing paperwork, saving money and fostering strategic partnership.

However, more recently, the commercialization of the Internet and its popular interface, the World Wide Web (WWW), has brought e-commerce to an entirely new level (see Berners-Lee, 1999). It has spawned some radically new ways of sharing information, communicating, trading and distributing products between consumers and organizations, between organizations, within organizations and even between consumers. In addition, it has also transformed some of the existing types of EC such as EFT and EDI (Roth, 1997; Tucker, 1997).

In the media, this revolution has gained considerable attention, particularly as new and agile start-ups with fresh ideas and business models begin to capture large revenues. This has started a cycle of interest, demand and expectation (Stroud, 1998). Thus, we have seen the market capitalization of very new EC-oriented companies such as Amazon.com soar to unprecedented levels despite lack of profits. In a more recent example, eToys.com was a first mover to the online toy retail market offering a clean, well-executed and easy-to-use Web site where customers can view products and purchase online. Its stock floated on Wall Street for $20 in May 1998 and has since rocketed to over $50 a share. It is now worth more than the traditional 'bricks and mortar' rival Toys R Us, with an estimated market capitalization of $6.1 billion. However, even though sales increased by 2000 per cent to July 1999, it is recognized that eToys will lose money for the 'foreseeable future', currently running at a loss of $0.17 a share (*Financial Times*, 1999b). The moral is that big gains will not necessarily happen overnight – these are massive, strategic investments requiring continuous innovation and considerable consumer critical mass – but the expectation is that they will happen in the longer term (Hagel and Singer, 1999).

Growth in electronic commerce is phenomenal and new estimates frequently outstrip old. The two key areas of trade are recognized as businesses selling to consumers and businesses selling to other businesses. Business-to-consumer (B2C) EC revenue, running at approximately $65 billion in 2000, will grow to $165 billion by 2003. Conservative estimates of worldwide EC revenue in the businesses-to-business (B2B) sector, around $200 billion in 2000, will grow to over four times that figure by 2003 (*Financial Times*, 1999c).

To some extent, although B2B revenues are considerably larger, a significant amount of attention has been given to the B2C sector in the press and academic literature; while B2B EC trade is well established, the B2C EC market is perceived as a new window of opportunity that has opened. This is where we pick up in this section. Here, we focus predominantly, but not exclusively, on the new environment and possibilities presented by B2C EC. The second section delves deeper and explores B2B relationships.

Electronic commerce (EC) is demonstrating its potential to turn the business world on its head. Few, if any, companies or industry sectors are protected from electronic commerce incursion, and there is little doubt that e-commerce will separate business winners and losers. The companies who face the toughest struggle to establish an electronic presence will be those that are already well established. According to Evans and Wurster (1999), 'Product suppliers and physical retailers still see the Internet as an arena for marketing and promotion: a new channel for doing old things. If they persist in that view, they will handicap themselves against new competitors'. E-commerce requires existing business models to be rethought radically. Companies whose business models are flexible or can be readily discarded stand a greater chance of e-commerce success. New business situations, such as e-commerce, merit new thinking. Companies risk being wrong-footed if they allow years of accumulated success in the real – rather than the virtual – business world to cloud their thinking. Operational matters, both tactical and strategic, need to be thought through. Often, processes and procedures for dealing with marketing, customers, suppliers and methods of payment need to be invented from scratch. In many ways it helps if these routines do not already exist.

This section provides a starting point for understanding the new environment provided by e-commerce. It recognizes the importance of new strategies and business models driven by technology, the power of controlling and streamlining information, and the need to build customer relationships and quality of service (Kalakota and Robinson, 1999). Chapter 1 provides an excellent introduction to the issues outlined above. On the basis of extensive research in the world's largest and best-known companies, it explores how firms are transforming to take advantage of this challenging new environment. Uppermost in the findings are the need for new business models to foster customer relationships and strategic change in pricing, promotion, placement and products. In terms of products, Chapter 2 examines a new and potentially very important set of items in electronic trade – online delivered content. It examines the nature and potential of these digital goods and services, including newspapers, music, video and other types of publishing.

Chapters 3 and 4 provide some of the business models sought in Chapter 1, while Chapter 5 offers some direction in evaluating such models. Indeed, Chapter 3 explores the dynamics of strategic change in industries and markets, providing some insight into how companies build a strong position in e-commerce. It shows how agile new EC entrants can push existing players out of a traditional market, but also how established players can fight back. Similarly, Chapter 4 examines the nature of virtual communities, which are currently espoused as an important competitive model for firms in the online world. Building relationships with customers can generate value in many ways for both consumers and businesses alike. Chapter 5 sheds some light on the issue of evaluating such e-commerce offerings, providing a tool for analysing the effectiveness of online businesses. As such, it uses two of the classic competitors in the online book trade, mentioned in Chapter 3, as pertinent examples.

Chapters 6 and 7 extend the discussion of e-commerce impacts to a sector of the economy that is often overlooked – small and medium-sized enterprises (SMEs). These businesses represent an important component of national economies and evidence suggests that they too can reap rich rewards. Chapter 6 explores the impacts of e-commerce on SMEs in general using a number of global examples. It presents a framework that is useful for understanding the issues involved. Finally, Chapter 7 raises the unit of analysis when it examines the impacts of e-commerce on SMEs at an industry level. The example chosen is the travel industry, predicted to be one of the largest areas of online B2C EC and in which SMEs play a significant part as intermediaries. Like the large businesses of Chapter 1, the prognosis is that SMEs need to transform their strategies and business models if they are to succeed in this new environment.

References

Berners-Lee, T. (1999). *Weaving the Web*. Orion Business.

Evans, P. B. and Wurster, T. S. (1999). Getting real about virtual commerce. *Harvard Business Review*, November–December, 84–94.

Financial Times (1999a). Information technology survey. 1 September, 1–18.

Financial Times (1999b). Information technology survey. 6 October, 1–18.

Financial Times (1999c). Electronic business survey. 20 October, 1–12.

Hagel, J. and Singer, M. (1999). *Net Worth: shaping markets when customers make the rules*. Harvard Business School Press.

Kalakota, R. and Robinson, M. (1999). *E-Business: roadmap for success*. Addison Wesley.

Roth, P. (1997). *Internet and Electronic Commerce: EDI, EFT and beyond*. Spiral Books.

Seybold, P. (1998). *Customers.com*. Times Books.

Stalling, W. (1990). *Business Data Communications*. Macmillan.

Stroud, D. (1998). *Internet Strategies: a corporate guide to exploiting the Internet*. Macmillan.

Tucker, J. M. (1997). EDI and the Net: a profitable partnering. *Datamation*, April, 62–69.

Turban, E., Lee, J., King, D. and Chung, H. M. (2000). *Electronic Commerce: a managerial perspective*. Prentice Hall.

1
Business transformation on the Internet
Soumitra Dutta and Arie Segev

Introduction

Despite many scepticisms and some hesitation, business on the Internet has taken off. Though difficult to account for accurately, growth in Internet sales has exceeded most expert estimates and is predicted to exceed US$1.2 trillion by the year 2002 (Activmedia, 1999).

There is also real money in the Internet revolution. Far from experimenting with a toy, organizations are reaping rich financial rewards from the Internet. Cisco is a case in point. Cisco played a pioneering role in building the Internet. Today the Internet is not only Cisco's business, but it is also its way of doing business. The Internet permeates every nook and cranny of Cisco's operations and makes a healthy contribution to its bottom line – annually more than half a billion dollars (Symonds, 1999). Dell first revolutionized the personal computer (PC) industry in 1983 by selling direct to customers. Today, the Internet presents the perfect medium for the next revolution in the PC industry: enabling customers to design their own PCs – online. As we enter the new Millennium, Dell's global online sales are approximately $16 million per day.

The Internet is creating a shared, real-time commercial space, the like of which has never been seen before. The degree to which corporations are leveraging the unique Internet market space is an interesting research issue. Despite the recent growth in electronic commerce figures, successful examples given in the popular media revolve around a relatively small group of companies – startups such as Yahoo! and E*Trade, and older (in relative terms) firms such as Cisco and Dell. Further, most of these exemplar firms come from the USA and from 'soft' information-intensive sectors such as software and financial services. The question of what is happening in other corporations – especially those from outside the USA and from other more 'hard' (such as automobile manufacturing or mining) sectors – thus looms large in this context.

The Internet genuinely provides corporations with an opportunity to do things differently. Dell has transformed its business model of direct selling to one of mass customization, in which each customer is encouraged (and supported) to design his own PC online. Cisco has successfully exploited the Internet to create new value for its existing channels – in fact to such a degree that most of Cisco's customers find it easier to do business with it online than through conventional channels. However, not all corporations show the same zeal in transforming their business models while leveraging the Internet. Many rest content with simply transporting their existing business models onto the Internet and treating it as just another business channel.

The quest to learn more about the degree to which large global corporations – the leaders of business today – are exploiting the unique potential of the Internet lies at the heart of this chapter.

A theory of cyber-transformation

Empirical surveys have been conducted (Dutta and Segev, 1998, 1999a) to evaluate the degree to which organizations across the globe – from a number of different sectors – are transforming their business models to exploit the unique capabilities of the Internet. The theory underlying these studies is the Marketspace model, which is depicted in Figure 1.1. The Marketspace model is built on two dimensions: (1) a *technological capability* dimension; and (2) a *strategic business* dimension.

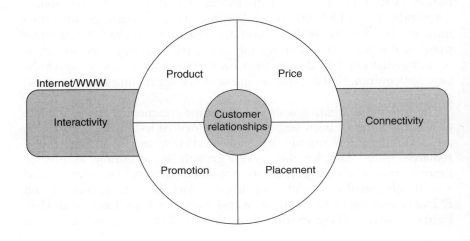

Figure 1.1
The Marketspace model

The first dimension – technological capability – comprises the following important elements:

- *Interactivity*. Owing to the real-time, online nature of the Internet, relationships between organizations and customers are becoming more interactive. This is enhancing the richness of customer relationships and creating new paradigms of product design and customer service.
- *Connectivity*. The open and global nature of the Internet is fostering the creation of a shared global market space. The radical increase in connectivity enabled by the Internet is giving rise to new communication and co-ordination mechanisms, both across organizations and customers and within groups of customers themselves.

The dual aspects of interactivity and connectivity are transforming the business models of organizations. This is brings us onto the next element of the model – the strategic business dimension. Here, the authors have chosen the classical strategic marketing model of the 'four Ps' (please refer to any major strategic marketing text, e.g., Kotler and Armstrong, 1999, for further details). In essence, this model consists of the following:

- *Product*. In this sense, the term is used to refer to both products (tangible and intangible) and services.
- *Price*. The cost at which the buyer obtains the product.
- *Promotion*. Encouraging the sale of the product, e.g., by advertising or securing financial support.
- *Place*. Distribution of the product.

This model has the dual advantages of simplicity and time-tested acceptance. We have augmented the 'four Ps' with one 'C':

- *Customer relationships*. This refers to building a connection, association or feeling with the customer. The 'four Ps' do not capture this aspect adequately.

Design of the study

The Marketspace model was used to design a questionnaire that probed into the following research question: 'to what degree are the elements of the Marketspace model (products, price, promotion, place and customer relationships) being transformed owing to the real-time interactivity and global connectivity of the Internet?'. More details about the specific aspects covered in the questionnaire are given in Table 1.1. Note that some questions referring to the technological sophistication of Web sites were included even though they are not explicitly contained within the Marketspace model – these provided useful context. Other questions evaluated the presence of a certain Marketspace feature. All questions required a binary (yes/no) answer. The binary responses minimize

Table 1.1   Questionnaire details

The overall evaluation for each dimension was obtained by aggregating a number of items related to the degree and extent to which specific features/aspects have been transformed/achieved:

Technological Sophistication
- The ease of navigation of the site
- The degree of customization possible of the Web interface
- Speed and ease of access to site features
- Advanced technological capabilities (such as video)

Transformation of Products
- The availability of product-related information online
- The customization of products for individuals or groups of customers
- The participation of customers in the specification and design of products

Transformation of Promotion
- The use of online advertising
- The use of online promotions such as sales and discounts
- The customization of online promotions
- The participation of customers in online promotions
- Links with other organizations in organizing online promotions

Transformation of Pricing
- The availability of pricing information online
- The dynamic customization of prices
- The availability of online price negotiation
- The possibility to charge customers for only proportions of products consumed

Transformation of Place
- The availability of online ordering
- The availability of secured online payment
- Distribution of products online
- The involvement of partner organizations in online distribution

Transformation of Customer Relationships
- The provision of online customer service
- The online identification and tracking of customers to provide customized services
- The provision of online communications to customers
- The creation of online communities for customers
- The solicitation of online feedback from customers

evaluator bias and thus provide an objective basis on which to rank the surveyed companies.

The evaluation of companies was randomized across different sectors – again in an effort to reduce evaluator bias. The companies selected for the study were chosen from the Fortune Global 500 list (see Appendix 1.1). To achieve a good representation across sectors, the list was classified into nine groups: Electronics and Computers; Media and Entertainment; Finance and Insurance; Retail and Wholesale; Manufacturing; Travel and Transport; Chemical and Pharmaceutical; Telecoms and

Utilities; and Mining, Oil Production and Refining. Fourteen of the leading companies (by revenue) from each of these sectors were chosen. However, only eight companies from the Media and Entertainment sector were present in the Global 500 list. Further, in the Manufacturing sector, all top fourteen firms were automobile manufacturers so, to get a more diverse profile, we selected the top seven companies and the next seven involved in manufacturing products other than cars. In total, 120 companies were selected for inclusion in the study.

Most of the firms surveyed are multinationals and hence it was very common to find different Web sites for each country, with possibly different languages and product offerings. Quite a few sites featured a global corporate homepage that led on to links to local subsidiary sites. Frequently, there were wide differences across the sites of different subsidiaries of the same company, or across different national sites. As much as possible, an attempt was made to evaluate the best features of the available sites.

Many of the surveyed companies – such as Akzo Nobel, BP, GE and Thyssen – also have proprietary intranets or extranets that are accessible only to employees and/or suppliers and business partners. Owing to the restricted access to these networks, they could not be evaluated.

Overall transformation is poor

The overall degrees of achievement of the surveyed companies along the dimensions of the Marketspace model are shown in Figure 1.2. A first observation is that corporations have a long way to go to exploit the transformational potential of the Internet. Except for the Customer Relationship dimension, all Marketspace elements are rated at less than 40 per cent; the surveyed firms earn a cumulative score of less than

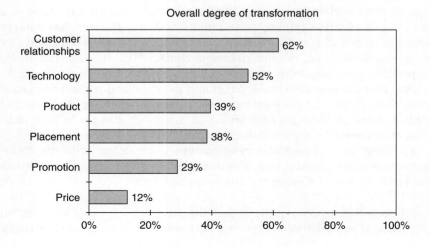

Figure 1.2
Overall degrees of achievement along the Marketspace model dimensions

40 per cent for all four Ps – Product, Place, Promotion and Price. This is important, particularly when one notes that the indicated scores are for the best site of a subsidiary or region within a firm. Thus, these are – in a way – the most generous ratings of the surveyed firms.

Few firms are rethinking their business models to take advantage of the unique interactive and connective capabilities of the Internet. Most firms are stuck in the first stage of exploitation of the Internet: publishing corporate and, in many instances, product information. Few have actually moved onto the next stage – conducting electronic commerce; only about one-third of the surveyed firms allow electronic ordering and payment. Even fewer have actively tried to shift gears into the third and most interesting stage of Internet exploitation: business transformation in cyberspace. In our study, less than 20 per cent of the surveyed firms allowed for the formation of cyber-communities among customers and very few were innovative in stimulating intra-community interactions.

Customer relationships is the priority

Despite the low levels of overall achievement, the focus is clear for all corporations: it is on using the power of the Internet to enhance customer relationships. Pharmaceutical firms, such as Merck, provide customer service online via product guides that inform consumers about the use of products. Media companies attempt to keep their customers constantly updated via e-mails about product and site updates. Computers and electronics firms such as IBM provide extensive online support and troubleshooting services.

This focus on customer relationships is not surprising given recent increases in the number of Internet users globally and the increasingly 'mainstream' profile of cyber-surfers. Recent evidence (Graphics, Visualisation and Usability (GVU) Centre, 1998) suggests that the percentage of female Web users has improved (to 38.5 per cent) and the average age of Web surfers has increased (to 36 years). In addition, there is a growing realization among corporations that the Internet has forever changed the traditional paradigm of marketing. Gone are the days of mass marketing and remote customer contact. The Internet has made it possible for companies to focus on building relationships with individual customers and to make direct and personalized contact with each customer. Even customer-savvy firms such as American Airlines and British Airways (BA) are now trying to reach out directly to each individual customer in a personalized manner via the Web.

The emphasis on customer relationships is consistent with the observations of other practitioners. For example, noted IT consultant Patricia Seybold, author of *Customers.Com*, is quoted as saying:

> I stumbled upon a pattern that the successful businesses were all focused on existing customers, and committed to making it easier

for them to do business, either via the Web, or through better information provision (Seybold, 1998).

Internet pioneers, such as Cisco, also note that nearly all of their Internet-related developments over the last four years have resulted from listening to customers and constantly utilizing their feedback to create innovative ways to use the Internet.

While a lot has been accomplished with respect to customer relationships, much remains to be done (see Figure 1.3). About half of all firms try to identify or track customers and about one-fifth of them offer to keep their customers informed by sending e-mail updates on product releases and other corporate events. Also, only a small fraction of all firms surveyed encourage the formation of communities among customers. This is despite evidence that shows that cyber-communities increase loyalty and sales and make customers feel more connected to organizations (Kannan *et al.*, 1998).

Simplicity is a virtue

Many leading firms have relatively simple sites that focus on providing easily accessible functionality at the expense of dazzling technical wizardry. They have realized that most Web users are not willing to wait for more than a few seconds for a page to load, something that is often not possible for pages rich in graphics and video. This is particularly true for users who access sites from locations outside the USA.

Despite the relatively lower emphasis on technological sophistication, many companies make effective use of technology to make their site more attractive and to retain the attention of customers. Shell UK, for example, uses Shockwave to provide the user with an animated outline of the whole process of exploring crude oil and getting it to the consumer as gas. Most media firms use a variety of video and audio tools to provide customers with a rich multimedia experience.

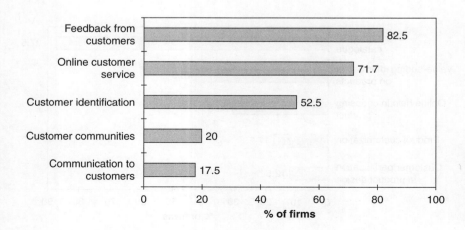

Figure 1.3
Use of the Internet for different aspects of customer relationships

While most of the surveyed Web sites provide useful navigational aids such as site maps (70 per cent) and search engines (92.5 per cent), very few give customers the ability to customize the site pages (5.8 per cent). Only about 15 per cent of the companies provide a 'text only' option, which benefits customers with less powerful PCs or individuals accessing the pages from locations with slow Internet access. Quite a few companies make their sites interesting by using animated graphics (84 per cent), audio clips (34 per cent), video clips (37 per cent) and Javascript (67 per cent).

Product customization is rare

A high proportion of the surveyed companies featured product catalogues in some form (see Figure 1.4), though with varying levels of detail. While most of the catalogues covered the whole product range (70 per cent), only a handful (5 per cent) provided information or comparisons with competitors' products. This is interesting, not least because there are many 'new' intermediaries on the Web who provide a free comparison of product offerings from competing firms. For example, virtual travel agencies such as Expedia.com provide comparisons of different airlines' ticket prices for any particular route.

Many companies make significant effort to provide value-adding information about their products. For example, Volkswagen provides tips for safe driving and helps consumers make the buy-versus-lease decision by guiding them through the relevant financial details. Most chemical companies provide detailed product specifications and information about the application of their products to aid the purchase decision.

About one-third of the surveyed firms provide expert systems, questionnaires, or other forms of online help in choosing a product. Insurance

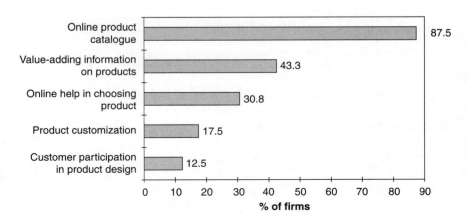

Figure 1.4
Use of the Internet for different aspects of the product dimension

companies, for example, encourage the customer to answer a set of questions and then suggest the right policy. General Motors (GM) asks potential customers for the features they look for in a car and then recommends a model to suit their tastes.

A smaller proportion of firms allow users to either customize products or to participate in product design online. Disney enables buyers to customize commodities such as mugs and mouse pads and to design custom greetings (via Design Online). Allyn and Bacon (the Viacom publishing division) allows college faculties – by selecting specific parts from available books – to build custom books as course material.

Promotions aim to seduce customers

Promotions on the Internet are similar in many respects to promotions in the 'traditional' marketplace: price reductions, discounts and prizes. Thus, many companies offer special discounts for Internet orders.

However, the interactive nature of the Web provides firms with a unique possibility to get customers to participate in promotions (see Figure 1.5). About one-third of all companies use online games and contests to retain the attention of customers. For example, Volkswagen advertises its New Beetle on its Web pages and encourages visitors to enter the New Beetle contest to win one. The United States Postal Service features contests allowing users to participate and submit entries for designing new stamps.

Promotions also come by way of links to related sites or sites which might be of interest to customers. For example, the Dutch financial powerhouse, ING Group, provides links to Dutch tourism sites from its homepage.

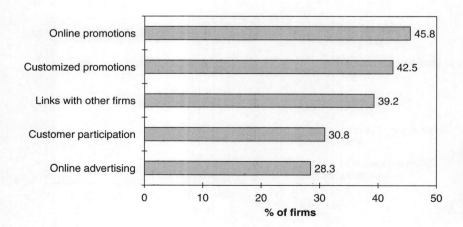

Figure 1.5
Use of the Internet for different aspects of the promotion dimension

Online ordering is hampered by poor progress in pricing

Less than half of all surveyed firms allow online ordering of products (see Figure 1.6). Of those that do, computers and electronics firms such as IBM not only have self-operated online stores but also provide links to other retailers that sell their products. Of course, given the physical nature of many products, they cannot be distributed online. However, 'soft' products such as software, media, music and financial services are good candidates for online distribution. Nevertheless, only a small proportion of firms are actively using the Internet for delivering 'soft' products in this way. Most firms distribute product-related information – such as dealer or store locations – online.

The majority of companies that allow online purchases ship goods via UPS or other air/surface mail. A small proportion (8.3 per cent) provides hot links to third parties involved in online distribution and delivery. About one-third of all firms allow for online payment.

Internet commerce and online ordering is hampered by the fact that most firms fare relatively poorly along the price dimension (see Figure 1.7). About half of all surveyed firms do not display prices for their own products, and less than 5 per cent of the surveyed firms display prices for competing products. Only a small fraction of all firms offer any form of dynamic price negotiation or customization to customers. The leaders along the pricing dimension appear to be airline companies; these progressive online traders dynamically vary prices and allow customers to make bids for specific tickets.

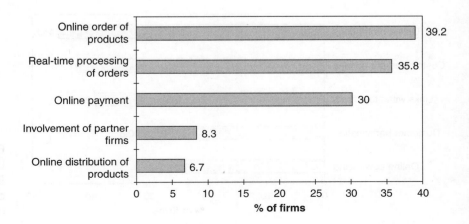

Figure 1.6
Use of the Internet for different aspects of the place dimension

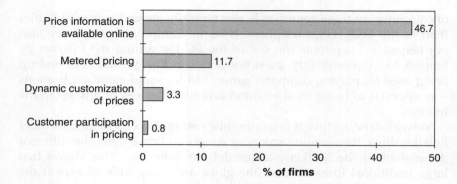

Figure 1.7
Use of the Internet for different aspects of the price dimension

Regional trends

The distribution of the surveyed firms across geographical regions is as follows: North America (42 per cent), Europe (40 per cent) and Asia–Pacific (18 per cent). Figure 1.8 depicts the regional variations in the scores of the surveyed firms along the different dimensions of the Marketspace model.

The relative lead of American firms is not surprising; the Internet was born in the USA and it still contains a dominant majority of all Internet transactions. Firms from the Asia–Pacific region, primarily Japan, are lagging significantly relative to their counterparts from Europe and North America along all aspects of the Marketspace model. The gap between European and North American firms is slightly less but still very significant.

American giants such as Microsoft dominate the high-technology sector in Europe and Asia. Statistics show that less than one-quarter of all households in Europe have PCs as compared with about half in the USA (Computer Industry Almanac, 1999; ET Forecasts, 2000). The situation is yet worse when one examines Asia – with only 17 per cent of households in Japan having PCs. Not only do most Europeans and Asians have less disposable purchasing power after taxes, but the prices

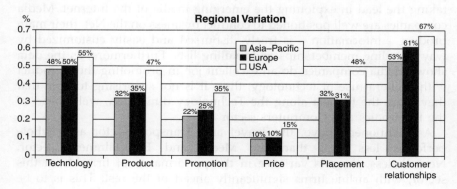

Figure 1.8
Regional comparisons along the dimensions of the Marketspace model

of computers in these countries is also typically about 30 per cent higher than in the USA. High telephone costs in Europe and Asia have also not helped to encourage the use of the PC for surfing the Internet by households. Consequently, most home PCs in Europe and Asia end up being used for playing computer games and for stand-alone applications – as opposed to being used as communication devices to link up to the Internet.

Notwithstanding this, it is worthwhile noting that except for Customer Relationships, the absolute scores of American firms along the different dimensions of the Marketspace model are quite low. This shows that large traditional firms all over the globe are doing little to exploit the unique transformational potential of the Internet. In such a situation it is possible for European and Asian firms to catch up with their American counterparts in the near future. This appears to be happening in some sectors. A recent study of 863 banks in Europe and 1676 American banks concluded that 55 per cent of European banks could be classified as intermediate or advanced 'cyberbanks' as compared with just under 15 per cent of US banks (Bluesky International, 1998). Also, Scandinavian companies such as Ericsson and Nokia are rapidly turning Scandinavia into a wireless society. Finland boasts the highest per capita penetration of the Internet in society among all countries in the world (GVU Centre, 1999).

However, much will have to change in Europe and Asia in order to avoid a widening of the gap with America. The penetration of the Internet in society will have to increase significantly. Further, management will have to show the right leadership for business transformation while moving online.

A comparison across sectors

Table 1.2 presents a summary of our results across sectors. Firms from the Media and Entertainment sector obtain the highest scores across nearly all dimensions of the Marketspace model – except for price, where Travel and Transport firms dominate. This is not surprising when one notes that these firms are skilled in exploiting traditional media such as print, radio and television; it is perhaps only natural that they are taking the lead in exploiting the emerging media of the Internet. Media companies are well positioned to conduct business on the Net: their main product – information – is freely disbursed and easily customized by way of online memberships and mailing lists. Furthermore, as the data show, Media companies do an excellent job in promoting their product with a liberal use of technology; thus, it is not surprising to note that they score the highest along the Technology dimension, well ahead of the Electronics and Computers sector.

As mentioned above, the Travel and Transport sector as a whole performs less well than the Media and Entertainment sector. Nevertheless, there is variance in the performance of firms from this sector, with airline firms significantly ahead of the rest. This is to be

Table 1.2 Ranked order lists of sectors across different dimensions of the Marketspace model

Technology	Product	Promotion
Media & Entertainment 75%	Media & Entertainment 50%	Media & Entertainment 66%
Electronics & Computers 63%	Travel & Transport 47%	Electronics & Computers 35%
Manufacturing 57%	Chemicals & Pharmaceuticals 44%	Telecoms & Utilities 34%
Telecoms & Utilities 53%	Manufacturing 43%	Travel & Transport 28%
Chemicals & Pharmaceuticals 52%	Telecoms & Utilities 40%	Retail & Wholesale 27%
Mining, Oil & Refining 50%	Electronics & Computers 39%	Finance & Insurance 26%
Finance & Insurance 45%	Finance & Insurance 32%	Chemicals & Pharmaceuticals 21%
Travel & Transport 41%	Retail & Wholesale 29%	Mining, Oil & Refining 20%
Retail & Wholesale 29%	Mining, Oil & Refining 28%	Manufacturing 18%

Place	Price	Customer Relationships
Media & Entertainment 64%	Travel & Transport 26%	Media & Entertainment 79%
Retail & Wholesale 56%	Retail & Wholesale 19%	Electronics & Computers 68%
Electronics & Computers 46%	Media & Entertainment 18%	Telecoms & Utilities 67%
Telecoms & Utilities 46%	Telecoms & Utilities 16%	Chemicals & Pharmaceuticals 66%
Travel & Transport 43%	Electronics & Computers 11%	Manufacturing 65%
Finance & Insurance 37%	Finance & Insurance 11%	Retail & Wholesale 58%
Manufacturing 31%	Manufacturing 9%	Mining, Oil & Refining 55%
Mining, Oil & Refining 26%	Mining, Oil & Refining 1%	Finance & Insurance 53%
Chemicals & Pharmaceuticals 13%	Chemicals & Pharmaceuticals 0%	Travel & Transport 52%

expected given that airlines have been sophisticated users of information technology for several decades. Most airline sites are not highly technology-intensive, yet they are rich in functionality. Enticing promotions and deals are advertised all over airline sites. Airlines such as Lufthansa and UAL allow for online ticketing. Lufthansa also auctions tickets online.

Being in the business of building the infrastructure of the Internet, both the Electronics & Computers and Telecoms & Utilities sectors do very well in exploiting the Marketspace, especially along the Customer Relationships dimension. Firms from these sectors provide extensive product-related information and make it easy for customers to interact with them. Online forums for consumers to exchange product-related information are often provided. Further applications are also available; firms such as BT guide customers through an interactive questionnaire to help them identify the product that best meets their needs, and subsequently to purchase the product online.

Turning to the retail sector, we note that the exploitation of the Marketspace is rather uneven. Some organizations such as Wal-Mart have transferred their entire business onto the Web, while others such as K-Mart have done little to exploit the Marketspace. Wal-Mart's Web presence is relatively simple from a technology point of view, but provides a very accessible offering – a neatly categorized and comprehensive product catalogue with detailed features and prices. Promotions and special deals in the online supermarket are similar to those found in a conventional Wal-Mart store. Tesco – a leading UK retailer – has a site very comparable with that of Wal-Mart, providing extensive value-adding information such as online recipes for each product and a free wine-selector software package available for download.

Companies in the Manufacturing sector are disadvantaged by the nature of their products. However, many companies – typically the auto-mobile manufacturers – do very well. GM has a good Internet presence, allowing customers to configure their dream car, add different features, get a price quote for the car, and also check for availability of desired models at a neighbourhood dealer. All automobile manufacturers manage to seamlessly integrate car financing into the car purchasing process.

Companies from the Finance and Insurance sector are rather disap-pointing in terms of market space transformation. Most banks – from Japan in particular (such as Bank of Tokyo-Mitsubishi and Nippon Life Insurance) – have a very elementary Internet presence. As such, they do not even attempt to conduct any business over the Net. Nevertheless, some banks stand out from the crowd. For example, Citicorp delivers many services online such as Internet Banking and financial tools to compute mortgage repayments.

Clearly, firms from the both the Chemicals & Pharmaceuticals and Mining, Oil & Refinery sectors cannot deliver their products online; they are physical, tangible products. Hence, the Web sites of many of these companies are little more than glorified corporate brochures. However, some firms have chosen to emphasize the delivery of information related to their products through their Internet presence. Merck, for example, presents detailed information about a variety of ailments, their symp-toms, remedies and relevant Merck pharmaceuticals. Additional features also add value to the Merck Web site; interactive quizzes keep the customer interested, whilst health care professionals can exchange infor-mation via online forums.

Conclusions

The results of this study are interesting and give a poignant message. While the media reports of increasing volumes of online commerce are encouraging, our study shows that most large corporations are doing little to exploit the unique transformational potential of the Internet.

It is worth reiterating that our research indicates that approximately two-thirds of the surveyed firms are simply treating the Internet as a publishing medium. Further, of the remaining one-third, most appear content with simply transporting their existing business models onto the Internet. Very few firms are actively using the Internet for launching new business models. Even the highest ranked firms in the study (UAL, Lufthansa, Time Warner, Viacom, BT and AMR) achieve an overall score of only 68 per cent, and there are just eight firms with overall scores higher than 50 per cent. While it would be wrong to evaluate the Internet strategies of the surveyed firms solely on the basis of these scores, these low figures do indicate that there is a lot of room for further exploiting the Internet within large, global firms who constitute the sample of our research.

The reasons for the lack of exploitation of the Internet by traditional large firms are both complex and varied. Such barriers are perhaps more organizational than technological in nature. Frequently, 'traditional' firms are hostage to the legacy of their own successes; management within such organizations have risen to the top on the basis of historical successes and it is very difficult for them to detach themselves from these and venture into new territory. For example, France Telecom has been credited with the successful launch of the Minitel videotext service in France more than a decade ago. Trapped by the success of the Minitel, France Telecom had a difficult time, until recently, in embracing the Internet (which threatened to eclipse the Minitel).

Regardless of what the reasons for the lag may be, large firms from all over the globe risk stagnation and competitive disadvantage. Agile new entrants are moving onto the Internet easily and fearlessly. Firms such as Yahoo! and Amazon are questioning the rules of entire industries. In just five years, Amazon has redefined the business of book retailing. Traditional leaders in book retailing such as Barnes and Noble and Bertelsmann were slow to move onto the Internet. Late in their move, these firms now realize that they have lost the game to Amazon; they see little hope of prospering except by joining forces.

Despite wide publicity about American firms as leaders of the Internet revolution, our results show that large American firms are not far ahead of their European and Asian counterparts. This is good news for European and Asian managers who often lament the lead of American organizations. Indeed, there are some indications that large European firms are catching up with their American counterparts in some sectors (such as banking), but real progress in this direction has yet to be witnessed. The real issue for all surveyed firms, American or otherwise, is their lag relative to agile new entrants; these new players are rapidly moving ahead with new business models and novel business practices.

As organizations look to exploit the Internet, there is recognition that the customer is an important area of business focus, and this is underlined by the survey results. The Internet allows firms to customize their products and services to each individual customer and to deliver a personalized level of service not previously possible. However, such developments do not happen overnight; providing customers with enhanced levels of service and involving them in product/service design requires significant changes within internal business practices. This is a difficult task. Much hard work lies ahead as firms learn how to make their customers' lives easier via the Internet.

Some businesses have a natural advantage in their transformation of the market space. Typically, firms from 'soft' sectors such as software, media and financial services can deliver most of their products and services online. However, while software and media firms have embraced the Internet for product delivery, sectors such as financial services have been reluctant. This reluctance may cost them dearly in the future – already

Yahoo! boasts the number one finance site as ranked in many surveys. Moreover, the physical nature of products need not necessarily be a stumbling block in embracing the Internet; Internet pioneers such as Amazon have a strong track record in trading tangible goods online. The potential strength of 'hard' sectors – such as electronics and computers – is also confirmed by the findings reported in this chapter. Firms in all sectors should actively question how to best exploit the Internet to transform their business practices for competitive advantage.

Note

The results described here are the output from ongoing research collaboration between the Research Initiative in Information Systems Excellence at INSEAD and the Fisher Center for Management of Information Technology at the Haas School of Business. This chapter is reprinted with permission from the *European Management Journal* (see Dutta and Segev, 1999b).

References

Activmedia (1999). Global e-commerce to top $95 billion in 1999. *Nua Online*, 28 June.
http://www.nua.ie/surveys/index.cgi?f=VS&art_id=905354987&rel=true

Bluesky International (1998). Advanced Internet banking explodes in Europe. *Bluesky Online*, 26 October.
http://www.blueskyinc.com/pressrelease1/

Computer Industry Almanac (1999). Over 364 million PCs in use globally. *Nua Online*, 2 April.
http://www.nua.ie/surveys/index.cgi?f=VS&art_id=905354817&rel=true

Dutta, S. and Segev, A. (1998). The global Internet 100 survey 1998. *Information Strategy Online*, June.
http://www.info-strategy.com/GI100/

Dutta, S. and Segev, A. (1999a). Transforming business in the market space. *Proceedings of the Thirty-Second Hawaii International Conference on Systems Sciences*, Maui, Hawaii.

Dutta, S. and Segev, A. (1999b). Business transformation on the Internet. *European Management Journal*, **17**, 466–76.

ET Forecasts (2000). PC market will continue to boom. *Nua Online*, 29 February.
http://www.nua.ie/surveys/index.cgi?f=VS&art_id=905355624&rel=true

Graphics, Visualisation and Usability (GVU) Centre (1998). *GVU's 8th WWW User Survey*. Georgia Institute of Technology.
http://www.gvu.gatech.edu/gvu/user_surveys/survey-1997-10/

Graphics, Visualisation and Usability (GVU) Centre (1999). *GVU's 10th WWW User Survey*. Georgia Institute of Technology.
http://www.gvu.gatech.edu/gvu/user_surveys/survey-1998-10/
Kannan, P. K., Chang, A. and Whinston, A. B. (1998). Marketing information on the I-way. *Communications of the ACM*, **41**, 35–43.
Kotler, P. and Armstrong, G. (1999). *Principles of Marketing*. Prentice Hall.
Seybold, P. (1998). *Customers.com*. Times Books.
Symonds, M. (1999). Business and the Internet: survey. *Economist*, 26 June, 1–44.

Appendix 1.1
List of companies surveyed

Travel & Transport	Telecoms & Utilities	Retail & Wholesale	Mining, Oil & Refining
US Postal Service	NTT	Wal-Mart stores	Royal Dutch/Shell Group
Japan Postal Service	AT&T	Sears Roebuck	Exxon
United Parcel Service	IRI	Metro Holding	Mobil
East Japan Railway	Tokyo Electric Power	K-Mart	British Petroleum
Deutsche Bahn	Électricité de France	Carrefour	Elf Aquitaine
AMR	Deutsche Telekom	Daiei	Texaco
Deutsche Post	RWE Group	ITO-Yokado	Sunkyong
La Poste	France Telecom	Dayton Hudson	ENI
UAL	ENEL	Kroger	Chevron
Nippon Express	BT	J.C. Penney	Total
SNCF	Kansai Electric Power	Tesco	PDVSA
Japan Travel Bureau	GTE	Koninklijke Ahold	Amoco
Japan Airlines	Chubu Electric Power	J. Sainsbury	Ssangyong
Lufthansa Group	Bellsouth	Promodes	PEMEX

Manufacturing	Finance & Insurance	Chemical & Pharmaceutical	Electronics & Computers
General Motors	Nippon Life Insurance	E.I.Du Pont de Nemours	General Electric
Ford	Allianz	Hoechst	IBM
Toyota	Dai-Ichi Mutual Life	BASF	Hitachi
Daimler-Benz	Insurance	Bayer	Matsushita Electricity
Volkswagen	Bank of Tokyo-Mitsubishi	Novartis	Industrial
Daewoo	Sumitomo Life Insurance	Johnson & Johnson	Siemens
Chrysler	State Farm Insurance Co.	Dow Chemical	Sony
Mitsubishi Heavy	UAP – AXA	Merck	Toshiba
Industries	Prudential Insurance Co.	Rhone-Poulenc	NEC
Robert Bosch	– America	ICI	Philips Electronics
Lockheed Martin	Deutsche Bank	Mitsubishi Chemical	Fujitsu
Thyssen	ING Group	Bristol-Myers Squibb	Hewlett-Packard
United Technologies	Credit Agricole	American Home	ABB
Manesmann	Meiji Life Insurance	Products	Mitsubishi Electric
Boeing	Citicorp	Akzo Nobel	Alcatel Alsthom
	GAN		

Media & Entertainment
Walt Disney
Bertelsmann
Viacom
Dai Nippon Printing
Lagardere Group
Toppan Printing
Time Warner
News Corp.
Havas

2

Online delivered content: concept and business potential

Claudia Loebbecke

Introduction

Electronically traded online delivered content (ODC) is data, information and knowledge traded on the Internet or through other online means. ODC includes online newspapers, magazines, music, education, searchable databases, consulting and, eventually, expertise and ideas.

When trading ODC, the full commercial cycle – offer, negotiation, order, delivery, payment – can be conducted via a network such as the Internet. In addition to the issues inherent in trading physical goods on the Web, trading ODC on the Internet raises concerns such as version control, authentication of the product, control over intellectual property rights (IPR) and the development of profitable intra- and inter-organizational business models.

This chapter outlines the growing importance and possible business models for ODC. It attempts to position electronic trading in ODC within the wider field of electronic commerce. It identifies the distinctive characteristics of ODC compared with other forms of trading content and compared with electronic trading in physical goods. Important ODC peculiarities are identified and analysed. Based on two case studies of medium-sized specialized publishers the benefits and problems of moving into the business of electronic trading in ODC are discussed.

Online delivered content – the core of the Intangible Economy

A major characteristic of the Internet Economy (also commonly referred to as the Digital Economy or Information Society) is its shift to the intangible. The creation and manipulation of dematerialized content becomes a major source of economic value (Wang *et al.*, 1998). This move to the intangible affects all sectors and activities. It profoundly transforms economic relationships and interactions, the way firms and markets are organized and in which transactions are carried out. However, the intangible economy is not limited to the Internet. Analogue technologies such as radio and television are also to be considered integral parts – these are used to an increasing degree and further media integration is foreseeable for the near future.

To some extent the intangible economy runs squarely against the conventional logic of economics. Intangible goods are not limited by physical constraints and are not limited to traditional economic characteristics, such as 'durable', 'lumpy', 'unique', and 'scarce'. Instead, intangible goods can simultaneously be 'durable and ephemeral, lumpy and infinitely divisible, unique and ubiquitous, scarce and abundant' (Goldfinger, 1998). The business of purely intangible goods is radically different from conventional electronic commerce areas, which focus on trading or preparing to trade physical goods or hybrids between physical and intangible goods. Trading intangible goods demands new business models and processes.

Classical economic theory does not usually address the issue of information, content, or knowledge as a tradeable good. The value of information is traditionally seen as derived exclusively from reducing uncertainty. In the Internet economy however, information/content is simultaneously a production asset and a good.

From a suppliers' perspective, the growing importance of intangible assets and the resulting complexity can be seen in the huge differences between book value and stock market values. These differences can partly be explained by the crucial role attributed to brands, content, publishing rights and intellectual capital, which may emerge via, be embedded in, or be stimulated by, ODC. The implied problem of pricing the value of information/content has so far received most attention in the context of managerial accounting when discussing the issues of: (a) consistent value measuring; and (b) the negligibility of costs for acquiring and creating intangible assets. In the rest of the chapter the concept of intangible assets will not be further pursued. However, suppliers' perspectives allow helpful insights into accounting and measuring aspects of intangible goods, and thus can well contribute to developing business models for electronically trading intangible goods and especially ODC.

The following focuses on intangible goods in general and ODC as one of its core representatives. Their inherent logic of dematerialization is outlined in the context of ODC peculiarities.

Online delivered content – a special kind of intangible good

ODC is a particular kind of intangible good. In the literature, the term 'intangibility' refers to two rather different concepts. Levitt (1981) suggests that the terms 'goods' and 'services' be replaced by 'tangibles' and 'intangibles', and hence observes that, in their production and delivery mode, intangible products are highly people-intensive. This does not really match with a more recent interpretation of 'intangibility' aiming at non-material goods (but not services), often expressible in bits and bytes (Meinkoehn, 1998). While today most products contain intangible aspects, such as know-how or brand recognition, this chapter considers ODC to be a counterexample of 'all products have elements of tangibility and intangibility' (Levitt, 1981: 101). ODC – by definition – has no tangible components.

Consequently, electronic infrastructure requirements for electronic trading (including delivery) in ODC are significantly higher than for electronic trading of tangible goods not delivered via the infrastructure (usually the Web). However, taking into account that no physical infrastructure is needed, the total infrastructure requirements for trading in ODC are comparatively low (and independent of the distance to be bridged).

Online delivered content – a special kind of experience good

Another common approach for clustering products is grouping them into 'search goods' and 'experience goods' (Peterson *et al.*, 1997). The quality of search goods can be determined without actually using them. With experience goods' quality is learned from experiencing the product, i.e., from using the good. Most forms of ODC belong to the group of experience goods – the quality of content is only learned from using/consuming it. However, treating ODC as an experience good (i.e., letting potential clients 'experience' ODC) implies giving the actual content away for free (i.e., not trading it) and, in all likelihood, counting on receiving revenue via some synergy mechanisms. Unfortunately, once a potential customer has experienced ODC, he has no more reason to buy it. Suppliers of ODC try to solve this dilemma by shifting ODC as much as possible into the category of search goods. Possible steps for this are establishing strong brand reputation for Web sites, publishers and so on, or offering abstracts, sample chapters or reviews as triggers to buy the whole product.

Towards a framework of online delivered content

The above definition of ODC is derived from investigating the range of instances covered by Choi *et al.*'s (1997) description of the 'core of electronic commerce', also termed 'fully digital business'. They differentiate three dimensions: 'products', 'agents' (or players), and 'processes', which all are divided into 'physical' and 'digital'. This is shown in Figure 2.1.

The distinction between *physical* and *digital products* appears self-evident. According to Choi *et al.* 'anything that one can send and receive over the Internet has the potential to be a digital product' (1997: 62). Similarly, *Agents* (or players) are 'sellers, buyers, intermediaries and other third parties such as governments and consumer advocacy groups' (1997: 17). Physical players show up in person, digital players communicate via an electronic interface. For instance, electronic shoppers are considered to be digital players. The distinction between physical and digital processes depicted on the third axes seems to be as easy as the product dimension: 'visiting a store is a physical process, whereas searching on the Web is a digital process' (1997: 17).

Regarding the product dimension, Choi *et al.*'s list of examples ranges from information in general, letters, postcards, credit card information, airline or concert tickets, to 'hybrid digital products' such as smart appliances. A good example for the latter is an intelligent alarm system.

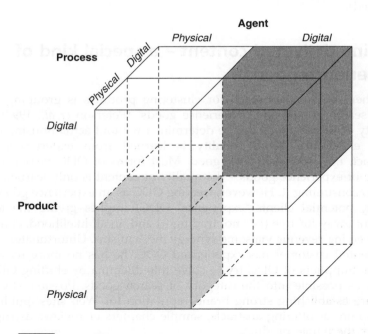

Figure 2.1
The core of electronic commerce (Choi *et al.*, 1997)

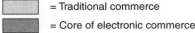

= Traditional commerce

= Core of electronic commerce

A more unusual, futuristic example is an intelligent toothbrush – this could take a sample of one's saliva, analyse selected aspects, transfer data to a connected server and start blinking in case of any unwanted bacteria.

In this context, the term 'digital' is clear. However, the term 'product' needs further clarification. As illustrated below, only some of the products falling under Choi *et al.*'s definition of digital products are also ODC.

To achieve this additional clarification of ODC, the introduction of a new dimension referring to the value of the digital product is suggested. It distinguishes 'bundled' or 'supported' versus 'unbundled' or 'stand-alone' digital products.

Traditionally, intangible goods were always bundled with some physical means. For centuries, content and physical medium were tightly linked, with the stronger value component being on the content side. Hence, the overall products were unique or reproducible only on a comparatively small scale (e.g., a theatre performance required a stage). Later storage and replication technologies have loosened the link between content and physical medium. As a result, goods with identical content appear in different forms and packages. For instance, certain songs appear on many different tapes and CD-ROMs; news items can be printed in newspapers and magazines, shown on television, presented on a radio network or be distributed via an online network such as the Internet. Thus, the importance of bundling content to a specific medium has decreased significantly with the emergence of the Internet.

The term 'ODC', as defined and applied here, is limited to 'unbundled', 'stand-alone' products consisting just of content/information. Hence, the term ODC implies that *only* the content is the object of a transaction, no physical product is shifted among suppliers, customers or other players.

The distinction between *physical* and *digital players* is more problematic. Even if players use a software-based agent, they are still a 'physical' legal entity (person, company or institution). Online shoppers are also to be viewed as physical shoppers, just not located inside the store. Following Choi *et al.*'s concept there cannot be any combination of a physical player executing a digital process; the example of the online shopper shows that running a digital process also makes the player digital. Since this still implies physical players (who may be supported by a software/digital agent), this dimension will be omitted when clarifying the term ODC.

Concerning 'processes', this author concurs with Choi *et al.*'s differentiation of *physical* and *digital processes*. In the following, the focus is only on those 'digital' processes that are part of a complete 'digital' cycle executed – or at least executable – over the electronic infrastructure. Off-line processes refer to those cases in which certain 'sub'-processes (e.g., product selection, production, market research, searches, ordering, payment, delivery or consumption) are not executed via the infrastructure.

Thus, the dimensions underpinning the proposed definition of ODC are as follows (see Figure 2.2). The 'product dimension' taken from Choi

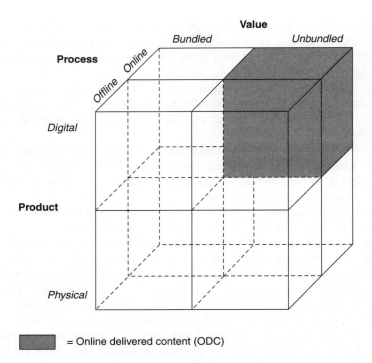

Figure 2.2
The concept of ODC

= Online delivered content (ODC)

et al. is retained. A distinction between 'bundled and unbundled value' of the product traded is added. The 'agent/player dimension' is dropped, as it has no relevance to digital players. Finally the 'process dimension' is kept, stressing that digital processes are those in which *all* sub-processes are executed online. Strictly speaking, the idea of unbundled value is implied in 'online processes' if the complete trading cycle also comprises product/value delivery. From a practical point of view, however, it is useful to stress the concept of unbundled product value separately. The following three examples further illustrate the ODC concept.

A first example is *music*. ODC refers to music that can be downloaded from the Web. Afterwards, if desired, it can be stored on a CD-ROM. ODC does *not* include the ordering of a CD-ROM to be delivered to one's home, since ODC – by definition – refers *only* to the content and excludes the need for any physical medium.

A second example is *databases* offered by online bookstores and various kinds of content offered on Web pages maintained by television stations. The information/content contained in those Web sites is a form of ODC, even if it is not usually traded separately (Loebbecke *et al.*, 1998). Possibilities for commercializing such content could be 'pay per view', 'pay per page', or 'pay per time' concepts. By trying to sell such content (instead of offering it for free and counting on positive impact on other product lines such as books or TV programmes) suppliers would rely on the actual value that potential customers associate with it (regarding pricing issues and limits of cross-subsidizing – see the next section).

The third example to be mentioned – *tickets to planes, trains or concerts* – is actually a counterexample. It clearly shows the difference between digital products as analysed by Choi *et al.* (1997) and ODC as introduced above. Choi *et al.* suggest 'digital products are not limited to information or "infotainment" products. All paper-based products, such as posters, calendars, and all sorts of tickets . . . can be converted into or replaced by digital counterparts' (1997: 20). Certainly, one can imagine ordering and receiving tickets for trains, planes or concerts online. In the near future, technology will allow individuals to print tickets (administered wherever) just as travel agencies or event agencies do today. However, for consumers this is not the full delivery cycle. Consumers do not pay for the piece of paper called a ticket, but for 'being moved' from A to B or for attending a concert/stage performance. Those services of 'being moved' or 'concert performance' are the actual values bought, and these will never be delivered via any technical infrastructure (at least not within the limits of current imagination). Therefore, a ticket, even if bought and – with regard to the specific piece of paper – delivered over the Web does not represent unbundled, stand-alone value of content. It does not belong to ODC as understood in this chapter. (For reasons of simplicity, this illustration leaves out the possibility of reselling a ticket and thus giving it a monetary function.)

Online delivered content – characteristics and classification

In general, ODC is characterized by three fundamental attributes (Choi *et al.*, 1997; Goldfinger, 1997):

1 *Indestructibility/non-subtractivity*. The same ODC can be consumed repetitively either by the same consumer or by a different one. Consumption by one person does not reduce anyone else's consumption.
2 *Transmutability*. ODC is easy to modify, thus leading to enormous product differentiation and customization.
3 *Reproducibility*. Fast and cheap reproducibility raises – among other aspects – issues of copyright protection and economies of scale.

As a consequence of these characteristics, exclusivity of ODC may be difficult to durably maintain. Sharing may be simultaneous or sequential and affects the allocation of property rights. While sellers of physical goods lose their property right, a seller of ODC may continue to hold it. Even 'illegally sharing' ODC often causes positive network externalities, which may even exceed the cost of sharing if caught. Once ODC has positive network externalities, control over reproduction and sharing is the primary objective of copyright protection.

Related to the issue of externalities is the issue of value generation. Often there is no direct link between a transaction and the generation of value. Furthermore, ODC value can hardly be measured solely in monetary terms. For instance, the appreciation of free television broadcasts could be measured in terms of viewing time and numbers, whilst appreciation of academic papers (increasingly provided as ODC) may be measured in terms of the number of citations. Indirect value creation and the related problem of ODC value measurement lead to the problem of adequately pricing ODC (discussed later in this chapter).

A next step is to *classify* ODC products, i.e., to look at different criteria for further distinguishing homogeneous kinds of products *within* the still rather broad category of ODC. Five dimensions for classifying general digital products are outlined by Choi *et al.* (1997): 'transfer mode', 'timeliness', 'intensity in use', 'operational usage' and 'externalities'. These are analysed below for their relevance to ODC.

Transfer mode: delivered versus interactive products

ODC is, by definition, delivered. However, the differentiation between delivered and interactive transfer mode is becoming increasingly difficult. Notwithstanding, as long as content consumption is initiated based on a 'pull-approach', this implies a certain degree of interactivity. Therefore, this chapter prefers to distinguish between ODC based on push- and on pull-approaches. Further, those ODC products delivered via a pull-approach can be further differentiated based on the degree of customization resulting from interactive communication. Clearly, these two dimensions are highly interdependent: push-based delivery excludes strong customization based on interactive communication; pull-based delivery allows for all degrees of customization.

Timeliness: time-dependence versus time-independence

ODC may be very time-dependent (e.g., stock market information), rather time-independent (e.g., dictionary information), or somewhere in the middle, e.g., street maps for drivers, hotel information and phone numbers. The criterion of 'timeliness' will be important for identifying homogeneous packages of ODC to be traded based on consistent business models.

Intensity in use: single-use versus multiple-use products

Similar to the previous criterion, 'intensity in use' is an important aspect for further classifying ODC. There is a significant overlap between 'timeliness' and 'intensity in use' – only rather time-independent ODC will be used more frequently, i.e., more intensively. However, the two criteria have different implications for trading.

Operational usage: executable program versus fixed document

Fixed documents delivered electronically are ODC. Executable programs are only counted as ODC if their focus is on the content execution provides. It may well be that a certain form of delivering content includes executable components. For instance, whenever users can determine the search function, the content includes some operational features in addition to the content in the narrow sense of the word.

Externalities: positive versus negative

Externalities refer to economic consequences that are not fully accounted for by the price or market system. Different kinds of externalities are a valid criterion for further classifying ODC. For example, positive network externalities imply that the value of the product increases the more people use it (e.g., academic papers, awareness-raising content about medical innovations). Negative externalities occur when the use of ODC is a zero-sum game. This means that whenever someone gains (from consuming ODC), someone else loses. Examples include all kinds of competitive content, e.g., for information related to research and development (R&D).

Online delivered content – issues of pricing

Conventional pricing and transaction mechanisms are barely suitable for capturing the economic value of ODC. The price of a product normally consists of three elements: production (and logistics) costs, co-ordination costs and the profit margin (Benjamin and Wigand, 1995). Co-ordination costs include the transaction (or governance) costs of all the information processing necessary to co-ordinate the work of people and machines that perform the primary processes (Malone *et al.*, 1987). It is now becoming clear that – with variable production (and logistics) costs near zero, drastically reduced transactions costs resulting from information and communication technology (ICT) usage and eroding profit margins in current business models – new concepts have to be put in place for determining ODC prices.

Production costs cannot be used as a guideline for pricing since there is no link between input and output. Mass consumption does not require mass production. Economies of scale are determined by consumption, not by production. Economies of scale in ODC production are limited, but economies of scale in ODC distribution can be significant owing to a combination of high fixed costs of creating the necessary infrastructure and low variable costs of using it. Economies of scale in distribution are accentuated by consumption characteristics: consumers tend to use the supplier with the largest variety even though they typically take advantage of less than 5 per cent of the choice (Goldfinger, 1994).

Traditionally the pricing of content has been based on the delivery medium – mostly measured in convenience – rather than on actual quality (Goldfinger, 1997). For instance, the price of a book depends heavily on its printing quality and the number of pages, while the price for an excellent book is often the same as for a poor one. Electronic trading in ODC implies unbundling: content can be priced separately from the medium, allowing for price differentiation based on the estimated value of the content. The unbundling, however, also raises problems. Administration becomes more complex, and cross-subsidies between profitable and non-profitable (but nonetheless desirable) content on offer diminish.

A consumer's willingness to pay is often influenced by the consumption or non-consumption of other consumers. Accordingly, it is not an adequate approach to assess the value of ODC, given the ease of replication/sharing and associated externalities. Further, it is often difficult for the customer to determine whether it is worthwhile to obtain a given 'piece of ODC' without knowing its content (Schlee, 1996).

Furthermore, the pricing of ODC raises the fundamental issue of inherent volatility of valuation when the value of ODC is highly time-sensitive. For example, stock market information may be worth millions in the morning and have little value in the afternoon.

The range of ODC pricing schemes is becoming broader and more sophisticated. The Internet provides a variety of possibilities for selling, sharing and giving away. Moreover, consumers can also be charged based on the actual 'use of ODC' or based on fixed access charges. In addition, pricing models may imply giving actual goods away for free and then charging for complementary services, updates and so on.

Offering ODC over an extended period of time may lead to the establishment of electronic communities. Following Armstrong and Hagel (1996), electronic communities are likely to create value in five different ways: usage fees, content fees, transactions (commissions), advertising and synergies with other parts of the business. Translating these opportunities for income to the narrower defined area of ODC, *usage fees* could be in the form of 'fixed subscriptions', 'paying per page' or 'paying per time period', independent of the quality of the content. *Content fees* would most likely be based on 'fixed amounts per page', but should tackle the issue of valuing the content (particularly for quality or relevance). *Commissions and advertising income* are triggered by attractive ODC on display. Strictly speaking, however, the subsequent income would not stem from ODC, but from either attracting customers to a page regardless of its content or from offering some 'empty space' for third party advertising in addition to the actual ODC offered (Loebbecke *et al.*, 1998).

Economists are developing theoretical solutions to the problem areas mentioned. However, some of the mechanisms developed (e.g., MacKie-Mason and Varian, 1995) demand an enormous amount of data, thus questioning the trade-off between allocative efficiency and operational cost-effectiveness (Mitchell and Vogelsang, 1991).

Online delivered content – impacts of abundance

While conventional logic of economics is concerned with scarcity, the dematerialization logic inherent in ODC is concerned with abundance (Goldfinger, 1997). ODC is extremely cheap to replicate and is not eliminated through consumption (i.e., it has non-subtractivity). The resulting abundance of production is followed by the abundance of accumulation leading to a dramatically expanding imbalance between supply and demand. Efficient management of ODC overload requires yet more information/content. Information about information is a growing business.

Abundance and resulting ODC overload – the huge variety of ODC available to almost everybody – confront consumers with a dilemma. Customers want to take advantage of the increased choice of ODC and, at the same time, they seek to minimize the costs of searching. In order to respond to the first objective, new modes of consumption have emerged: 'zapping', 'browsing' or 'surfing'. These are characterized by a short attention span, latency, high frequency of switching and capriciousness. The distinction between consumption and non-consumption becomes difficult, rendering pricing problems even more intractable. The expanded choice of content makes consumer choice more difficult, thus continuously raising the cost of acquiring information about the content. To minimize these costs, choice is increasingly determined by criteria other than product characteristics, e.g., brand familiarity or fashion (Goldfinger, 1997).

The traditional rationale for the existence of companies, as articulated by Coase and others, is the minimization of transaction costs (Coase, 1974; Williamson and Winter, 1993). This analysis is no longer generally valid. Not only has ICT dramatically reduced transaction costs, but also the growing volume and importance of ICT-based intangible assets and artefacts has changed the nature of markets (Peterson *et al.*, 1997).

While traditional inter-firm linkages may be modelled by input–output analyses to measure the economic impact of each player in an inter-organizational value chain or network, the intangible economy introduces another linkage among companies – the 'monitoring' linkage (Goldfinger, 1997). Low transaction costs lead to an excessive volume of transactions that generate 'noise' rather than useful content. An abundance of products and services stimulates the development of activities whose purpose is to monitor, evaluate and explain their characteristics and performance.

Case studies: the publishing industry

The following two case studies analyse the situation of and the business implications for specialized, traditional, medium-sized publishers on the verge of entering the ODC business. As such, they help to put some of the theory discussed above into practice.

Krak – a Danish directory publisher

This case study of Krak, a Danish directory publisher, focuses on a special segment of ODC publishing (see Loebbecke, 1999a). Directory publishers such as Krak are somewhat different from other publishers that are considering going online – their traditional business model relies heavily on advertising-based income.

Krak's core business (since 1770) has been business information, starting with basic trade information that is now enriched with more detail such as names of board members and directors, key figures and customers. Another important product line is city and country maps for all over Denmark and a complete street-name index.

Krak's publishing is built on a database that serves their various product lines. Examples are: their original business directory, *Krak's Vejviser* (which contains entries for about 60 000 companies); a CD-ROM version (*Krak Direct*); Krak's *Export Directory of Denmark*; sector-orientated catalogues (for instance for the metal industry, construction, graphics and marketing, data/IT, textiles and transportation); their *Foundation Directory*; a *Farm and Forest Directory*; and *Krak's Blue Book* (a 'Who's Who' type document). Krak also produces city maps and tourist guides. However, Krak sells only its maps, *Krak Direct*, the *Foundation Directory*, the *Farms and Forests Directory* and *Krak's Blue Book*. The other products are given away free and the business model relies on advertising in the reference guides to cover costs and profits.

Today, the database consists of 'self-gathered' as well as purchased data. Of the 60 000 data records documented in the printed version of the business directory, only about 10 per cent are purchased. Of the 400 000 records represented in the online version, almost 80 per cent are acquired externally and then improved internally by Krak. This differentiation is crucial when it comes to developing a sustainable business model for trading in ODC. Repurposed information must also be rethought for the Web. Indeed, Krak has substantially supplemented its database to meet the demands of Web users. While the content base is Krak's most important business asset, the company credits four other factors for its position in the Danish market: (1) the company's 200-year tradition; (2) its brand name and reputation; (3) its sales force; and (4) the quality of its information.

Towards electronic trading in ODC

Krak perceives a key problem in selling its database as ODC – most of the content in its traditional printed package has already been given away free (against advertising income). Thus, the company decided to start by developing a business model that exploits various trajectories of business on the Internet in order to build market share and gain experience for the subsequent approach of electronically trading in ODC.

As of early 1999, 25 per cent of Krak's total income is generated from new media (CD-ROM and Internet). About 35 per cent of this comes from selling information goods – either packaged on CD-ROM or paper-based – and processing those transactions directly over the Web. Of the remaining 65 per cent of Krak's new-media-related income, 30 per cent stems from selling advertisements on the Web and 70 per cent from designing and maintaining home pages for business customers. Important business areas of Krak's Internet section include: Internet-related activities such as in-house development of Web sites, providing Internet services under the domain 'www.krak.dk', customer database solutions and e-commerce sites for customers.

The change in business focus from selling content and advertise-ments to selling Web site design and maintenance seems to have evolved naturally. The business concept of traditional directory publishing has always been to sell advertising space in the publications. Online-advertising sales, however, presented Krak with a business opportunity. When the directories were put on the Internet, some of the advertisements had to be made Web-site-compatible. Krak's advertisers soon realized that adverts on the Web should also be linked to profes-sional company home pages, and they began to ask Krak for design suggestions, followed shortly by requests for programming and main-tenance.

In addition to its Web services, Krak still sells adverts in its electronic directories. The income that is generated from these sales has three components (in 1999 prices):

1 Selling banner advertisements and thus offering marketing for busi-ness customers. The price for having a banner is either a fixed price per year based on the location of the banner, or DKK0.15 per click (page impression).
2 Selling links. In particular, having those companies pay DKK1000.00 per year to link from their sites to Krak maps.
3 Showing business locations on the Krak maps, costing DKK40 000 per company per year.

Krak's Internet section also offers several Krak products – maps, the business directory, the export directory and the coupon catalogue – directly on the Web. In 1999, the company made about 1 per cent of its total turnover from selling its traditional printed products in its online shop. Thus far, the Internet business has not led to decreasing sales in traditional outlets. On the contrary, actual sales via traditional channels have increased slightly since the products have also been sold via the online storefront.

The additional distribution channel for Krak information services has several other implications for the company. Initially, Krak updated the Internet site only once a month. At that time, it outsourced Web design and database design, and Krak's sales force sold Internet adverts to be placed in special sub-domains under Krak's home page. Later, as the company began selling products on the Web, the yearly information update that had sufficed for paper, and the monthly update that worked when Krak began its Internet service, had to be changed into an almost real-time operation. New figures are incorporated and visible on the Web maps once a month. Directories are updated once a week. Needless to say, that requires a significantly higher level of staffing. Almost constant updating also puts additional pressure on the approximately twenty employees who are involved in maintaining the core database, but who are not members of the Internet section.

Krak's next ODC product will be different from its traditional line of goods. The company has developed a search engine that is integrated into its Web site. This search engine can make the Krak site a portal to the business sites linked to it through its Internet services business and through its advertising sales. Krak plans a major marketing campaign to herald the benefits of the search engine – bringing users to the site and from the search engine to the businesses connected to it. The original business concept was to finance the marketing campaign and the follow-up maintenance of the search service by charging for featured search words and banner advertisements. However, over time, Krak has recognized that this approach will not work because of an insufficient number of listings.

Lessons learned

One crucial difference between directory publishers and other publishers has to be kept in mind: in most instances, directory publishers give their printed products away for free, based on a business model that generates income from selling advertising space. Hence the shift to ODC could be considered comparatively minor – most content on the Web is provided free. Where cost recovery is anticipated, it is expected to come from advertising income (Choi *et al.*, 1997).

Offering content online for free has become extremely popular in the Internet era. However, only a few companies are prepared to take advantage of their vast content archives to participate in electronic trading, i.e., they are aiming at 'making money' from it. In the near future, new market structures will emerge as a consequence of the Internet (or whatever may succeed it) and of the feasibility of providing electronic content commercially. The field of directory and reference publishing provides enormous opportunities for originality and creativity. New products may still be invented even though competition is constantly growing and the field is populated with more publishers and more innovative products than ever before.

The endless possibilities of electronic formats have opened the directory business anew. In acknowledging these new possibilities it is very important not to lose sight of market needs and of the editorial function, both of which have brought success in the past. Technology will continue to change and, in future years, today's electronic formats will look archaic. The challenge is to create content for the future inspired by the current technology. Krak has done that, and its lessons are worth heeding.

Rentrop – a German publisher of consultative journalism

This case of ODC focuses on a quite different area of publishing (see Loebbecke and Powell, 1999). Founded in 1975, Rentrop Publishing (RP) is headquartered in Bonn, Germany. With a stable of about 300 authors and 160 other employees, RP is one of the most important German business-focused publishers. It only disseminates content that is exclusively written for RP. RP's core business is consultative journalism for entrepreneurs and individuals with entrepreneurial responsibilities. Traditionally, the company has considered printed media as the only possible means of conveying valuable know-how and consulting at fair prices. RP's product range includes magazines, loose-leaf services, newsletters and books. Typically, books cover topics such as public speaking, money management, taxation and social security, human resources and personnel law.

The RP consulting pyramid (see Figure 2.3) is at the core of RP's publishing philosophy. Classical one-to-one consulting services offered by consulting companies at a cost of around DM2000 per day are judged to be prohibitive for young entrepreneurs. Even consulting seminars with about ten participants and costs of about DM800 per head per day are considered too expensive. RP therefore concludes that the only afford-able possibility in which a start-up company can obtain appropriate consulting services is by buying a specialized publication (published consulting) – where the total cost for the expert advice is shared by a large number of interested parties (see Gumpert, 1982).

Over the past twenty years, RP has achieved rapid growth through expansion on the basis of a holding-structure organization. This has allowed the company to develop from its core business of being a specialized publisher into an internationally operating publishing and media group.

In its effort to expand internationally, RP focuses on the concept of licensing certain products. In Europe, various RP consulting products have been available for a number of years, partly as licensed products. Entry into the US market was achieved through joint ventures with

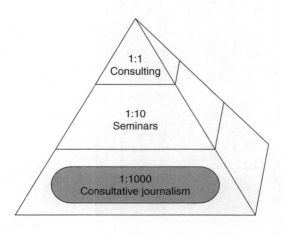

Figure 2.3
Rentrop consulting pyramid (Rentrop, 1997)

renowned partners and with products that had already been successful in Europe. In 1997, with around 600 employees and roughly 1000 authors, RP achieved a turnover of about EURO80 million in seven countries. The Internet offers the possibility to develop and market new products – ODC – to new customers.

Towards electronic trading in ODC

The entry into electronic trading in ODC could enable RP to further extend its successfully applied business concept of the consulting pyramid. By offering products and services electronically, most likely via the Internet, this would be equivalent to the expansion of their current pyramid – currently consisting of three layers – by an additional base layer (see Figure 2.4). ODC (consulting provision) via the Internet could vastly increase the number of potential customers per service to approximately 100 000. In spite of these numbers, RP is currently still unsure about the expected role of the Internet on its business model in the near future.

In its traditional business model, RP's core competence is the creation and provision of first-class, focused, almost unique content. In order successfully to distribute its product lines and, of course, also to provide appropriate customer support, RP needs to continue operating as a publishing house.

Potential roles in electronic trading in ODC

In order to determine the best opportunities, it is useful to analyse various activities potentially to be performed by RP in the context of electronic trading in ODC. The following value chain outlined for the electronic publishing (EP) trade differentiates between two layers (see Figure 2.5; for the original value chain concept see Porter, 1985; Porter and Millar, 1985). The content-related layer addresses 'content creation', 'content packaging' and 'market making'. The infrastructure-related layer comprises 'transportation', 'delivery support' and 'end user interfaces'.

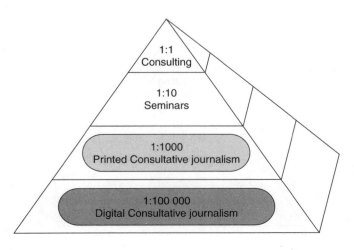

Figure 2.4
Rentrop consulting pyramid (adapted from Rentrop, 1997)

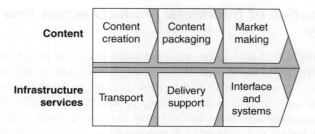

Figure 2.5
Electronic publishing
value chain
(European
Commission, 1996)

Within this framework, a report from the European Commission (1996) suggests the following strategic roles to be played (see Figure 2.6):

- Online network. Managing a full electronic marketplace.
- Community organizer. Focusing on an interest-centred target group.
- Interactive studio. Creating content with new levels of functionality.
- Content rights agency. Managing rights and matching content to market needs.
- Platform provider. Creating an end-to-end easy to use technical platform for authors, publishers and/or end users.

For a mid-sized, content-focused, traditional publisher like RP, however, none of these specific roles look attractive. RP, in conjunction with its editors, sees its strengths in the fields of 'Content Creation', 'Content Packaging' and 'Market Making'. RP aims at transferring its current core competencies into the ODC area. However, physical distribution, technical delivery support, and interface design are – on a small scale – considered barely feasible and not profitable. The outsourcing strategy already in place in the conventional business should certainly be continued for necessary competencies in the EP era, such as cryptography, platform management, billing, inter-publisher clearing house functions and vendor transactions management (Cronin, 1995). If RP becomes active on the Internet with its products, it will clearly focus on ODC creation and packaging.

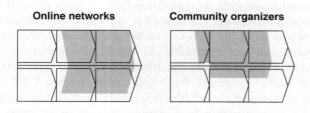

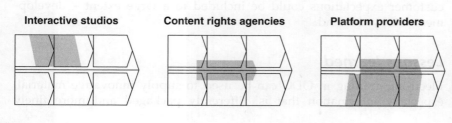

Figure 2.6
Strategic roles in
electronic publishing
(European
Commission, 1996)

Digitalization of traditional products versus new products

Another angle that should be analysed is the choice of products for ODC. Importantly, RP is faced with the decision of whether to adjust and digitize existing products or to create new content to be delivered online.

The first option is to take existing products, especially information letters, magazines and loose leaflets, and to prepare them (without significantly changing the content) for presentation, trading and distribution on the Web. While this approach is comparatively inexpensive and technically not demanding (Ellsworth and Ellsworth, 1996), RP awaits the answers to three major questions:

1 Is there a sufficient interest from its customers in ODC? (How soon will current customers become active on the Web?)
2 Will the issue of copyright protection have a significantly stronger negative impact on ODC than it has on print media?
3 Will the issue of product-line cannibalization reduce print media sales or can separate customer groups be maintained for the same product offered through different media?

Currently, except perhaps for university graduates considering starting their own business, the majority of RP's customers are not Internet users. However, RP expects this to change within the next two years. More importantly, RP sees the problems of copyright protection and the issue of forbidden reselling of digital products. While technologies to support both issues are under development (Kalakota and Whinston, 1996), they are not yet available. The question – what degree technical solutions will offer sufficient protection? – is still under debate. These issues are particularly relevant if RP digitizes existing products, since this could increase the general risk of product-line cannibalization. Furthermore, even though copyright protection may become less of a technical problem in the near future, there is no regulation that limits reading (Choi et al., 1997) and the marginal cost to further disperse ODC is negligible.

The alternative option is to develop a separate ODC business line. RP could focus on leveraging its core competencies from print. Its new business line would consist only of new ODC developed by additional editors and their teams in order to serve rather diverse customer needs. Since ODC delivery costs are negligible, RP could aim at developing legislation- and culture-independent products attractive to potential customers around the world. Further, the significantly higher ODC interaction potential – in comparison with conventional publishing – would allow more precise customization to customer needs (Gerdy, 1996). Therefore, customer expectations could be included to a large extent – development-led by demand.

Lessons learned

Electronic trading in ODC can be used to supply innovative material, especially information that is differently packaged and more finely targeted. It combines communication with content, thus leading to higher quality and added value for customers. Furthermore, ODC customers are much more in control of how much and what kind of content they want to obtain. When substituting print products by ODC, customers will request additional value such as availability (e.g., newest information, access to data from any location), format (e.g., multimedia such as video clips and sound), transparency and interactivity (e.g., user-friendly downloading and search functions), as well as innovative content. These ideas are shown in Figure 2.7.

Whereas in many business areas the significance of time and speed will further increase, this is not likely to be the case for many of RP's current products. Almost the same applies to video and sound elements. The company sees much more ODC market potential in offering increased interactivity – providing its customers with access to various consulting services (e.g., extended hotline features) as well as to detailed archives equipped with intelligent search agents. As RP aims at leveraging its core competencies into electronic trading in ODC, the company sees a definite need to create innovative content. Otherwise, it assesses the risk of cannibalization as higher than the additional profit potential.

Last, but not least, RP would need to adapt the role of revenues from advertising in its cost–benefit calculations to the common market principles of electronic trading in ODC. One of the most important sources of revenue in electronic commerce is the selling of advertising space (Choi *et al.*, 1997). RP has advertising in only three of its publications. However, selling advertising space is difficult since RP sells more than 98 per cent of its publications directly to a comparatively small customer group. As long as RP keeps its business model of selling published consulting targeted to a comparatively small customer group, trading in ODC will not fundamentally change the lack of attractiveness for advertisers.

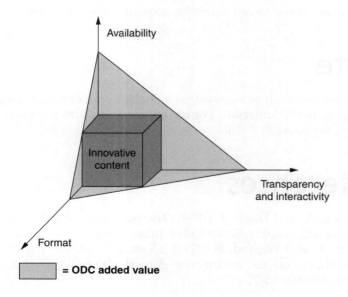

Figure 2.7
Dimensions of ODC added value

Conclusions

This chapter makes the point that within the wide field of e-commerce there are many fundamentally different products – both physical and digital – traded via various business models. One type of product defined here – online delivered content (ODC) – is particular interesting. ODC is a good that is manufactured, delivered, supported and consumed via the Internet or similar networks. Typical examples of OCD are music, information and expert knowledge.

Traditional economic models based on scarcity and uniqueness leading to a market based on demand and supply do not apply to these types of products. Once created, ODC is extremely easy/cheap to replicate. Furthermore, distribution costs are almost zero, and most other transaction costs – except perhaps marketing and sales – barely exist.

ODC characteristics and classification criteria have been discussed in some detail in this chapter. The purpose is to warrant a careful investigation of the nature of ODC. Such an investigation is important either for preparing a business plan for a new offering or researching the nature of a particular ODC.

While the free offering of ODC has become extremely popular in the Internet arena, only a few companies have started trading. The solutions offered by two companies have been briefly discussed in the chapter. Both of these companies have taken advantage of their existing content archives and have taken the first steps towards offering customers (new as well as established) the possibilities of buying ODC. This raises a number of questions about pricing mechanisms, security, protection of intellectual property rights and so on, for which solutions still have to be found in order to make ODC a viable business proposition. Answers to those questions promise significant theoretical advancement and attractive business opportunities. With the steadily increasing volume of material on the Web – information, content and knowledge – it seems an economic waste to not profitably exploit these untapped resources.

Note

The author gratefully acknowledges valuable comments and suggestions from Niels Bjørn-Andersen. For an earlier and shorter version of this text see Loebbecke (1999b).

References

Armstrong, A. and Hagel, J. (1996). The real value of online communities. *Harvard Business Review*, May–June, 134–41.

Benjamin, R. and Wigand, B. (1995). Electronic markets and the virtual value chains on the Information Superhighway. *Sloan Management Review*, Winter, 62–72.

Choi, S.-Y., Stahl, D. and Whinston, A. (1997). *The Economics of Electronic Commerce.* Macmillan Technical Publishing.

Coase, R. (1974). The market for goods and the market for ideas. *American Economic Review*, **64**, 384–91.

Cronin, M. (1995). *Doing More Business on the Internet: how the Electronic Highway is transforming American companies.* Van Nostrand Reinhold.

Ellsworth, J. and Ellsworth, M. (1996). *The New Internet Business Book.* John Wiley and Sons.

European Commission (1996). *Strategic Developments for the European Publishing Industry Towards the Year 2000 – Europe's multimedia challenge.* DG XIII/E. European Commission.

Gerdy, G. (1996). Dow Jones business information services on the Internet. In M. Cronin, ed., *The Internet Strategy Handbook.* Harvard Business School Press, pp. 51–68.

Goldfinger, C. (1994). *L'utile et le futile, l'economie de l'immatériél.* Editions Odile Jacob.

Goldfinger, C. (1997). Intangible economy and its implications for statistics and statisticians. *International Statistical Review*, **65**, 191–220.

Goldfinger, C. (1998). Trading intangible goods. *Workshop on Electronic Commerce of Intangible Goods.* European Commission.

Gumpert, D. (1982). Entrepreneurship: a new literature begins. *Harvard Business Review*, March–April, 50–60.

Kalakota, R. and Whinston, A. (1996). *Electronic Commerce: a manager's guide.* Addison-Wesley.

Levitt, T. (1981). Marketing intangible products and product intangibles. *Harvard Business Review*, May–June, 95–102.

Loebbecke, C. (1999a). A case study at the reference frontier. *Journal of Electronic Publishing*, **4**, 4, available online.
http://www.press.umich.edu/jep/04-04/loebbecke.html

Loebbecke, C. (1999b). Electronic trading in online delivered content. *Proceedings of the Thirty-Second Hawaii International Conference on Systems Sciences*, Maui, Hawaii.

Loebbecke, C. and Powell, P. (1999). Electronic Publishing: assessing opportunities and risks. *International Journal of Information Management*, **19**, 293–303.

Loebbecke, C., Powell, P. and Trilling, S. (1998). Investigating the worth of Internet advertising. *International Journal of Information Management*, **18**, 181–93.

MacKie-Mason, J. and Varian, H. (1995). Pricing the Internet. In B. Kahn and J. Keller, eds, *Public Access to the Internet.* Prentice Hall.

Malone, T., Yates, J. and Benjamin, R. (1987). The logic of electronic markets. *Harvard Business Review*, May–June, 166–72.

Meinkoehn, F. (1998). Electronic trade of intangible commodities: a technological and legal challenge. In P. Timmers, B. Stanford-Smith and P. Kidd, eds, *Electronic Commerce: opening up new opportunities for business.* Cheshire-Hensbury, pp. 81–86.

Mitchell, B. and Vogelsang, I. (1991). *Telecommunications Pricing.* Cambridge University Press.

Peterson, R., Balasubramanian, S. and Bronnenberg, B. (1997). Exploring the implications of the Internet for marketing. *Journal of the Academy of Marketing Science*, **25**, 329–46.

Porter, M. (1985). *Competitive Advantage*. Free Press.

Porter, M. and Millar, V. (1985). How information gives you competitive advantage. *Harvard Business Review*, July–August, 149–60.

Rentrop, N. (1997). *Der Verlag, der Sie berät*. Rentrop Company Brochure.

Schlee, E. (1996). The value of information about product quality. *RAND Journal of Economics*, **27**, 803–15.

Wang, R., Lee, Y., Pipino, L. and Strong, D. (1998). Manage your information as a product. *Sloan Management Review*, Summer, 95–105.

Williamson, O. and Winter, S. (1993). *The Nature of the Firm*. Oxford University Press.

3
Digital intermediation in electronic commerce – the eBay model

Alina N. Chircu and Robert J. Kauffman

Introduction

Interactions between buyers and sellers in a market normally reflect the existence of a *transaction process*, in which goods or services are exchanged between customers and suppliers (Bakos, 1991). This process may involve none, one or several intermediaries, depending on the kind of goods or services that are involved in the transaction and other situational factors (see Figure 3.1).

New technologies for electronic commerce on the Internet dramatically change the spectrum of possibilities for making transactions in the marketplace. Such technologies also change the manner in which the various players are able to interact (Rayport and Sviokla, 1994; Benjamin and Wigand, 1995; Whinston et al., 1997). Consider such well-known players in electronic commerce as Priceline.com, Amazon.com and eBay (see Appendix 3.1 at the end of this chapter for information on all

Figure 3.1
The transaction process

organizations mentioned). Priceline.com provides a buyer-driven market-place for leisure travel services, putting some control over pricing back into the hands of the consumer. Amazon.com embeds collaborative filtering technology that enables the 'right' book titles to be shown to the 'right' potential buyers, in effect 'digitizing' the expertise the firm has with respect to the market for books and consumer demand. In addition, eBay aims to improve market liquidity for collectible goods, which do not always transact as easily as other commodity goods such as books, CDs and new cars. Investors, recognizing the basis for a new age of industrial transformation, have conferred huge (cynics would say 'unwarranted') value upon the stocks of these firms.

In fact, David Baltaxe, industry analyst for the Web-based e-journal, *Current Analysis*, has noted the high levels of investor exuberance, but he also cautions:

> You have no idea how many companies come in with a five-minute pitch: 'We want to be the eBay of blank.' Just fill in the blank for a country. That's the entire business plan. (Baltaxe, 1999)

Even with Baltaxe's words ringing in our ears, still all the market indicators point toward the high values that the new forms of digital intermediation will achieve in the financial marketplace. This is evidenced by the recent market capitalization of some of the best known firms – even though there may not be a rational basis for such value estimates of a single firm in the traditional terms an investment banker might understand (see Table 3.1).

In this rapidly changing environment of innovation, there are many products and services that could not be offered in the way they are offered today without these technologies. Along with eBay, First Auction, Onsale.com and UBid amongst others – the new electronic consumer auction markets of the Internet – come to mind. These digital intermediaries create opportunities for transactions to occur that simply did not previously exist in the marketplace (Bailey and Bakos, 1997). They also offer – and sometimes require – new roles not previously taken on by intermediaries. Furthermore, the traditional processes associated with transacting may be fundamentally changed. As a result, some existing intermediaries may see their roles threatened by new competitors that have appeared in the market. There are also many opportunities for new, IT-focused middlemen (Bakos, 1998; Stepanek, 1998).

Although the buying and selling process may be transformed, at the time of writing this chapter there still were few cases in which Internet intermediaries provided completely new products and services to the market. Instead, most intermediaries support the interaction of buyers and sellers on the Internet. As a result, we see the emergence of a new organizational form that moves in to fill a gap in the existing organization of various industries: the *digital intermediary* or *cybermediary* (Sarkar *et al.*, 1996; Kane, 1999b). This digital support role – emphasizing *buyer/seller intermediation* – generally is not immediately assumed by traditional players and, as a result, we often see new entrants to the market acting in this capacity.

Table 3.1 Stock price ranges and market capitalizations of leading e-commerce firms (27 May 1999)

Intermediation niche Firm names	52-week stock price range ($)		Market capitalization (Millions of US$)
	Low	*High*	
Bookselling Intermediaries			
Amazon.com	13.37	221.25	18 799.80 (@115 1/4 per share)
BarnesandNoble.com	22.75*	26.50*	615.62 (@24 5/8 per share)
Electronic Auction Market Intermediaries			
eBay	8.43	234.00	21 259.82 (@169 3/4 per share)
OnSale.com	10.62	108.00	335.80 (@17 1/2 per share)
Priceline.com	58.00	165.00	15 584.04 (@109 1/8 per share)
Sotheby's Holdings	15.00	47.00	2032.44 (@35 7/16 per share)
UBid	30.00	189.00	312.40 (@35 1/16 per share)
Electronic Brokerage Intermediaries			
Ameritrade	5.62	188.37	4996.83 (@85 5/16 per share)
DLJDirect.com	28.25*	45.62*	3251.25 (@38 1/4 per share)
E*Trade	2.50	72.25	9861.42 (@42 9/32 per share)
Charles Schwab	18.50	155.00	42 438.49 (@104 7/16 per share)
Miscellaneous Internet Firms			
AutoByTel (automobiles)	15.50	58.00	387.31 (@21 11/16 per share)
CDNow (compact disks)	7.00	39.25	503.07 (@17 1/16 per share)
DoubleClick (advertising)	6.75	176.00	3463.25 (@87 1/2 per share)
MarketWatch (financial data)	45.50	130.00	587.50 (@50 per share)
Net Perceptions (personalization)	18.50*	35.00*	351.80 (@16 1/2 per share)
Preview Travel (travel reservations)	9.75	44.00	236.34 (@17 7/16 per share)

- Certain Low and High prices (those marked with *) do not reflect a 52-week period. The initial public offering (IPO) of DLJDirect.com occurred on Wednesday, 25 May 1999. Net Perceptions' IPO is similarly recent; it occurred on Friday, 23 April 1999. BarnesandNoble.com completed its IPO offering on 25 May 1999.
- The traditional basis for evaluating equity prices fails in the case of Internet stocks. Equity values are typically computed using two bases: discounted current and future earnings and the present value of growth opportunities (PVGO). Since future growth opportunities are so uncertain for the companies listed, one expects to see large variances in Internet firm asset prices over time. The price ranges that are observed indicate the extent to which variations in value are observed, driven to a large extent by under-informed (but certainly interested) investors with 'great expectations' of performance. For additional information on equity evaluation in this area, the interested reader should see Burnham (1999).

Source: Castonguay (1999); PR Newswire (1999); Quicken Excite (1999).

Analysing digital intermediation

According to the Gartner Group, there were about 300 electronic market-places operating on the Internet in 1999, but there are predicted to be around 100 000 by the year 2001 (Kane, 1999a). With such growth expected, what kinds of benefits will digital intermediaries create along the way? These include: matching buyers with suppliers, providing a level of trust that no other party to the transaction can deliver, offering product-related and transactional expertise and informational support, and supplying assurance that transactions are successfully completed (Bakos, 1998). However, a number of interesting questions are posed by these new players. Can digital intermediaries on the Internet successfully compete with more established players in the marketplace? What kinds of strategies might they bring to bear in order to be successful? Is the role of the cybermediary defensible in most marketplaces? If so, then what theories, frameworks and perspectives are appropriate to help senior managers develop useful ways to think about the issues that their companies must confront in this arena?

We will argue that *digital intermediaries* – in their roles as new Internet-focused competitors – can apply various approaches to achieve short-run competitive advantage and maintain long-run competitive parity. However, there are very few strategies that will provide sustainable competitive advantage. Unfortunately for many firms, long-run competitive advantage is likely to be based more on how well these Internet intermediaries leverage their *first-mover advantage*, 'stealing the march' (while established market leaders are still only dimly aware of the competitive threats) and then creating a foundation for longer-term gains. Let us continue by formulating a basis for analysing the strategies of digital intermediaries. Here we present a framework that describes the context of competition among traditional and digital intermediaries. We begin by laying out the core terminology we will use in the remainder of this chapter.

Intermediation 101

Intermediation is the process by which a firm, acting as the agent of an individual or another firm (a buyer or a seller), creates value by leveraging its middleman position to foster communication with other agents in the marketplace that will lead to exchange transactions. There are a number of roles that an intermediary can play that lead to the creation of value in the marketplace. They include: *aggregation of information* on buyers, suppliers and products; *facilitation of search* for appropriate products; *reduction of information asymmetries* through the provision of product and transactional expertise; *matching buyers and sellers* for transactions; and *trust provision* to the marketplace to enhance transactability (Bakos, 1998; Chircu and Kauffman, 1999a).

Traditional and digital intermediaries

We find that it is useful for analytical precision to distinguish among several different kinds of intermediaries. *Traditional intermediaries*, for instance, tend to rely upon their capabilities to deliver products to customers efficiently and to foster close interactions and communication with customers. In contrast, *digital intermediaries* tend to rely upon the communication-enhancing capabilities of the Internet, and through it are able to project aggregation, expertise, search, facilitation, matching and settlement capabilities into the virtual space of the new marketplace.

Linking intermediaries and information intermediaries

The technology-enhanced version of intermediation itself involves two somewhat different functions:

- a *linking function*, which enables relationships between buyers and suppliers to be created for transactions involving physical goods and services;
- an *information function*, enhancing the movement of information between counterparties in a transaction, creating trust and increasing the likelihood of transactional liquidity.

These different functions give rise to two distinctly different kinds of digital intermediaries that one can observe in the marketplace. A *digital linking intermediary* typically profits by reducing the transaction costs associated with the life cycle of a transaction that involves the exchange of goods or services. Insight.com is an example of such an intermediary. Insight advertises in such well-known computer industry periodicals as *Computer Shopper* and *PC Week*, among others, but in addition, it makes all its listings of computer hardware, software and peripherals available via the World Wide Web. Similarly, Optimark, Inc. fits this model, a firm that has created a new mechanism that it calls 'three-dimensional trading', enabling buyers and sellers of large blocks of equities – so typically institutional traders – to specify the prices, quantities and different levels of willingness to transact for each. The NASDAQ Stock Exchange in New York City adopted this kind of approach as a basis for some of its equity trading in the second half of 1999. In fact, NASDAQ itself is another good example of a digital linking intermediary: it creates value in the marketplace by linking buyers and sellers of stock and cutting transaction costs to the minimum.

In contrast, a *digital information intermediary* profits by controlling or enhancing the flow of information. For example, in the estate agency industry, estate agents profit as information aggregators for homebuyers, controlling the latter's access to residential multiple listing service (MLS) information. However, in the past couple of years we have seen the emergence of digital substitutes, e.g., Owners.com and upstart FSBO.com, that are chipping away at the traditional estate agents' control of information. FSBO.com is especially interesting: the value proposition it promotes is to create a place on the Internet so that potential sellers can make 'For Sale By Owner' (FSBO) listings, enabling the *bypass* of estate agents and saving commission expenses. The same kind of thing is occurring in the financial markets where fixed income securities and related derivatives – especially government and corporate bonds and bond futures – are traded. New competitors such as Cantor Fitzgerald's Cantor Exchange, Trading Edge's BondExpress and the Bank of New York's

BondNet aim to *bypass* existing traditional intermediaries (e.g., Wall Street's inter-dealer brokers), who have historically exerted significant control over the mechanism for trading such financial instruments. They enhance the flow of information in a marketplace where best bid and best offered prices have been difficult to discover.

Disintermediation

Disintermediation occurs when a middleman is pushed out by other firms or when the services it provides become irrelevant, particularly as other ways to perform transactions become available. Ten years ago, senior managers at well-known securities industry firms such as Merrill Lynch, Paine Webber and American Express Financial Advisors would have been hard-pressed to predict that a large portion of the retail stock trading business would rapidly move to the Internet. However, since then, traditional intermediaries, such as the brokerage and advisory firms mentioned above, are challenged by the new business models that are seen among emerging electronic commerce firms that compete head-to-head with them. Moreover, disintermediation is occurring almost everywhere: in the travel industry, diminishing the value of travel agents; in the home financing business, as mortgage lending specialists' offerings are eclipsed by Internet-based loan rate listings; and among other industries in the new digital economy.

Current theory in the field of information systems predicts that this will be the case in the presence of electronic communication technologies. Over a decade ago, in what has come to be recognized as a seminal article, Malone *et al.* (1987) wrote that such technologies would create the basis for an *electronic brokerage effect*. This effect is important because it predicts that *non-specific assets* and *commodity-like products* would transact more easily in *electronic marketplaces*. Their insights from that time, it turns out, enable us to explain a range of intermediation and market-related phenomena as they emerge and capture the attention of the marketplace. As search costs in the presence of IT fall, intermediaries are no longer needed. Only those middlemen with sufficient market power will manage to remain in the value-added chain (Hess and Kemerer, 1994), while the others will be disintermediated.

The financial services industry is a hotbed of innovation in this respect, providing an apt demonstration of the theory. In fact, technology-led 'Darwinian competition' is overtaking the more traditional 'sports competition' of similarly configured players in what once was a highly regulated marketplace (Wunsch, 1997); it is so no longer. For example, as long ago as 1969, Instinet created agent brokerage services to support institutional block trading, supplementing the 'upstairs trading' practices of the major Wall Street firms. Instinet's capabilities later developed into a full-blown electronic mechanism and today it is owned by Reuters, which has a vested interest in promoting the evolution of electronic trading systems. Other examples include Steve Wunsch's now defunct Single Price Auction Works (SPAWorks) and his newer Arizona Stock Exchange (AZX); J. P. Morgan's failed electronic bond issuance market, Capitalink; and, most recently, New York City-based Spring Street Brewery's move to raise capital for its business expansion via the Internet. The latter resulted in a real world 'eBay of Blank': Wit Capital. Today, this firm is widely recognized as the first Internet-based investment bank.

Reintermediation

In spite of the picture we have painted about the forces that will lead to disintermediation, we do not mean to imply that this is the only outcome that traditional intermediaries face. In fact, in our view, in the long run all the signs point towards *reintermediation*. This is the process by which a competitor that has once been disintermediated, or pushed out of a profitable market niche as an intermediary, is able to re-establish itself – typically by exploiting the capabilities of technology to become a *electronic commerce-able* (EC-able) *intermediary*. Looking through the lens of Malone *et al.*'s theory, we expect to see *biased and personalized electronic markets*, operated by large firms with significant standing in their industries (subject to their continuing strategic commitment to a given marketplace). In practice, as we shall see, this has certainly been the case!

The emergence of *electronic commerce-only* (EC-only) *intermediaries* in the travel industry – for example, Priceline.com, Internet Travel Network and Preview Travel – has led to the creation of new ways to make reservations on the World Wide Web. Notwithstanding, one expects that major industry players such as American Airlines, Northwest Airlines and American Express Travel Related Services would reply in kind after a time, with biased and personalized electronic markets of their own – which is exactly what we observe in the marketplace. In 1997, Cathay Pacific Airlines was first to use the Internet to conduct a 'fire sale' of excess airline ticket inventory. Today, however, many of the major competitors in the airline industry have followed up with their own direct reservation and ticketing Web sites (e.g., Northwest Airlines), a direct supplier link that affects both the traditional intermediary (the travel agent) and the EC-only intermediary.

In addition, building on the success of its SABRE computerized reservation system (CRS) subsidiary, American Airlines has been highly successful with Travelocity.com, one of the most used reservation-making sites on the World Wide Web. Furthermore, Delta Airlines, which currently tickets 43 per cent of its volume electronically, has just announced its new E-Delta unit. This will serve fifty US national accounts that spend more than $1.2 billion per year on Delta with the new distribution capabilities of an EC-able intermediary (Campbell, 1999). In a similar vein, American Express Travel Related Services, which emphasizes corporate travel management in its spectrum of 'blue box' services, launched American Express Interactive (AXI). AXI, a Web-based corporate travel reservation and planning tool, is a joint venture that brings together the technological capabilities of Microsoft Corporation with the travel industry expertise of American Express.

Understanding the IDR cycle

In tackling the above issues, a number of important questions are raised. When are we likely to see disintermediation and reintermediation occur, changing the structure of competition in an industry? How do EC-only intermediaries themselves formulate strategy to be successful? What situation factors need to be in place that one could use to predict the occurrence of digital intermediation and disintermediation? And, once they succeed, how can traditionally powerful firms recapture the high ground, leverage the opportunity to reintermediate, and effectively compete with new market entrants? The following analysis sheds some light on these issues.

The IDR cycle

Our view is that evolution of firm strategy in the presence of electronic innovations occurs in three distinct, but related phases. We call this the *intermediation–disintermedation–reintermediation cycle* (IDR cycle) (Chircu and Kauffman, 1999a, b). We next describe the three phases in terms of the strategies and value propositions that we observe in the marketplace.

The intermediation phase

Firms in this phase typically pursue pure electronic intermediation strategies. They identify a product, service or information flow gap that no traditional provider currently fills. Then, through technological innovation, they become an EC-only intermediary, and thus create value in the marketplace by delivering something that has not been available there before. eBay is a wonderful example of this kind of intermediation. Never before had there been a large-scale solution for trading non-commodity collectible items, such as Beanie Babies, collectible porcelain dolls and sports cards, other than through occasional and fragmented regional markets. *The value proposition that eBay brought to its marketplace was to give life to liquidity for non-commodity items, which had never been available previously market-wide to small-scale collectors and hobbyists.* Indeed, eBay's play in the market was to 'fill in the blank' for liquidity, a remarkable entrepreneurial insight, but one that was only possible with the technological innovations associated with the World Wide Web.

The disintermediation phase

In this phase, as EC-only intermediaries attract customers, their next logical strategic step is to disintermediate traditional middlemen, if they exist, and capture broader market share. By unbundling the financial advice from the trade execution, e-brokers such as E*Trade have put tremendous pressure on the full-service brokers, effectively disintermediating them in various segments of the market. *The value proposition that E*Trade brought to the marketplace with its Internet-based retail trading solution was to reduce the commission costs for trading stocks by nearly an order of magnitude for the typical retail brokerage customer.*

We may also observe some EC-only players who choose voluntarily to disintermediate themselves. This occurs when EC-only intermediaries realize that they can become IT providers to the industry. They recognize that they can earn higher profits as providers of a technological solution or an emerging IT standard than if they were to continue to compete head-to-head with traditional players who invest in IT to make themselves EC-able.

The reintermediation phase

In the final phase, the focus shifts to firms whose interests have been harmed by the entrance of digital intermediaries to the marketplace. One expects to see traditional intermediaries fighting back, making themselves EC-able. An example of this occurred when the large traditional bookseller, Barnes and Noble, beaten to the Internet market by the bold business strategies of Amazon.com, launched an EC-able company, BarnesandNoble.com, in May 1997, moving into the Internet channel. *The value proposition that Barnes and Noble delivered to the marketplace was to interact with customers through the new channel of the Internet, speeding product distribution through regional inventory maintenance, while maintaining the immediacy of the physical shopping experience in local stores.* However, as the market capitalizations listed in Table 3.1 show (as of 27 May 1999), Amazon.com's first-mover advantage has been considerable, enabling the firm to amass market value over thirty times that of BarnesandNoble.com. Apparently the market's perception of Amazon.com is that it is not just a bookseller but also a mechanism for selling a variety of goods, such as compact discs and other commodity-like products, whereas BarnesandNoble.com is merely an extension of Barnes and Noble's physical bookselling operations.

Of course, developments do not stop here. We expect that future change in the market structure of industries that are impacted by the EC-only strategies of new entrants and the EC-enabling strategies of incumbents will be characterized by some of the things we have described.

Conditions for reintermediation in the IDR cycle

Of the three phases of the IDR cycle, the reintermediation phase is the one that is least understood by academic researchers and senior managers. In previous research (Chircu and Kauffman, 1999a) we proposed that there were three conditions for reintermediation: *ownership of co-specialized assets* for both market intermediation and electronic commerce innovations; *weak appropriability* of electronic commerce innovations; and *economies of scale*. Let us consider each in turn.

Ownership of co-specialized assets

Reintermediation occurs when electronic innovations are imitable by competitors. *Firm-specific assets*, including IT, reputational, relational and other assets, are likely to play a major role in determining a digital intermediary's competitive position. These are things that actually can create disadvantages for most newly entering EC-only intermediaries, because they start out with little more than a Web page and an entrepreneurial vision. To be successful in creating sustainable competitive advantage, technological innovations require *complementary assets* to be put in place as well. However, EC-only intermediaries may find it hard to acquire the necessary complementary assets. For example, as long as profitability is uncertain, suppliers will tend to stay with traditional intermediaries for distribution (Clemons *et al.*, 1993). Oracle's purchase of E-Travel.com is a case in point. In lieu of building expertise in EC application development, Oracle chose to shortcut the path dependencies (Teece, 1992) associated with creating their own solution for the travel industry.

If traditional intermediaries exist in the value chain, they often already have significant *complementary assets*: their expertise, customer base and relationships with suppliers (Teece, 1987). Notwithstanding, they may not have the appropriate expertise to rapidly succeed in electronic commerce. However, traditional intermediaries often have the resources to buy into appropriate solutions. The Bank of New York, a major commercial banking player in the fixed income securities market, obtained an important complementary asset through an alliance with BondNet, when the latter was an independent electronic trading software solution innovator operating out of Connecticut, USA. The bank had the fixed income securities market operational expertise but, prior to its purchase of BondNet, did not have the EC application development expertise in place.

Traditional intermediaries cannot afford to rely too much on their pre-existing assets and *not* adopt electronic commerce innovations. If they want to stay in the game, they need to start the reintermediation process as quickly as possible to prevent EC-only intermediaries from acquiring or building their own co-specialized assets. Even if a traditional intermediary has all the necessary co-specialized assets for market intermediation, it still may lack those related to the development of electronic commerce applications. Here, technology investments become a strategic necessity. To prepare for reintermediation, a firm can either develop the requisite technologies itself or acquire them from existing providers. In both cases, the idea is to acquire co-specialized complementary assets necessary to appropriate benefits from technological innovations in an electronic marketplace.

A good example is American Express Travel Related Services, which possessed many well-established corporate travel management relationships (complementary assets), but which chose to rely upon Microsoft's capability with software development for electronic commerce to create American Express Interactive. This Web-based reservations system for business travellers has benefited from a number of co-specialized complementary assets, including the IT development experience of

Microsoft and American Express' travel industry experience. Although the exclusive access to Microsoft's technology negotiated by American Express lasted only two years (McNulty, 1999b), this kind of asset is still hard to imitate since it relies so heavily on Microsoft's experience with developing its Internet Explorer browser and its own Web-based reservation system, Expedia.

More broadly, co-specialized complementary assets may consist of industry-specific expertise and transaction data, in addition to customer and supplier relationships. Another related example makes this point well. In the 1980s, strong airlines were able successfully to capture the benefits of airline computer reservation systems by offering these systems to travel agencies (the co-specialized complementary assets). Travel agents, in turn, made the CRSs an integral part of their business process, transforming the operational mechanics of the industry (Duliba *et al.*, 1999).

Economies of scale

EC-only intermediaries will not succeed if they cannot achieve economies of scale. However, many traditional intermediaries will have achieved economies of scale in traditional markets, and can use this advantage to leverage their attempts to reintermediate. Thus, the problem that senior management will face is in effectively implementing an electronic commerce solution.

The perspective that we recommend emphasizes that an important way for an EC-only intermediary to maintain its first-mover competitive advantage is to become a technology provider. For example, it can become a technology provider for traditional intermediaries, if they exist, or for suppliers and customers, if the traditional market structure does not contain intermediaries. Thus EC-only intermediaries may welcome reintermediation, but only if they can benefit from it and not be pushed out of the marketplace themselves. Here, broad agreement in the marketplace about whether a technology provider's solutions will reach critical mass or become a *de facto* standard is critical.

Weak appropriability

An innovation's weak appropriability (Teece, 1987) is amplified by the independence of an EC application from the customers' installed software and hardware base. As long as the application resides on the intermediary's Web site, switching costs are almost zero. Since the same browser software can be used to access any Web site, customers can easily switch to a competitor, without being required to make extensive investments in proprietary hardware and software. Therefore, relying solely on their technological innovation cannot be a source of sustained competitive advantage for firms doing business on the Internet. This seems true for first movers (such as Amazon.com) who implemented electronic commerce innovations but had limited industry expertise when they began. Established players (such as Barnes and Noble or Borders) were able quickly to imitate the first mover's innovation, and provide similar services on their own Web sites. Moreover, firms that control *co-specialized complementary assets* – that only have value in association with other assets – are in a better position to appropriate benefits where dependence on the technological innovation exists (Teece, 1987).

Relevant competitive strategies

There are four characteristic competitive strategies that firms are observed to use in the IDR cycle (see Table 3.2). They include *partnering for access, technology licensing, partnering for content* and *partnering for application development*. Each strategy varies in the extent to which it confers upon the firm that employs it the ability to achieve sustainable competitive advantage.

Partnering for access

This strategy is used not only by EC-only intermediaries, but also by traditional competitors who become newly EC-able. This approach involves contracting for exclusivity agreements with high-traffic Web sites, such as search engines, browser providers and Internet Service Providers (ISPs). Because this strategy is readily available to other intermediaries, however, its success depends on the success of the chosen partners. Consider America Online's (AOL) partnerships with CDNow, DVDExpress and Amazon.com. The latter three firms pay AOL for direct links to their Web pages from AOL's home page on the Web (see Figure 3.2).

Figure 3.2
Amazon.com and CDNow partner for access with AOL.com (America Online's Web site, 27 May 1999)

Table 3.2   Four strategies for sustainable competitive advantage for Internet middlemen (after Chircu and Kauffman, 1999b)

Strategy	Description	Conditions for sustainable competitive advantage	Environmental conditions under which the strategy is appropriate
Partnering for content	The intermediary becomes an aggregator for products and services.	The digital intermediary can customize and brand the content, as well as retain control over customers' transactions.	Market niches are not yet stable; market search costs are too high; and insufficient value is available for firms to be able to appropriate it with individual offerings via the Internet; opportunities to create value through product or content aggregation still exist.
Partnering for access	The digital intermediary becomes the provider of services for other agents involved in electronic commerce, e.g., search engine and Internet service providers.	The partner is a leading online service provider with whom the digital intermediary has an exclusivity agreement.	Cost pressures begin to favour rationalization of Internet-focused software development; some Internet services begin to achieve dominance or become *de facto* standards; but service provision may be incompletely covered.
Partnering for application development	The digital intermediary forms alliances with established industry participants.	The right combination of assets (e.g., technological and industry-specific expertise) is obtained by the digital intermediary through partnering.	No technology standards have been established yet, but establishing them would confer significant value upon participants in the coalition of organizations promulgating the standard; firms may have formed agreed estimates of the value of Internet marketplace.
Technology licensing	The digital intermediary becomes a technology provider for other Web sites, either by selling them the technology or by sharing the profits resulting from transactions referred by other Web sites.	The digital intermediary is continuously innovating and licensing, moving value to the marketplace as rapidly as possible.	The profits from providing products or services online are lower than the profits from being a technology provider for other EC-only and EC-able intermediaries.

By placing their logos and links right at the portal, CDNow and Amazon.com maximize the likelihood of being able to take advantage of AOL's huge installed base of 13 million users (as of 1998). In the absence of such key partners, this approach is probably not a means to achieve sustainable advantage.

Technology licensing

This strategy may be the most compelling reason why voluntary disintermediation of EC-only intermediaries occurs. This is appropriate where the benefits from intermediating individual transactions are lower than the benefits from providing the technology for other industry players. However, licensing software and various hardware technologies cannot by themselves create a basis for sustainable competitive advantage. When licensing is used in combination with a continuous innovation strategy, it is possible for the innovating firm to become a supplier to other firms that would otherwise disintermediate it.

Technology licensing occurs in the emerging electronic bill payments segment of the financial services industry. Transpoint (previously called MSFDC, a joint venture between Microsoft and First Data Corporation), for example, works with banks to create electronic bill presentment and payment systems for the utilities industry, and then licenses its technology. Checkfree, another early entrant in the electronic bill payment arena, pursues a similar strategy.

A second example of this is the approach that the Internet Travel Network (ITN) pursues in the travel industry. If ITN were only to focus on disintermediating traditional travel firms, then it would eventually be subject to the threat of an industry-wide response, diminishing its likelihood of success. However, ITN now attempts to license its technology to major corporate travel and other reservation-making firms and smaller regional agencies, thereby creating a basis for getting potential competitors to 'buy in' to what could become a standard in the industry. For example, CNN is a well-known name in the news arena that also offers its services online through CNN Interactive. Instead of building a reservation engine itself, CNN Interactive's travel unit outsourced this function to ITN, which offers the same software and the expertise to build e-commerce sites around it to many firms. In fact, ITN lists more than sixty licensees on its Web site (see Figure 3.3 and Table 3.3). An even bigger play of this sort for ITN is its recent agreement with SAP, which will license the ITN booking engine, making it a part of the SAP enterprise resource planning system (ERP) software (McNulty, 1999a).

Of course, this approach is not new in the marketplace among technology firms. For example, Clemons (1991) reported that Merrill Lynch made a similar play with its investment in Bloomberg Financial in the pre-Internet marketplace of the 1980s. Merrill initially held back from making its financial information delivery capabilities available market-wide, but later maximized the value of its Bloomberg investment by licensing the use of the information to competitors. This strategy continues to pay off for both Merrill Lynch, and market leader Bloomberg.

Partnering for content

This approach involves product and information aggregation, another widely used strategy by EC-only intermediaries. This strategy is likely to work best for first movers. However, sustainable competitive

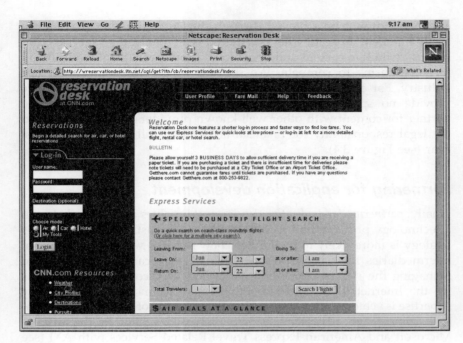

Figure 3.3
CNN's Reservation Desk licenses technology from the Internet Travel Network (Internet Travel Network's service Web site for CNN Travel Reservation Desk, 21 July 1999)

Table 3.3 Internet Travel Network's software licensing partnerships (Internet Travel Network, 1999)

Corporate travel licensees	Leisure travel licensees	
BSG Inc.	Airlines.com	Hot Office
Chevron	Airlines of the Web	InfoGear
PeopleSoft	Apex Travel	Infohiway
Maritz Travel @ Sun Microsystems	Arctic Travel	IVillage
Procter & Gamble	Atevo	Leisureweb
Schering Plough Corp.	Big Yellow	Maritime Marlin Travel
Silicon Graphics	CANOE – Canadian Explorer	Mindspring
Stanford University	Cardoza Travel	Morrison Travel
Texas Instruments	Casto Travel	Nequity.com
United Technologies	Cendant Travel Inc.	Rand McNally
United Airlines	Choice Travel Systems	Shopperzone
University California Berkeley	CitySearch	T@p Online
University of Iowa	CMPnet's Netguide	Ticketmaster Travel
Verifone	CNN Interactive	Travel and Transport
WorldBank	EGo Travel	Travel Quest
	European Travel Network	Trade Show Central
	Exploration.net	Travel Source
	Global Online Travel	Travel.com
	Global Shopping Club	Traveline Travel Agencies
	Go Explore	Travelnow
	Golf Travel Online	Uniglobe Travel Online
	Guthy Renker's	Windows on the World
	Hoffman Travel	Wyndham Travel

advantage cannot be achieved through this strategy: other players can easily imitate it. Instead, what is required is an amalgam of service capabilities, definitive content and operational prowess that makes it difficult for other firms to compete. We see this in the electronic brokerage industry. For example, e-brokers such as Charles Schwab and E*Trade provide no specific financial advisory services, choosing instead to partner for content with other well known providers and thereby avoid the legal responsibility for financial advice that full-service firms must bear (see Figure 3.4).

Partnering for application development

Finally, *partnering for application development* involves an alliance between a technology provider and a well-established industry participant. This strategy is more likely to be used for new services where no traditional intermediaries have been present. This strategy can also be used for managing the risk of developing large and very complex applications for the Internet. If the right combination of technology and industry expertise is achieved, this strategy has the potential of generating sustainable competitive advantage, as we discussed earlier in the case of Microsoft and American Express Travel Related Services with AXI (see Figure 3.5).

A second example involves Travis Tanner, previously CEO of Carlson Wagonlit Travel (CWT), and now CEO of Luxury Travel, Inc., a leisure travel market-focused startup. In 1999, Tanner was recognized by *Business Travel News* (BTN) in its 'Hall of Fame' of twenty-five top industry leaders. Prior to some more recent developments, Tanner's

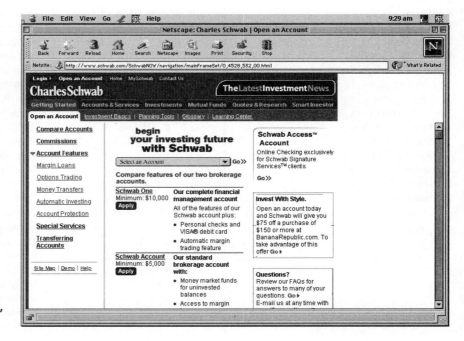

Figure 3.4
Charles Schwab partners for content with other financial information providers (Charles Schwab's Web site, 'News and Research', 27 May 1999)

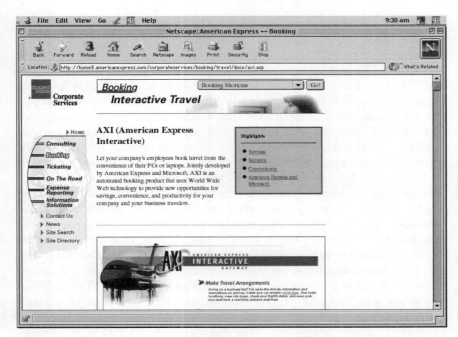

Figure 3.5 American Express Travel Related Services partners for application development with Microsoft (American Express Travel Related Services' Web site, 27 May 1999)

approach at CWT was to use third-party software solutions instead of building everything within the firm. His innovative approach involved using the TravelNet booking engine in order to support moving travel management tools onto corporate intranets (Rosen, 1999).

Conclusions

Numerous researchers have studied competition among traditional and electronic market players (Bailey and Bakos, 1997; Bakos, 1991, 1998; Bakos and Brynjolfsson, 1993; Clemons *et al.*, 1993; Hess and Kemerer, 1994; Sarkar *et al.*, 1995; Steinfield *et al.*, 1995). Among the things that we learn from this and related work (Mata *et al.*, 1995) is that IT alone is rarely a source of sustainable competitive advantage. To become an 'eBay of Blank' takes far more in the way of business vision, entre-preneurial marketing skills and operational and corporate finance capabilities (combined with the luck of doing things in the right place and at the right time).

However, IT can help leverage critical firm resources, such as the expertise of specific human capital, experience in a market niche and understanding of how to fine-tune manufacturing and services business processes to create sustainable competitive advantage (Clemons, 1991; Clemons and Row, 1991). We expect that this same view should apply in the arena of digital intermediation, so that the current and future 'eBays' of the electronic commerce world will be subject to all the same forces as most market leaders in traditional business have been.

Another important thing that senior managers must keep in mind when trying to achieve long-term competitiveness in electronic commerce is that their firm must either create or control relevant complementary assets to its EC technology innovations. We have argued in this chapter that this is a crucial element, and that it is as important for EC-only intermediaries who seek to sustain their position in the marketplace as it is for traditional intermediaries who wish to reintermediate and reinvigorate their business strategy in the emerging marketplace. The four strategies we discussed – partnering for access, technology licensing, partnering for content and partnering for application development – each, in their way, provide a foundation for creating complementary assets.

Finally, apart from securing ownership of necessary co-specialized assets, digital intermediaries need to renew organizational skills, resources and functional competencies to sustain the advantages that they build (Teece *et al.*, 1997). As a result, current innovation must be the wellspring for further innovation, as new technology replaces the old. Eventually, this must become systemic for the firm, but it requires more tightly coupled business processes (Chesbrough and Teece, 1996). In this context, Teece (1992) has pointed out the importance of *strategic alliances for interorganizational process coupling* in sustaining competitive advantage. This is likely to be true among various kinds of intermediaries (digital linking and information intermediaries, and EC-only and EC-able intermediaries) that we have discussed in this chapter.

Further reading

For the previous research into this area forming the intellectual basis for this chapter the reader is invited to refer to Chircu and Kauffman (1999a, b) and Kauffman (1999).

References

Bailey, J. P. and Bakos, J. Y. (1997). An exploratory study of the emerging role of electronic intermediaries. *International Journal of Electronic Commerce*, **1**, 7–20.

Bakos, J. Y. (1991). A strategic analysis of electronic marketplaces. *MIS Quarterly*, **15**, 295–310.

Bakos, J. Y. (1998). The emerging role of electronic marketplaces on the Internet. *Communications of the ACM*, **41**, 35–42.

Bakos, J. Y. and Brynjolfsson, E. (1993). From vendors to partners: information technology and incomplete contracts in buyer-supplier relationships. *Journal of Organizational Computing*, **3**, 301–28.

Baltaxe, D. (1999). Industry analysis. *Current Analysis*, March.

Benjamin, R. and Wigand, R. (1995). Electronic markets and virtual value chains on the information superhighway. *Sloan Management Review*, **36**, 62–72.

Burnham, B. (1999). *How to Invest in E-Commerce Stocks*. McGraw-Hill.

Campbell, J. (1999). E-Delta opens shop – Delta unit to share savings of e-commerce with corporate buyers. *BTN Online*, 17 May.
http://www.btnonline.com/db_area/archives/1999/05/99051701.htm

Castonguay, G. (1999). Focus – DLJ sets $320 million online unit offering. *Reuters/Quicken Excite*, 25 May.
http://quicken.excite.com/investments/news/story/rtr/?story=/news/stories/rtr/18/n25238818.htm&symbol=amtd

Chesbrough, H. W. and Teece, D. J. (1996). Organizing for innovation. *Harvard Business Review*, **74**, 65–73.

Chircu, A. M. and Kauffman, R. J. (1999a). Analysing firm-level strategy for Internet-focused reintermediation. *Proceedings of the 32nd Hawaii International Conference on Systems Science*, Maui, Hawaii.

Chircu, A. M. and Kauffman, R. J. (1999b). Strategies for Internet middlemen in the intermediation–disintermediation–reintermediation cycle. *Electronic Markets – The International Journal of Electronic Commerce and Business Media*, **9**, 109–17.

Clemons, E. K. (1991). Evaluation of strategic investments in information technology. *Communications of the ACM*, **34**, 22–36.

Clemons, E. K. and Row, M. C. (1991). Information technology at Rosenbluth Travel: competitive advantage in a rapidly growing global service company. *Journal of Management Information Systems*, **8**, 53–79.

Clemons, E. K., Reddi, S. P. and Row, M. C. (1993). The impact of information technology on the organization of economic activity: the 'move to the middle' hypothesis. *Journal of Management Information Systems*, **10**, 9–35.

Duliba, K., Kauffman, R. J. and Lucas, H. C., Jr. (1999). *An Evaluation of the Indirect Impacts of Computer Reservation Systems on Airline Performance*. Working paper. Stern School of Business, New York University.

Hess, C. M. and Kemerer, C. F. (1994). Computerized loan origination systems: an industry case study of the electronic markets hypothesis. *MIS Quarterly*, **18**, 251–75.

Internet Travel Network (1999). ITN's portfolio: online travel excellence, 28 May.
http://www.itn.com/cgi/get?portfolio:JPgQlw_Kl8u*itn/ord=927901554.13696,itn/agencies/itnpublic

Kane, M. (1999a). Cybermediaries: the Net's new kings. *ZDNet Tech News*, 28 May.
http://www.excite.com/computers_and_internet/tech_news/zdnet/?article=zdnews3.inp

Kane, M. (1999b). Who will rule the new middlemen? *ZDNet Tech News*, 31 May.
http://www.zdnet.com/zdnn/stories/news/0,4586,2265313,00.html

Kauffman, R.J. (1999). *The New Electronic Markets of the Internet*. Presentation to MIS Research Center, Carlson School of Management, University of Minnesota, 23 April.

Malone, T. W., Yates, J. and Benjamin, R. I. (1987). Electronic markets and electronic hierarchies. *Communications of the ACM*, **30**, 484–97.

Mata, F. J., Fuerst, W. L. and Barney, J. B. (1995). Information technology and sustained competitive advantage: a resource-based analysis. *MIS Quarterly*, **19**, 487–505.

McNulty, M. A. (1999a). ERP portals add travel booking. *BTN Online*, 17 May.
http://www.btnonline.com/db_area/archives/1999/05/99051756.htm

McNulty, M. A. (1999b). AXI hits open market. *BTN Online*, 7 June.
http://www.btnonline.com/db_area/archives/1999/06/99060725.htm

PR Newswire (1999). NetPerceptions announces initial public offering. *Quicken Excite*, 23 April.
http://quicken.excite.com/investments/news/story/pr/?story=/news/stories/pr/19990423/hsf036.htm&symbol=netp

Quicken Excite (1999). Investment quotes. 27 May.
http://quicken.excite.com/investments/quotes/

Rayport, J. F. and Sviokla, J. J. (1994). Managing in the marketspace. *Harvard Business Review*, **72**, 141–50.

Rosen, C. (1999). The Business Travel News hall of fame: top of the top 25s. *BTN Online*, 17 May.
http://www.btnonline.com/db_area/archives/1999/05/99051759.htm

Sarkar, M. B., Butler, B. and Steinfield, C. (1995). Intermediaries and cybermediaries: a continuing role for mediating players in the electronic marketplace. *Journal of Computer-Mediated Communication*, **1**.
Available online: http://jcmc.huji.ac.il/vol1/issue3/sarkar.html

Steinfield, C., Kraut, R. and Plummer, A. (1995). The impact of electronic commerce on buyer–seller relationships. *Journal of Computer-Mediated Communication*, **1**.
Available online: http://jcmc.huji.ac.il/vol1/issue3/steinfld.html

Stepanek, M. (1998). Rebirth of the salesman. *Business Week*, 22 June, pp. 146–48.

Teece, D. J. (1987). Profiting from technological innovation: implications for integration, collaboration, licensing and public policy. In D. J. Teece, ed., *The Competitive Challenge*. Harper & Row, pp. 185–219.

Teece, D. J. (1992). Competition, co-operation, and innovation: organizational arrangements for regimes of rapid technological progress. *Journal of Economic Behavior and Organizations*, **18**, 1–25.

Teece, D. J., Pisano, G. and Shuen, A. (1997). Dynamic capabilities and strategic management. *Strategic Management Journal*, **18**, 509–53.

Whinston, A. B., Stahl, D. O. and Choi, S. Y. (1997). *The Economics of Electronic Commerce*. Macmillan.

Wunsch, S. (1997). Letter to Jonathan G. Katz, Secretary, United States Securities and Exchange Commission. Arizona Stock Exchange, 15 September. http://www.azx.com/pub/katzwuns.html

Appendix 3.1–An overview of leading firms in electronic commerce

Firm name (home page)	Business description
Amazon.com (www.amazon.com)	First mover in the online market for books and has used its strong brand name to expand in online markets for a variety of products such as CDs and electronics.
American Express Travel Related Services (www.americanexpress.com)	Major corporate travel firm that partnered with Microsoft to create American Express Interactive (AXI).
America Online (www.aol.com)	Leading Internet service provider (ISP) in the USA.
Arizona Stock Exchange (www.azx.com)	Low cost, single price auction (call) market for US equities based in Phoenix, Arizona.
AutoByTel (www.autobytel.com)	First highly successful Internet-based referral service for retail purchases of new and used motor vehicles.
Bank of NY BondNet (www.bondnet.com)	A live, screen-based electronic market for fixed income securities owned by a money centre bank.
BarnesandNoble.com (www.bn.com)	Leading traditional bookseller's brand name extension to electronic commerce; late to market.
Bloomberg (www.bloomberg.com)	A leading provider of news and information for financial markets operations.
Bond Express (www.bondexpress.com)	A provider of electronic trading systems for bonds and of a database with information about bond trading.
Bond Net (www.bondnet.com)	A real-time, automated electronic market for the professional bond broker/dealer community.
Cantor Exchange (cx.cantor.com)	The provider of an electronic single-price auction system for the US Treasury futures market.
Cathay Pacific Corporation (www.cathaypacific.com)	The first airline to provide electronic ticket auctions on its Web site.
CDNow (www.cdnow.com)	Internet-only distributor of popular and classical music compact discs; merged with Music Boulevard.
Charles Schwab (www.schwab.com)	Discount stockbroker from the 1980s that recently transformed its strategy to emphasize the Internet.
Checkfree (www.checkfree.com)	One of the first companies to provide electronic bill payment and bill presentment services in the USA.
CNN Interactive (www.cnn.com)	The online news service of Cable News Network (CNN), a leading news provider.

DVD Express (www.dvdexpress.com)	First Internet-based retailer to sell 'digital virtual discs' (DVDs); now the market-leading vendor in the USA.
eBay (www.ebay.com)	Highly successful digital intermediary for Internet-based auction market for collectible items.
E*Trade (www.etrade.com)	The fastest growing Internet-only electronic brokerage in the USA.
E-Travel (www.etravelsystems.com)	A leading provider of Web-based reservation systems for business travel, now part of Oracle Corporation.
Expedia (www.expedia.com)	Microsoft's booking engine for travel, hotels and rental cars.
FSBO.com (www.fsbo.com)	For Sale By Owner, for Internet-based sales of real estate without the involvement of estate agents.
Insight Inc. (www.insight.com)	Traditional reseller of computer hardware and software, with a major presence on the Internet.
Instinet Corporation (www.instinet.com)	A leading agency brokerage company that provides electronic trading systems for its clients.
Internet Travel Network (www.itn.com)	One of the leading electronic travel agencies in the USA.
NASDAQ (www.nasdaq.com)	A leading securities market well-known for its technological innovations.
Northwest Airlines (www.nwa.com)	International airline; early adopter of the Internet for direct air ticket sales.
Onsale.com (www.onsale.com)	Internet-only wholesaler and auction Web site for computer peripherals.
Optimark Technologies, Inc. (www.optimark.com)	A provider of confidential electronic markets that has introduced the concept of optimal matching using its patented 'three-dimensional trading' technology.
Owners.com (www.owners.com)	Residential real estate listing service for 'for sale by owner' properties.
Priceline.com (www.priceline.com)	Buyer-driven marketplace for leisure travel ticket purchases.
Preview Travel (www.previewtravel.com)	One of the leading electronic travel agencies in the USA.
Spring Street Brewery (www.interport.net/witbeer)	First American company to raise capital with an initial public offering of stock via the Internet.
Trading Edge Bond Express (www.bondexpress.com)	Internet-only electronic screen-based trading mechanism for fixed income securities for retail investors.
Transpoint (www.transpoint.com)	Joint venture of Microsoft and First Data Corporation for electronic bill payment services.
Travelocity (www.travelocity.com)	A leading Web-based reservation system for leisure travel, developed by SABRE, a computerized reservation system (CRS) owned by American Airlines.
UBid Inc. (www.ubid.com)	An Internet-based auction house for excess, refurbished and limited-run merchandise with live-action bidding.
Wit Capital (www.witcapital.com)	The first Internet-based investment bank in the USA.

4
E-business and the intermediary role of virtual communities

P. K. Kannan, Ai-Mei Chang and Andrew B. Whinston

Introduction

While the term 'virtual community' may be relatively new, the concept is not. Such a conception existed even in the early days of e-mail when researchers used the online medium to exchange ideas and information and to collaborate on research projects. For example, the Unix operating system and its derivatives, Sendmail software, and other similar products were developed collaboratively as 'open source software' on the online medium (e-mail, Usenet discussion boards) by researchers and programmers who hardly interacted with each other face-to-face. Many online services also provided local bulletin boards for special interest groups (SIGs) to exchange content. Later, as the World Wide Web environment began to grow, many off-line communities (for example, those centred around magazines) started gravitating towards the Internet to take advantage of its connectivity and reach to help their communities grow. In addition, many unique communities began to form on the Internet itself. These early communities were centred mainly on non-commercial interests and activities. However, as commercial use of the WWW increased, many Internet communities have been formed that cater to members' or organizers' commercial interests. Thus, there are communities on the WWW that are formed, organized and maintained by members themselves (with or without any commercial focus); some that are organized and controlled by marketers; and some that are organized and maintained by third parties who act, on the one hand, as intermediaries between the members and, on the other, as marketers and advertisers. Given the empirical evidence and trends, it is clear that communities will be playing a very important role in the growth of electronic commerce. The focus of this chapter is to explore this potential of virtual communities – to complement e-business – viewing them as important intermediaries. We describe how virtual communities organized for business motives differ from other types of communities and explore conditions under which such business-oriented virtual communities can evolve successfully. We argue that, in order to ensure a healthy growth, virtual communities should increasingly take on the role of an intermediary in

1 exchange relationships between community members, and
2 exchange relationships between community members and marketers and advertisers.

Drawing parallels from extant research in financial intermediation and drawing upon social exchange theory, we postulate conditions and market mechanisms under which virtual communities could provide great impetus for the growth of electronic commerce on the Web. Wherever possible, we provide empirical examples to support our argument.

In the next section we provide a brief introduction to virtual communities and discuss how value is created within a business-oriented community. We follow this up in the third section with a discussion on how virtual communities can act as intermediaries and provide services to both community members and corporate clients. In the fourth section, we present a model for an intermediary and our postulates regarding the conditions under which virtual communities can evolve and thrive. Finally, we round off the chapter with some concluding comments on the future of virtual communities.

Virtual communities and value creation

Types of virtual communities

In their narrowest form, virtual communities can be defined as:

> *social* aggregations of a *critical mass* of people on the Internet who engage in public discussions, *interactions* in chat rooms, and information exchanges with sufficient *human feeling* on matters of common interest to form webs of *personal relationship*s (Rheingold, 1993).

According to this definition, virtual communities are made up of individuals who aggregate into a critical mass driven by common needs, which are mainly social in nature. This common bonding is strengthened by personal relationships that ensure some degree of loyalty of the members to the community. However, commercial interests are a part of the individual-level needs, and it is not uncommon to find communities for business transactions focused on individual and organizational needs – communities of buyers and sellers, such as GE Information Services' Trading Process Network (GEIS-TPN), a community of GE suppliers and other buyers. These business communities consist of a critical mass of members whose needs are mainly *commercial* in nature and who use the communities mainly for *networking* and building *business relationships*. While these communities may lack the human feeling element and the social interactions, there is such significant informational exchange and communication that we consider these business-to-business communities as virtual communities.

Extending our analysis, we find that there are essentially four types of virtual communities in existence on the WWW, depending on the types of consumer needs they meet (Armstrong and Hagel, 1995, 1996). Thus, communities could be transaction-oriented, interest-oriented, fantasy-oriented or relationship-oriented. It is also possible that some virtual communities meet several of the above needs. Let us consider each category in turn.

Transaction-oriented communities primarily facilitate the buying and selling of products and services and deliver information that is related to fulfilling those transactions. These communities do not address the members' social needs in any manner; the focus is on interaction between members either to transact business or provide informational leads or consultations about other possible participants in transactions. Examples of communities of transactions include: Virtual Vineyards, where consumers get information tips from the vendor and buy products at the Web site; Levis.com, where consumers can chat about latest fashion; Amazon.com, where visitors can get reviews about books from other readers; and, business communities such as GEIS-TPN, VerticalNet, Aeneid and CommerceNet, which meet members' transactional and/or informational needs. Although communities of transactions could be organized by anyone, the organizers are usually the vendors themselves. For example, GEIS-TPN, which is now an independent entity, began as a community owned by GEIS.

The second type of community is a community of interest. Here, members have significantly higher degrees of interactions than in a community of transactions and the interactions are usually on topics of their common interest. Examples include: Café Utne, a community of hip urbanites; Motley Fool, a community for financial investors; the Well, one of the oldest communities; and BioMedNet, a professional community for physicians. These communities usually have chat rooms, message boards and discussion groups for extensive member interaction. Thus, they are characterized by a significant amount of user-generated content.

The third type of community is a fantasy-oriented community where users create new environments, personalities, stories and role-play. For example, some online applications create fantasy environments in which groups of users can interact by typing special commands and messages (often referred to as Multi-User Dungeons or MUDs). The popular fictional works of writers such as J. R. R. Tolkien (author of, for example, *The Hobbit* and *Lord of the Rings*) and William Gibson (author of, for example, *Neuromancer*) often influence such environments. Examples include ESPNet, Sony.com, and many of the fantasy communities within America Online.

The fourth and final type of community is the community of relationship built around certain life experiences that are usually very intense and lead to personal bonding between members. Examples include the Cancer Forum, a community for cancer patients and their close friends and family, as well as communities that focus on religion, divorce and other topics.

Many virtual communities have an overlap of several of the above orientations. For example, communities such as GeoCities and Tripod have allocated 'concept spaces' where members with similar interests can put up Web sites, transact business with each other, play out their fantasies, and build relationships through interactions. These are meta-communities or 'portals', which organize several smaller, focused, virtual communities centred on common interests and relationships. Similarly, in the business-to-business realm, VerticalNet and Aeneid are vertical mega-portals that organize a number of tightly focused virtual communities in vertical industries. In this sense, the concept of a virtual community is still evolving. In the discussions that follow we use the term virtual community to encompass all of the above interpretations. All of the different types of virtual communities that we have discussed – transaction, interest, fantasy and relationship communities – can be organized as for-profit communities. The non-profit communities, however, generally tend to be less transaction-oriented.

Value creation

Figure 4.1 provides a snapshot of how value is created in a community, based on the work of Kannan *et al.* (1998). Members' input to the community consists of information content in the form of comments, feedback, elaborating their attitudes and beliefs and informational needs. Members may provide such content unsolicited, or in response to queries by other members or the organizer of the community. Thus, members provide useful information that is retrieved and used by other members of the community. The community organizers may also put in their own content which members may find valuable. For example, the organizers of BioMedNet provide content in the form of information on the latest medical research and techniques, which the physician members would find very useful. In such communities, the members would also be willing to pay *subscription fees* to become members of the community since they may value highly the information they receive from the community. People pay subscription fees in order to become members of communities such as America Online or CompuServe. Such subscription fees may be viewed as a charge that members need to bear to be part of an exclusive community or for accessing the content in the communities that they value.

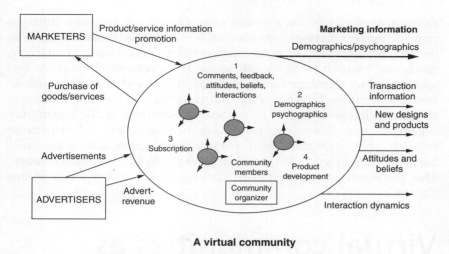

A virtual community

Figure 4.1
Value creation
in electronic
communities
(Kannan *et al.*, 1998)

Another possibility for value creation in virtual communities arises from the fact that a community brings together consumers of specific demographics and interest. This presents opportunities for transacting business and communicating messages about products and services that are of interest to consumers, and which marketers and advertisers value and are consequently willing to pay for. In as much as business transactions take place in communities, value is created. In addition, virtual communities can attract advertisement-revenues from advertisers eager to communicate their messages to community members (which is currently a significant source of revenue for virtual communities). In addition to business transactions and advert-revenues, there are also other opportunities for value creation. These arise from the marketing information that is generated within communities, which the environment (marketers and advertisers among others) would find valuable. Such information includes the demographics and psychographics of members, their attitudes and beliefs about products, services and issues, their behaviour data with regard to business transactions within communities and information on their interactions and interaction dynamics. If members do not object, such information could be sold to marketers and advertisers.

Research communities working on software projects such as Linux OS kernel, Apache server software and Perl also add value by designing and creating new software products and extensions. Although none of these communities are formed with for-profit motives, members derive value from each other's contribution and work towards the common good of the researcher and user communities.

The exact manner in which value is created in virtual communities also depends on who organizes the community and who owns it. Transaction-oriented communities are generally organized, controlled and run by marketers. In such virtual communities, value is created mainly though transactions rather than through advert-revenues. The marketing information generated in the communities may also reside with the marketers who may or may not sell such information. In many cases, marketers who own virtual communities can use such information to derive synergies for other related business functions, such as better customer service, mass customization in service and delivery, marketing research feedback and so on. If the community is controlled and owned by members themselves, the main focus of such communities is to derive sole benefits for the members and value is created in content exchange and/or through subscription fees. If the community organizers and those who run it are not marketers, advertisers or members but unrelated third parties, such communities are in a better position to leverage the full range of possibilities of value creation. This intermediary role of virtual communities is a key focus of this chapter.

Virtual communities as intermediaries

One of the main reasons for focusing on the intermediary role of virtual communities is that they are increasingly called upon to undertake that role in order to achieve a healthy growth. As an illustration consider Parentsplace.com. This is a community started by a Californian couple interested in bringing parents together in cyberspace to discuss issues of mutual interest. The community was begun with the objective of selling children-related products to the community members, particularly as they ventured out of the chat rooms and into the retail sections of the community. As the community grew in the chat rooms and discussion rooms, the members were more interested in their common interests, getting tips and information on child-rearing, rather than on transacting business. The organizers quickly realized this and, in order to keep the community growing, they adopted the business model of an advert-revenue supported community rather than a transaction-revenue supported community. This was achieved by selling advertising space to advertisers and removing the retail section of the community, thereby pushing the community into more of an intermediary role than a marketer's role.

Another illustration of a similar role transition involves GEIS-TPN. This business-to-business community was started by General Electric's lighting division in order to manage their supply chain efficiently by bringing suppliers to a Web-based transaction system. The supplier community grew, more buyers joined the community and, at the appropriate time, GE spun off the venture into a separate entity that helped both buyers and suppliers build relationships and transact business. While GE's brand name and buying power were necessary to start the community, once a critical mass was reached an intermediary role better suited TPN.

In addition to the above examples of role changes of virtual communities, many analysts, manufacturers and community members are increasingly questioning the idea that businesses can easily 'build' a community to sell their products/services. While some marketers with strong brand presence may be able to sow the seeds for forming a community and encouraging its growth, it is not possible for them to control and manipulate what happens in the community in the manner that they may envision. This increasingly supports the notion that communities grow essentially through members' initiatives and through mutual trust and respect between community organizers and members. If members begin to question the motives of organizers or perceive a pushy agenda of marketers, it may adversely affect the communities. These arguments lend credence to the following proposition.

> *Proposition 1:*
> *Electronic communities increasingly will have to adopt the role of an intermediary between marketers and members to ensure a healthy growth of the communities.*

In order to understand the specific issues involved in performing the above role, it will be useful to list the services that virtual communities provide to members on the one hand and to marketers and advertisers on the other. Let us consider each in turn.

First, consider the members of communities. Typically, members enrol in a community for one or more of the following reasons:

1 To extract or download content from communities with the assurance that the content is of 'good' quality and is not 'junk'. This could be, for example, input from other community members such as opinions and experiences with products or services; input from community organizers which could be investment advice, or tips on health and so on; and input from marketers and advertisers such as product and service information, information about loyalty programmes and so on.
2 To provide content of their own that could be of use to other members – these could be their own opinions and experiences about products, services and issues.
3 To forge 'useful' relationships with other members of the community and/or with marketers and advertisers without compromising their privacy. We define 'useful' in terms of meeting social needs or commercial needs without opening the way for 'spamming' or 'stalking' on the Web.

Second, we turn to corporate clients. Typically, these could consider virtual communities useful for the following reasons:

1 To gain access to consumers of a specific demographic and psychographic profile on the Web in order to communicate their messages such as advertisements, product or service information and so on.
2 To transact business with community members and provide personalized offerings using information on their demographics and psychographics. To forge long-term relationships with them and earn their loyalty.

3 To buy information from virtual communities on members' attitudes and preferences, their interactions with other members, their transaction information, and demographics and psychographics for marketing research purposes.

This creates a number of implications. Specifically, given the above needs of members and corporate clients, a virtual community must maintain the following two conditions to be an effective intermediary. It must:

1 Ensure that the content input by community members, advertisers and marketers is of 'good' quality.
2 Ensure that members' privacy is protected even as appropriate relationships are forged between community members and marketers.

This leads us on to several issues involved in ensuring the above conditions – the absence of which could lead to a meltdown of a virtual community.

Content quality

If members join a virtual community for its content – whether member-, organizer- or marketer-generated – then one of the major tasks of that virtual community is to ensure that all content made available meets some quality standards. This could be an easy or difficult task depending on the content in the community. For example, if content is generated by community organizers (as in BioMedNet) then their editorial staff is responsible for maintaining its quality. However, if content is member-generated then maintaining quality may not be an easy task. Such member input could vary from opinions to experiences and reviews where it may be difficult to judge the quality. There is nothing preventing a community member from inputting deliberate lies or misrepresentations about their experiences of products or services, thereby misleading other community members. In most cases, virtual communities can make a disclaimer regarding the member-generated content. Typically, disclaimers state that communities cannot fully vouch for the quality of the content, suggesting that they are the opinions of individuals and so on. Notwithstanding, unless there is some intervention to assure quality, the community can easily disintegrate, as serious community members will start looking elsewhere. The intervention can be in the form of moderators in chat rooms or editors who will continuously monitor the nature and quality of input and interactions and take action against members who continuously disrupt the community. Ensuring the quality of information from advertisers and marketers may also be difficult, but in most cases the virtual community can rely on the corporate image and reputation of such advertisers and marketers as proxies for their information quality. Virtual communities can thus ensure that their community members are not subject to the manipulations of 'fly-by-night' operators and their schemes.

Free-riding members

For a community which relies on members' input for value generation, members who 'free-ride' can be a problem. For example, consider a virtual community devoted to vacation travelling. Members can access useful information from travel agents and other marketers of vacation packages, but can also refer to other members' reviews of and experiences with different packages – which can be much more useful. If community members participate in a community only as 'lurkers' and do not contribute any useful information (by trying out a package or service themselves), then the community can suffer (Choi *et al.*, 1997). Over time, such free riding can lead to paucity of useful content in the community. Thus, as an intermediary, virtual communities have to ensure active participation of members. In some cases, this may come through economic incentives.

Members' privacy

Members who join virtual communities usually provide demographic, lifestyle and interest information to the community organizers. This information is usually needed to better meet member needs for social and commercial interactions, e.g., a senior citizen may like to interact with other senior citizens who have similar interests and concerns, and they may be interested in learning about new medical insurance plans that they may want to enrol in. The community organizers also need the information to maintain the relative homogeneity of the community in terms of interests and/or demographics. In addition, a virtual community can also generate significant information regarding members' interests through chat rooms and discussion groups where they interact with other members. Virtual communities can also track members' transaction information. While all such information has value for marketers and advertisers, most members expect virtual communities to respect their privacy and safeguard their personal information and not let advertisers and marketers use the information indiscriminately to 'spam' members. Members also expect similar privacy in dealing with other members. Thus, virtual communities may choose to use *aggregated* personal information to provide to marketers and not divulge individual-level information. Any serious breach of privacy can lead to litigation, negative publicity and ultimately to the disintegration of the community.

Corporate clients' needs

Advertisers and marketers expect value for the revenue that they provide virtual communities by way of advertising fees and commissions. They derive such value through communicating their messages to the right target segment, forging long-term relationships with members and getting information on how best to meet members' needs. This implies that corporate clients expect to get 'good' quality demographic and interest data from virtual communities that do not contain deliberate falsifications and misrepresentations. In addition, they would like to focus on individual consumers and their specific needs to take advantage of the one-on-one marketing opportunities that the Web facilitates. This implies that corporate clients may demand individual-level data from virtual communities – even as virtual communities are concerned about protecting members' privacy. If virtual communities cannot deliver significant value to corporate clients, advertising and commission revenue may dry up quickly, thus adversely affecting virtual communities' financial status.

Maintaining the critical mass

For any community to thrive it needs to achieve a critical mass. If the chat rooms and discussion rooms are empty or do not have new content, membership dwindles quickly. Business-to-business communities are also similar in this respect. For example, Industry.Net was never able to attain the critical mass in time for the community to thrive. Since many businesses adopted a 'wait-and-see' approach, the community never took off. Critical mass is necessary for membership growth and for healthy revenues from corporate clients. As intermediaries, virtual communities have a special role to play in maintaining a critical mass.

In the next section, we focus on a model of intermediation, and the economic and incentive mechanisms that are needed to maintain a healthy virtual community while considering the various trade-offs among the issues identified above.

A model of intermediation

We use the principal-agent framework to model intermediation (see, for example, Diamond, 1984, 1996). Consider a cybermarket with two players – consumers who are risk averse, and marketers who are risk neutral. Assume that consumers possess demographic and psychographic information about themselves that is of significant value to the marketer. This information has value for marketers as it can help them design products and services tailored to consumer needs and thereby increase the chances of a significant earning. We also assume that consumers value their personal information – either because they know marketers value it and/or because they value their privacy. If their personal information becomes easily available it could be potentially costly for them in trying to avoid or stop unnecessary 'spamming'. Thus, consumer information has value for consumers, just as monetary assets have value. While monetary assets have value that is practically homogeneous across consumers, the valuation, v, of consumer information can vary across the consumer population. For example, marketers may value demographic and psychographic information about certain consumers more than about others. For now, let us assume that each consumer's information, prior to being obtained, is valued at the distribution's mean, $E(v)$. Without any loss of generality, let us assume that $E(v) = 1$.

In the absence of intermediaries, marketers have to go directly to consumers in search of appropriate consumer information. Also, they will need personal information from a significant number of consumers, say, m. Using information from the m consumers, the marketer would be able to realize a return that could include increased profits through personalization of their products or services, increasing customer loyalty and so on. The marketer could then share this profit with consumers as a return on their information. When consumers provide information to marketers in exchange for some future return as just explained, they would like to monitor what the marketer does with the information and ensure that the marketer uses the information properly to generate a return for their investment of personal information. There is a cost involved in monitoring, denoted by K. Realistically, there is no available mechanism on the Internet for consumers to monitor what marketers do with personal information, other than through their experience and interactions with the marketer over time (say, through loyalty programmes or through finding product offerings tailored to their interest, all of which may provide indications as to how their personal information is being used; or indications of misuse if they are subject to spamming). Thus, the cost of monitoring can be assumed to be prohibitively high, that is, $K \gg 1$, which is the expected valuation of information. There are also savings, S, associated with monitoring. These savings could be interpreted as the benefits arising from the information remaining private.

Let us assume that a marketer enters into contracts with consumers for obtaining their personal information. If there is no monitoring by consumers of what the marketer does with the personal information, then the nature of the optimal contract will depend on the actual realization (or perception) of profits through the use of personal information. Let the profits earned be $Prf = m*1*f(m)$ where $f(m)$ is a function of m that takes a value of zero for values of m less than some critical mass, and takes on a value greater than 1 beyond the critical mass, increasing at a diminishing rate. That is, the marketer cannot make a profit from the information if the marketer has less than the critical mass signing up, and the exact profit level depends on the number of customers beyond the critical mass. One could specify the function form of $f(m)$ and the probability distribution of m but, for now, let us assume a discrete distribution for Prf: $Prf = m(1.6)$ with a probability $p = 0.6$, whilst $Prf = 0$ with $p = 0.4$. Assume that this information is common knowledge for the marketer as well as for consumers. What does this information imply for the consumers? The probabilities indicate that consumers give the marketer a 60 per cent chance of succeeding in getting a return on their personal information (in whatever form – better products, longer term relationships, lower prices, better services and so on). On average, if they are expecting a 10 per cent return on their information invested, valued at 1, then the optimal contract payment, Cp, that the marketer needs to offer can be calculated from the equation $0.6*Cp = 1.1$, which results in Cp to be 1.833, a 83.3 per cent return. (In fact, since we have assumed consumers to be risk averse, the value of Cp will be even higher.)

Thus, based on the uncertainty faced by the consumer regarding the success of any venture that requires their personal information, the marketer will have to promise a significant return for the consumers in exchange for their personal information. If the marketer fails to generate the return that the consumer expects, or fails to share the realized profit with the consumers, then the consumers can blacklist the marketer and refuse to deal with the marketer in the future. This ensures that if the marketer profits then there is an incentive to honour the contract. How do concerns about privacy impact the contract? At present there is no mechanism to stop the marketer from reselling the personal information to others for profit. This is an added impediment for consumers to share their personal information. It should be noted that even for a contract with an optimal Cp, there will be consumers who will not enter into such a contract: these are the consumers who have valuations in the upper tail of the distribution of v (those who value their privacy and information much more than does the average consumer). Since Cp is designed with the average consumer's valuation $E(v)$, these consumers will not find Cp sufficiently attractive to exchange their information. On the basis of the above modelling framework, the following proposition can be made.

Proposition 2:
Marketers will incur a significant cost in obtaining personal information directly from consumers in cyberspace. This cost will be higher: (1) for marketers with lower reputation; (2) as the return for information is less concrete; and (3) as the percentage of consumers in the target population who already share information with other marketers is lower.

This proposition follows by noting the effects of the above factors on the variables that determine the optimal Cp. When a marketer's reputation is low, consumers' perception of overall success of the marketer's project will be low. This effect will be felt through a lower mean of the distribution of m, that is, consumers perceive that the marketer cannot gather information from a significant number of consumers. The probability of success decreases and the optimal contract Cp increases, sometimes even so far beyond the level of believability that marketers cannot approach the consumers. If the return for information is in an abstract form – better service and better quality that cannot be easily perceived – then, given the risk-averse nature of consumers, they may seek higher returns (say, more than the 10 per cent assumed in the model). By the same token, if consumers already share their information with other marketers, the marginal return they may seek from sharing the same information may be much lower than otherwise (that is, their marginal costs of sharing their private information are much lower now).

The above proposition has many implications for a community of transactions. It implies that marketers with established reputations in other channels have an advantage over Internet startups with lower reputations in building a transaction-based community. At the same time, startups have a better chance of collecting information from consumers who are already cyberspace savvy and have shared information with other firms and by providing concrete monetary rewards – discounts, coupons, money – for information sharing.

What can marketers do to reduce the costs of acquiring consumer information without the intervention of any intermediary? One way to reduce costs is to increase the probability of a larger community membership base, m, through several value-added measures. They can provide chat rooms and discussion groups, which can meet consumers' social needs and increase the chances of a larger community base. These may lower the return they would seek for exchange of information as they are already obtaining some value in the social dimension. Value-added content on marketers' Web sites also has the same effect. In order to lower costs further the marketer may have to take on the role of an intermediary. The impact of intermediaries in the value-chain is discussed below.

Impact of intermediaries

In financial intermediary theory (see Bhattacharya and Thakor, 1993), intermediation is often justified on the basis of avoiding duplication of monitoring efforts. Using the notation introduced earlier, if m consumers spend K (cost of monitoring), then the total cost of direct monitoring is mK. S is the total savings from monitoring (that is, keeping all information private) and, if there is no monitoring, S is also the cost without monitoring. If the total cost of monitoring with an intermediary is less than the minimum of mK and S, then intermediaries create value in the transaction. With the intermediary, the total cost of monitoring is K plus a cost of monitoring the intermediary, T. Thus, if $K + T < \min (S, mK)$, then having an intermediary is cost effective (Diamond, 1996: 54). In the context of our application, if T – the cost of monitoring the intermediary – is as high as mK, that is, if the intermediary is just like another marketer to the consumers, then intermediation will not create any value. Thus, T has to be much less than mK. Under what conditions can T be small? T can be small if: (1) the community that is providing the monitoring function is controlled by the members themselves; and (2) if the community is run by a third party who has a vested interest in keeping the community alive, i.e., the third party has no ulterior motive in running the community. We explain below the intuition behind this result in the context of our application.

When consumers provide their private information to the intermediary, the intermediary has a conflict of interest with the members. That is, the intermediary can do whatever they want with the information. How can consumers avoid having to monitor the intermediary? This can be done through the intermediary entering into contracts with the consumers, providing an attractive return in exchange for their information. If the intermediary fails to do so, the intermediary will face the disintegration of the community. This threat of disintegration is sufficient incentive for the intermediary to honour the contracts, since not doing so will threaten its well being.

Proposition 3:
Electronic communities taking on the role of intermediaries can signifi-
cantly lower the costs of obtaining consumer personal information and
access for marketers.

The impact of intermediaries on the costs of obtaining consumer information can be gauged through an understanding of how the different
variables such as consumers' expected return on investment of information, the distribution of expected profits, membership base and
consumers' perception of probability of success, are affected.

The first advantage that intermediaries can provide is diversification.
That is, consumer information is provided to multiple marketers and,
therefore, the probability of an eventual success increases significantly.
This can be viewed as a reduction of uncertainty through the law of
large numbers. This increase in the probability of successful return
reduces the magnitude of Cp, the optimal cost of the contract.

The second impact is through protection of privacy. Intermediaries
are in a good position as third parties with no connection to marketers
to provide mechanisms and assurance for consumer information
protection. By crafting clever mechanisms for consumer privacy and
securing members' trust intermediaries can lower the expected return
of consumers for their private information (say, from the 10 per cent that
we had assumed earlier in this section to 5 per cent).

Third, given the different relationships that the intermediaries can
forge with multiple marketers, they would be in a much better position
than individual marketers to provide value to members in terms of
product or service information content and varied choice. This also
enables them to secure members' trust in less time than would be possible
for an individual marketer, as they would not be hindered by an agenda
of pushing a specific product or service at members. For the same reason,
intermediaries can better fulfil the social needs of members through chat
rooms, discussion rooms and content compared with marketers. As intermediaries can effectively provide a variety of services to members of a
virtual community, they are also in a better position to maintain the critical mass of members and help grow the community. Meeting members'
needs in multiple ways also impacts the probability distribution of
m positively (that is, consumers will be more certain about the ability
of the community to attract members) and this leads to a perception of
higher profits and, thus, the return promised in the contract is more
believable.

The net effect is that those consumers who prefer to remain on the
sidelines when a marketer approaches them for private information are
more likely to join a virtual community because of the increased probability of success with their information. The protection of privacy also
increases their likelihood of joining the virtual community.

The preceding discussion provides a clear understanding of how, even
though intermediaries incur a significant cost in monitoring marketers
(K), the overall cost of obtaining consumer information can be much
lower. Intermediaries can incur additional costs in monitoring the quality
of content entering the community, whether from members or marketers.

The costs of monitoring quality from members could be significant – moderating chat rooms, discussions forums and so on. If there are still serious problems, then the intermediary could even charge subscription fees from members to weed out unwanted input, to keep membership exclusive and to sustain a high quality of input. Some virtual communities charge a nominal fee of US$0.25 for members to post their messages in the discussion forums to prevent frivolous messages. If members derive significant value from the content generated in the virtual community (for example, in BioMedNet), then subscription fees act as a mechanism to maintain the quality of content and contribute towards a healthy virtual community.

Subscription fees can also help in reducing the enrolment of purely 'free-riding' members as they incur a cost in enrolling. Such fees can be set high for initial enrolment and as members remain for a longer time the fees could be gradually reduced. It is to be noted that such charges are possible only if members value content sufficiently to enrol. However, revenue from marketers and advertisers could be used to subsidize these fees significantly, with those members who have been loyal for a longer time reaping the benefits.

We have seen that maintaining the privacy of consumers can bring the costs down appreciably. At the same time, however, intermediaries have to meet the needs of marketers to keep revenue flowing into the virtual communities. Such a trade-off can be accomplished by clever mechanisms such as FireFly's Passport (www.firefly.net). FireFly collects demographic and psychographic information from those consumers who apply for the passport and offers them full control over their personal information as to what could be shared and what not, who to share with and who not and so on. When members enter the Web sites of marketers who are clients of FireFly, they provide their passports which, depending on their previous consent, provide the appropriate personal information to the marketer. The marketer uses this information to personalize his service and product offering to the members, develop a relationship with the customer, direct the customers to their own communities with like-minded members and so on. FireFly also provides content to members and reviews on things of interest to them from other community members. In addition, FireFly provides opportunities for marketers to build relationships among themselves (for example, airlines, hotels and car rentals) centred on FireFly members' interests.

Concluding comments

In this chapter we have focused our attention on virtual communities from the perspective of how they can contribute to electronic commerce rather than viewing them as a pure social phenomenon. We have made arguments as to why virtual communities need to take on an intermediary role to keep the communities healthy. Obviously, this argument is valid only when we view virtual communities from a commercial perspective. It is not necessary for a relationship-oriented community to take on this role if revenue generation is not one of the objectives of the community. What we have shown is that virtual communities can offer a win-win situation for both members and marketers. Based on our exploratory work it could be hypothesized that for virtual communities to thrive as a part of a digital economy, they need to transform themselves as intermediaries. GEIS-TPN started off as a community owned by GE largely for the purposes of using GE's brand equity to help initiate the community. It was spun off as an intermediary once it attained a critical mass. Communities run by marketers will have limitations in terms of offering members variety. Such communities may not be able to take criticism from members easily. Controlling such a community will not be easy; these are not issues when virtual communities are in the hands of intermediaries. In addition, as we have shown, there are strong economic arguments for their existence based on the value they create. Still, there are many interesting issues that need exploring. How do virtual communities diffuse in cyberspace? What are the mechanisms – social, economic, cultural or otherwise – that lead to their formation? What is the future scenario for virtual communities? We hope that the thoughts expressed in this chapter will contribute to this exploration.

References

Armstrong, A. and Hagel, J. (1995). Real profits from virtual communities. *The McKinsey Quarterly*, **3**, 127–41.

Armstrong, A. and Hagel, J. (1996). The real value of online communities. *Harvard Business Review*, **74**, 134–40.

Bhattacharya, S. and Thakor, A. V. (1993). Contemporary banking theory. *Journal of Financial Intermediation*, **3**, 2–50.

Choi, S.-Y., Stahl, D. and Whinston, A. B. (1997). *The Economics of Electronic Commerce*. Macmillan Technical Publishing.

Diamond, D. (1984). Financial intermediation and delegated monitoring. *Review of Economic Studies*, **51**, 393–414.

Diamond, D. (1996). Financial intermediation as delegated monitoring: a simple example. *Federal Reserve Bank of Richmond Economic Quarterly*, **82**, 51–66.

Kannan, P. K., Chang, A. and Whinston, A. B. (1998). Marketing information on the I-way. *Communications of the ACM*, **41**, 35–43.

Rheingold, H. (1993). *The Virtual Community: homesteading on the electronic frontier*. Harper Perennial Publishers.

and thus lead to the emergence of electronic markets. Electronic markets are, first and foremost, markets – institutions or mechanisms which serve the market participants to allocate resources (Williamson, 1983; Schmid, 1995). In these domains, information and communication technologies are used to establish marketplaces in cyberspace, to enable buyers and sellers to meet, evaluate offerings and negotiate digitally with little or no restrictions of distance or time.

Moreover, it has long been established that information technology has a significant impact on industrial organization as well as on individual organizations. Malone *et al.* (1987; see also Porter and Millar, 1985; Nault and Dexter, 1995) suggest that companies are changing the way they operate owing to significant reductions in the cost of obtaining, processing and transmitting information. A myriad of examples from different industrial sectors, such as clothing, books, wine and tourism, show the trend towards direct sales by the supplier or manufacturer to the final customer (e.g., Belz *et al.*, 1991). However, the same emerging electronic marketplaces offer revenues and profits for specialized intermediaries. Technical and institutional obstacles, high information costs, missing transparency and security flaws – distinctive features of the Internet at present – all provide a huge field for intermediation, in some cases even reintermediation (Sarkar *et al.*, 1996; Lee, 1997).

The purpose of this chapter is not to explore these changes in depth. However, it is important to note that these alterations imply a continuous evolution of the firms' value chains and industry value systems (Porter and Millar, 1985; Rockart and Scott, 1993), as IT transforms not only intra-organizational structures and processes but also the nature and structure of linkages between them, the interaction patterns with customers and the transaction process as described in the next section.

Transaction phases

A market transaction may be divided into three phases (Schmid, 1993; Zbornik, 1996): information, agreement and settlement.

- *Information phase*. In the information phase, customers collect information on potential products and services. They look for possible suppliers, asking for prices and conditions. The information phase covers the initial satisfaction of a consumer's need for information to reconcile his or her demand for a product or service with the offer.
- *Agreement phase*. Negotiations between suppliers and customers take place in the agreement phase. The phase serves to establish a firm link between supplier and buyer that will eventually lead to a contract, fixing details such as product specifications, payment, delivery and so on.
- *Settlement phase*. The last of the conventional steps is called settlement phase. The (physical/virtual) delivery of the product ordered will take place during this phase. Also possible are after-sales interactions such as guarantee claims or help desk services.

In virtual environments, however, a further degree of interaction becomes a central issue. A reader who buys a book at Amazon.com is automatically a potential source for reviews. If many readers with similar tastes and preferences join her efforts, an online community of similarly minded people comes into existence. The notion of community lies at the heart of the Internet revolution.

Community component and personalization

The concept of 'community', which has been discussed in recent literature (Parks and Floyd, 1995; Schuler, 1996; Hagel and Armstrong, 1997; Schubert, 1999; Schubert and Selz, 1999), serves as an essential tie between two transactions. The communication that takes place among customers, and between customers and the firm, links the product more firmly to them. Shared interests allow for the building of communities that generate a certain level of trust among their respective members (Armstrong and Hagel, 1996; Erickson, 1997; Iacono and Weisband, 1997; Figallo, 1998) thus inspiring a fertile electronic commerce environment. The collection of shared community knowledge facilitates the personalization of the user interface and the product offering. Collaborative filtering methods generate suggestions for individual users based on the data of a community of like-minded people (using statistical techniques such as nearest neighbour algorithm). When a user selects a home page, an EC Web site identifies the user and presents an individual welcome screen with pre-selected product suggestions. It is even conceivable to customize new products which are tailored to the needs of special sub-communities (e.g., insurance products for people who participate in sports activities in the high-risk category; Elofson and Robinson, 1998).

Classical trading rules may prove not to be effective in a world where people (consumers) are anonymous and empowered to create their own (deliberately chosen) identity. Spar and Bussgang (1996) point to the fact that an absence of established business rules on the Internet may result in a commercial environment affected by insecurity. Virtual communities that set standards (e.g., Netiquette), will generate confidence and allow for the constitution of 'Trusted Intermediaries'. Trusted intermediaries will guarantee generic services such as contracting, payment, logistics and security, and will serve as an entity transforming the anonymity and anarchy of the Internet into a market with identifiable customers and recordable transactions.

Technology and media-inherent characteristics

As mentioned above, the Web Assessment Model examines characteristics that are inherent to the Internet, such as 24-hour worldwide availability. Table 5.1 lists the core characteristics that were used to develop the Web Assessment criteria.

Marketing: performance system

In marketing, the term performance marketing (Belz *et al.*, 1991) defines the quest to offer a customer not just the product itself, but to propose

Table 5.1 Media-inherent characteristics

Media inherent characteristics

Hypermedia presentation
Database interface (expert system)
24-hour access (time)
Anonymity
Ubiquity (space)
Asynchronous communication
Configuration possibility (interactivity)
Transfer of cost benefits to the customer

a specific solution for each individual customer need. Why should a company turn away from mass marketing to individually tailored solutions? Customers today show a very rational and price-sensitive behaviour. A company thus cannot just offer the genuine product or service itself, but needs also to offer integrated solutions embracing the following elements in order successfully to differentiate itself from the competition:

- core product/service
- a product system
- bundling
- complementary external offerings
- price and quality arrangements
- delivery
- set-up and training
- continuous service agreements
- an emotional customer experience.

To illustrate, a sample resulting performance system – the case of an airline – is shown in Table 5.2.

Table 5.2 Retail (airline) example of a performance system

0	Product/service system	Flight from Zurich to New York with Swissair or packaged Swissair offer, e.g., flight Geneva–Amsterdam–Zurich
1	External bundling	Combination of onward flight with partner airline, hotel arrangement, theatre tickets, etc.
2	Generic services	Integration of payments, logistics systems, e.g., airline credit card, city check-in, etc.
3	Customer specific: additional services	Focused offers, e.g., youth fares, package holidays, business packages, adventure trips, etc.
4	Emotional customer experience	Youth club, forum for frequent flyers or leisure travellers focusing on special destinations, e.g., Big Apple Club

The Web Assessment tool

Developing the tool

The Web Assessment tool was designed and programmed in order to collect assessment data. The list of criteria was implemented into an online WWW form. The outline of the questionnaire was developed in accordance with the requirements listed in Kromrey's work (Kromrey, 1998) about models and methods for the gathering and evaluation of empirical data; and guidelines for the development of computer-supported questionnaires by Möhrle (1997). The questions were derived from the Internet-inherent characteristics listed in Table 5.1.

In order not to overload the questionnaire we decided to restrict the number of questions for each transaction phase to the most important. Thus, not all of the media-inherent characteristics are represented in every transaction phase. This helps keep the questionnaire short, thus motivating assessors to proceed to the very end. The assessment scale varies from 'I strongly agree' to 'I strongly disagree', encompassing four different values. Respondents often tend to choose the middle option of a given set of answers so we decided to implement an even number of values to encourage assessors to unveil their preferences either in favour or against the criterion. In addition, there is a 'zero option' denoting 'not applicable'. This should be used whenever the criterion is not relevant for the Web site (e.g., logistics are not relevant in the case of digital products). Figure 5.1 is an excerpt from the online assessment form.

Each assessment question is accompanied by a detailed explanation which can be accessed via a hyperlink. The Web Assessment tool has been designed using Lotus Domino technology. The tool is part of the NetAcademy project, which aims at the design of a system for the structuring, acquisition, mediation and dissemination of domain-specific scientific knowledge on the basis of a generic, Internet-based platform (Lincke *et al.*, 1998; Schubert *et al.*, 1998).

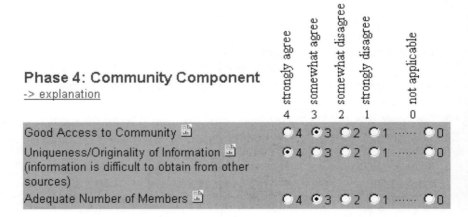

Figure 5.1
Excerpt from the Web Assessment questionnaire

In a final section assessors are asked to rank the overall quality of the Web site. Remember that the best profile is not simply the one that includes the highest scores. The success of an electronic commerce site has to be judged separately according to financial success (from the vendor perspective) and fulfilment of customer needs and expectations (from a consumer perspective). The consumer perspective is examined in a final question where participants evaluate the general quality of the Web site. Finally, assessors are asked to unveil their level of experience with EC Web sites.

Web Assessment criteria

The following section describes the Web Assessment criteria that were implemented into the online questionnaire.

Community component

A commercial Web site should help to establish a relationship among customers on the one hand and between customers and the company on the other hand. It thus facilitates the means to establish a community of people sharing common interests. Customers interact and exchange information, for example, about experiences with company products or services. The information from customers to customers provides an additional level of confidence. The company gets the chance to respond directly to customer requests and needs, thereby strengthening the bond between the company and its clients.

The criteria set forth in Tables 5.3 to 5.6 are intuitive but not necessarily exhaustive. To validate this particular set, it is necessary to develop survey measures that capture these factors and then correlate individual criteria measures with overall Web site assessment ratings. To date, we know of no comprehensive study assessing this or any other criterion set. We present this set as a first pass to stimulate discussion in the important area of developing metrics to evaluate Web sites.

Selected findings

During 1999, we asked a number of people (researchers as well as practitioners) to use the Web Assessment tool in order to assess their favourite Web sites, focusing especially on *online auctions* and *bookstores*. The resulting data sheets were collected and processed. So far, we have been able to collect seventy data sheets from more than fifty-five different assessors. We asked participants to evaluate only sites with which they are really familiar. Since each user usually has a limited set of favourite Web sites most people only made one or two assessments. The data thus represent a small sample of highly qualified user opinions.

The following section describes different ways of graphically evaluating the Web Assessment data and preparing them so that they can be

Table 5.3 Information phase

No.	Criterion	Explanation
1	Good user interface	The 'user interface' assesses ease of use for frequent users as well as for first time visitors. This also comprises loading times of pages and guidance in the interaction process with the Web site when completing a transaction.
2	Good structure of content	The 'structure of content' measures ease of access as well as first and second impression of the logical structure of the content. Tables of contents, navigational frames or image maps are typical features to facilitate navigation.
3	Reasonable information quantity	The 'quantity of information' focuses on the range of information on company, product and services.
4	Apparent benefits from stored customer profile (e.g., client-specific offers)	Most Web sites require customers to register or at least to supply some basic personal information. Good Web marketers should remunerate their customers for 'revealing' this kind of information. This could be via: • directly crediting money or services, examples are www.bonusmail.com and www.cybergold.com • granting discounts for product sales.
5	Good products/service combination possibilities (cross-selling: combine products and/or services)	'Combination possibility' examines the breadth of the product range and the possibility to combine various product offerings (either to the company's own products, or third-party goods or services) online. It measures the amount of cross selling, i.e., the combination of various goods or services (such as an airline ticket and a hotel reservation).
6	Good availability/performance of the system	'Availability/performance' (with respect to geographical aspects) measures the global availability of the system. It judges the availability to customers regardless of their geographic location (e.g., different language versions). Special mirror sites could, e.g., improve global performance. Since this aspect is one of the main advantages of the Internet it gains special consideration. 'Availability/performance' (with respect to time) measures the loading times, which are of great importance for user comfort.
7	Cost benefits passed on to the client	The use of electronic sales channels often reduces transaction costs. Provided that margins remain unchanged vendors should be able to offer products on their Web site at a lower price than in a comparable physical store.

used to analyse strengths and weaknesses of existing Web sites. First, we look at the single company profile which gives an overview of the overall performance of a single Web site. We then compare different profiles of companies operating in the same business for an inter-company comparison.

In the following diagrams the x-axis represents the assessment criteria within the different transaction phases. The value range is from +2 (I strongly agree) to –2 (I strongly disagree). It is important to mention

Table 5.4 Agreement phase

No.	Criterion	Explanation
1	Adjustable customer profile (e.g., payment information)	Business transactions usually require customers to reveal some basic personal information, e.g., payment information. For a greater comfort this kind of information can be safely stored for reuse in a subsequent session.
2	Guided ordering according to profile (personalized services)	In order to receive a higher degree of personalized services customers could be willing to reveal additional information. Besides, the system might track user activity. A detailed user profile containing personal information such as age, gender, hobbies, preferences and so on helps to treat each customer differently. This could result in guiding mechanisms, enable the system to come up with suggestions or even grant special client discounts.
3	Possibility of customized products	Some customers might be interested in buying combinations of products (product systems) or only fragments of a product (e.g., only parts of a magazine or newspaper). The Web site could support the customization of user-designed products.
4	Transparent, interactive integration of business rules	The underlying business rules should be transparent to the user. Business rules are general terms and conditions, guarantees, possibility for returning products, etc. Click buttons to accept terms and conditions and guided interaction are helpful in this context.
5	Good implementation of security issues (digital signature, secure server)	Good Web sites should offer reliable security features (such as Secure Sockets Layer (SSL), digital certificates, etc.) or implement accepted standards (e.g., Secure Electronic Transactions (SET), TRUSTe, Platform for Privacy Preferences (P3).
6	Good contact possibilities with vendor (help desk for problems during order process)	'Contact possibility' examines the various ways to establish communication with the vendor. It may comprise the implementation of a help desk or a call centre. The Web site could offer: ● the opportunity to write and read questions of common interest (Frequently Asked Questions or FAQs) ● a feedback possibility via e-mail or Web forms (i.e., via the electronic medium) The feedback response times must be adequate to the medium used.

that the values do not represent the quality of the Web site (overall high scores do not equal a high-quality Web site). Rather, the values indicate, on the one hand, that the company did a good job in implementing certain Web Assessment criteria (0 to 2); or, on the other hand, that there is still room for improvement (0 to –2).

Single company profile

Amazon provides a unique case to illustrate how the Internet is actually changing the way consumers buy and sell products and services. The

Table 5.5 Settlement phase

No.	Criterion	Explanation
1	Easy selection of generic services	'Generic services' are software modules that are available on the entire Web platform and always present themselves in a uniform interface. Generic services support an electronic transaction (such as the purchase of a book online). Examples are electronic payment systems, logistics services, electronic contracting modules and so on. Their bricks-and-mortar counterparts are power sockets, telephone hooks, water taps and the postal system that should be the same wherever you are (this applies at least within the same country). An easy selection of such services means that they are integrated into the settlement process. Examples are the selection of different choices for, e.g., payment systems (Ecash, credit card, SET, cheque, bill) or logistics services (UPS, FedEx, US Post). The tracking of order information should also be supported.
2	Good integration of generic services	A good integration of such services means that they are sensibly used wherever necessary, comforting the user by their common interface and their routine operation. Typical generic services in EC applications are payments, electronic contracting (dealing with prices and conditions) and logistics. Other generic services are, for example, shopping trolleys, one invoice for multiple shops and shopping lists.
3	EC-application makes effective use of customer profile (e.g., payment and logistic information)	During the settlement of a business transaction some basic personal information needs to be revealed (e.g., payment information or delivery address for physical goods). For a greater comfort this kind of information could be safely stored for reuse in a subsequent session.
4	Good tracing and tracking (e.g., direct access to personal order information)	A good example for an integration of a logistics service (in this case of a third party), can be found at www.amazon.com. After ordering, customers are provided with information on how to trace their order at the UPS tracking site.
5	Good IT-integration (connection with customer's infrastructure)	Especially for small and medium-sized businesses (SMEs) an export filter (a link to their accounting system) for financial data could be of great value (e.g., information can be exported into Microsoft Money, the financial package).
6	Convenient after-sales support	The Web site should also support the handling of after-sales services (e.g., guarantee form, feedback form).

case of Amazon is well documented (e.g., *The Economist*, 1997; Kotha, 1998). Today, Amazon sells books worth US$600 million (*The Economist*, 1999) out of total book retail sales in the USA of about US$25.5 billion in 1995. Recently, Amazon began to sell videos, music, gifts and has even started a new Web site for online auctions.

Amazon differs from a physical bookstore. Customers can browse the online catalogue containing over 2.5 million books – about ten times as many as the largest physical bookstore. The reviews and comments

Table 5.6 Community component

No.	Criterion	Explanation
1	Good access to community	The following definition applies to the notion 'virtual community': 'Virtual communities describe the union and the communication between individuals who share common values and interests and who use electronic media to get in touch with another. Their communication is independent from restrictions of time and place'. These 'virtual communities' may be loosely or more closely attached to a special Web site. A high value of the 'access to community' criterion indicates a good link between the product offer and the community component of the Web site.
2	Uniqueness/originality of information (information is difficult to obtain from other sources)	This criterion evaluates the value of the information that can be obtained from the community area. A community that includes experts who actively contribute to the community area might supply information that cannot be retrieved from other sources. A TV guide, for example, features online interviews between community members and movie stars and stores them on its Web site. In this case, the community area is really worth visiting.
3	Adequate number of members	The value of a community is its members. There must be some 'key members' who show a special dedication to the community. Nevertheless, as the numbers of members increase so does the probability of good questions, answers, reviews and other contributions and hence a rich community experience.
4	Well-implemented personalization and collaborative filtering mechanisms.	When joining a community, members are usually looking for people with similar tastes or interests. There are two main kinds of user profiles that can be stored in a community database: • personal information about interests and tastes entered by the user (self-assessment) • tracking of interactions performed by the user (activity log). The self-assessment should contain a selection of pre-defined categories (e.g., gender, age, favourite music, etc.). This information is not subject to many changes whereas the activity log is meant to trace dynamic information (page accesses, market transactions). After a while the system may use the dynamic information to derive patterns of users' interest and behaviour. Customers with similar tastes or needs are identified according to commonalties in their preference profiles. Based on these preference patterns mutual recommendation from customers to customers can be derived, sometimes even for new products that the customer was not previously aware of (e.g., a new CD by a favourite pop group or a completely new product tailored to the needs of a special sub-community).
5	Member may choose his or her appearance within the community (e.g., choosing a personal avatar)	Some Web sites offer the possibility to choose a representation of one's self (e.g., Worlds Away, Ultima Online). These representations are called 'avatars'. They appear in the form of animals, people or characters from comic strips. Sometimes it is even possible to assemble the character, choosing from a given set of heads, bodies, arms and so on.

Table 5.6   continued

No. Criterion	Explanation
6 Privacy is sufficiently protected	Sometimes access to a community forum might be gained without revealing personal information. There are clients who prefer the anonymity of the Web to the face-to-face encounter in a bricks-and-mortar shop.
7 Perceived real added-value from membership	This criterion assesses the value of membership. Besides the information that can be obtained from the community area there might be an additional value creation, e.g., in the establishment of personal relationships with other members. According to Armstrong and Hagel (1996) there do exist so-called 'communities of relationship'. Specific shared experiences of life are the basis of these communities. ParentsNet is one example for this type of community.
8 Good, customized push mechanisms (information is automatically being sent to members)	There are two different mechanisms to establish a customer relationship via e-mail, push and pull. • Push-technique. Here the Web system automatically supplies the customer with information. Either the customer chooses to receive specific information updates or the information provider sends unsolicited information which might be of interest to an established or possible customer. Customers can customize push mechanisms. The information provider may offer different categories of information updates where the client can check boxes in order to receive the information required (examples are Netscape's In-Box Direct and Amazon.com).
9 Good pull mechanisms (member can ask for information updates)	• Pull-technique. The customer actively seeks information and retrieves this information on his/her own whenever needed. Pull effects are typically the result of advertisements, discounts or a good (visible) place in store shelves.

represent a unique attraction of the Web site. Professional reviews from newspapers such as the *New York Times* and more informal reviews from readers are added to the system on an on-going basis. Unlike most physical bookstores, the firm competes as information broker and not just as a retailer of books. Collaborative filtering mechanisms allow the company to propose suggestions for suitable books. The company collects reviews from customers thus adding much of the editorial content of their site. As this content grows, it attracts others to add to the richness of the mix and thus creating a virtuous cycle. In essence this is an explicit attempt to create a community around the needs of transaction (see Schubert, 1999). We will discuss in more detail the importance of the community component for Amazon.

Orders for best-sellers are shipped immediately, whilst other books are ordered directly from publishers. Amazon consistently undercuts the list price by as much as 40 per cent. The company fulfils core value propositions such as convenience, selection and service. Competition on price is fierce and competitors regularly even undercut Amazon's keen prices.

Table 5.7 is an example of the aggregation of eight user opinions assessing the information phase of the Amazon Web site. The mean value displays the aggregated ratings. The deviation column illustrates the degree of consensus among the assessors. The zero value represents complete agreement, values higher than 1 indicate a high degree of discrepancy. Figure 5.2 depicts the mean value graphically.

The sample shows complete agreement for the 'quantity of information' (item number 3) offered on this site as well as for the overall 'performance of the system' (item 6). The criteria for 'design of the user interface' (item 1) and 'structure of content' (item 2) are also almost equally valued. Nevertheless, there is a discrepancy for 'cost benefits' (item 4) and 'combination possibilities' (item 5). A possible explanation could be that the assessors developed their opinions based on different experiences with product offerings. There may be products on this server which are apparently cheaper than usual, making the benefit transfer obvious to the client. On the other hand, other products may already be sold at a very low margin in a bricks-and-mortar business that does not allow for even lower prices on the Web site. The same applies to 'combination possibilities' which might be appropriate only for a limited range of products.

Amazon received high values for the *information phase*. It offers a good user interface, good structure of content and a rich amount of useful information. In the case of Amazon, stored customer profiles allow the company to suggest books that the reader might be interested in. The

Table 5.7 Single company profile for the information phase – Amazon.com

No.	Information phase	A 1	A 2	A 3	A 4	A 5	A 6	A 7	A 8	Mean	S.D.
1	User interface	2	2	2	2	2	2	1	2	1.88	0.33
2	Structure	2	2	2	2	1	2	2	2	1.88	0.33
3	Information quantity	2	2	2	2	2	2	2	2	2.00	0.00
4	Benefits	2	2	−1	2	2	2	2	2	1.63	0.99
5	Combination possibility	−2	0	2	−2	−1	0	−1	2	−0.33	1.48
6	Performance	2	2	2	2	2	2	2	2	2.00	0.00
7	Cost benefits	2	2	2	1	2	−1	2	2	1.50	1.00

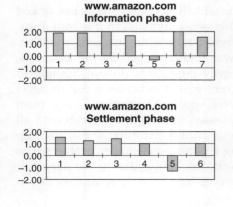

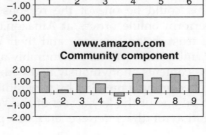

Figure 5.2
Single company profile of Amazon

profile also supports the online order process, as some information (such as address) does not need to be retyped. The delivery and payment information is used for all repeating transactions. Except for the combination of books and music on one single Web site, there is no product bundling with complementary services. The system usually shows a good performance. Low prices imply a certain level of transfer of cost benefits to the customer.

The *agreement phase* shows positive results for all categories with a lower mark for 'contact possibilities' (item 6). The ordering process is well structured and the assessors were generally satisfied with services offered in the agreement phase. The lower mark for 'contact possibilities' is most likely explained by the fact that if something goes wrong, people prefer a real (telephone) contact to resolve the situation. Amazon lacks this facility. To keep costs low (a call-centre is an expensive undertaking) most interaction is carried out by e-mail.

The lowest mark in the *settlement phase* is the 'IT-integration' (item 5). Amazon properly manages all the information and immediately transfers this to its enterprise resource planning system and to business partners. However, there is no possibility directly to integrate this information on the customer's computer system. People need to retype their orders into their own systems. A direct interface to the customer's IT environment might not be necessary for business-to-consumer transactions but it could represent an asset in business-to-business relations.

The *community component* appears to be one of the company's key assets for generating loyalty and repeat purchases. Amazon offers a good access to the community of book readers (item 1). Although the contents (summaries, comments, reviews and so on) are, principally, also available from different sources, the positive values of the second criterion show that the combination of 'book reviews' (via editors, newspapers, famous people) and 'customer comments' (via other readers) are valued by the customers. The number of active community members (item 3) yielded fairly high values, an advantage that differentiates Amazon from its competition (cf. following section). The implemented mechanisms for collaborative filtering (item 4) also received good grades. The possibility of choosing the personal appearance of representation of the user (item 5) is apparently not important for a Web site that sells books (indicated by negative values). Customers give their names when adding their comments but since the system does not examine their real identity these could well be false. The benefit from comments is not linked to the real identity of the author. This is not unusual in the book business: authors often use pseudonyms without forfeiting readers' attention. The protection of privacy (item 6) was highly judged by the assessors. This could be one of the reasons why customers do not hesitate to perform online orders at Amazon.com, which indicates a certain level of trust in the company and their Web site. The criterion 'benefit from membership' was also favourably assessed. Although users can read all the contents anonymously and without prior registration, the actual step of becoming a member by generating a personal customer profile seems to be one of the key assets of the Web site. This is due to the personalization of the interface and the profile-based book recommendation (e.g., 'instant recommendations'). Push (item 8) and pull (item 9) mechanisms are additional strong features (see Figure 5.3).

Summarizing the results, the emerging picture shows that Amazon covers the information phase very well, does a good job in the agreement and settlement phases and provides unique community services that are valued by their customers.

Inter-firm comparison

In order to identify general success factors, it will be necessary to look at Web sites that are actually yielding profits. For this reason, each assessor was asked to classify the Web sites according to the business for which it was designed. Profiles of less successful EC applications can then be compared against more profitable ones. The comparison of profiles and differences identified may suggest important aspects for improvement.

The following section presents a comparison between the Web sites of Amazon and Barnes and Noble. The bars in Figure 5.4 indicate that both Web sites follow a similar strategy for their community component. The key strength of Amazon comes in the form of the 'recommendation centre', book reviews and book comments. These services might be an explanation for why Amazon received higher values for almost all of the criteria.

Amazon versus Barnes and Noble

Figure 5.4 lists the three transaction phases and the community component drawing a direct comparison between Amazon and Barnes and Noble. Barnes and Noble is the largest book retailer in the USA. After an initially slow start on the Internet, this Web site is trying to catch up with Amazon. Early anecdotal evidence suggests that although the largest book retailer puts considerable resources into its online venture it is finding it difficult to win back business from its online rival.

The first observation when comparing the aggregated assessments of the two sites is the similarity of the results. Both sites seem equally to please or displease. Both are doing a fairly good job in the information phase with the exception of item 5 – 'combination possibility'. Barnes

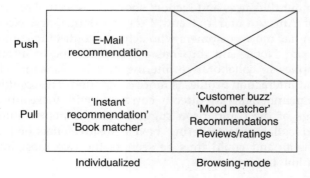

Figure 5.3
The Amazon.com 'recommendation centre'

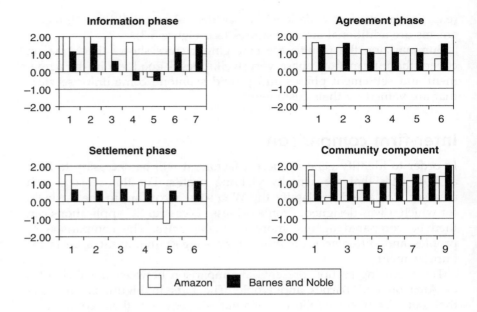

Figure 5.4
Inter-business
comparison –
Amazon versus
Barnes and Noble

and Noble, however, ranks lower for criterion 3, 'information quantity', and criterion 4, 'customer profile'.

Both companies emphasize services in the information and the community phase. They are obviously not interested in bundling their products with external partners, choosing instead to focus on low prices. In the beginning of Barnes and Noble's online business, their community approach was different from that of today. Amazon always made use of an open-community approach where everybody has access to all information. On the Barnes and Noble site, users first had to contribute to the system before access to the community area was granted. The higher number of members reflects that the Amazon approach is the more successful way of establishing a long-term relationship with the customer. Meanwhile, all big booksellers (e.g., also Borders Books and BOL) have almost identical strategies for personalization and community building.

Amazon offers more additional information than does Barnes and Noble. This becomes apparent in the number of stored book comments. A sample taken in March 1999 for three popular books from the categories 'Computer, Business and Fiction' showed respective results of 41, 18 and 78 for Amazon and 1, 1 and 2 for the Barnes and Noble Web sites. Amazon has more customers who actually contribute content than does Barnes and Noble and thus has a broader scope of information. The same applies to collaborative filtering because Amazon's basis of preference and interaction profiles is more compound. The resulting high benefits from membership are directly correlated with these advantages.

The findings of the comparison suggest that the items 'numbers of members' and 'collaborative filtering' have a positive effect on perceived customer benefits and could thus be seen as the two most important criteria for online bookstores.

Overall appraisal

The Internet makes it easier and much cheaper for people to contact a company. The easier the interaction, the more likely it is that people will interact on the Web site. This establishes a closer bond with the customer than at any given time in the past. It is fair to claim that in the online world services eclipse products, and effectively and successfully managing the customer relationship is more important than profit margins. As it is fairly easy and cheap for everyone to copy best practice Web sites and the features they offer, it becomes vital to create a solid relationship with customers beyond the initial contact. Successful players will become, in effect, types of portal owners similar to Amazon in books, eBay in auctions and Charles Schwab in finance.

However, few business-to-consumer Web sites are profitable today, and even high-profile sites such as Amazon do not expect to become profitable soon. Some of the auction sites report profits, albeit at very low levels. Business-to-business Web sites are a possible area to look for future avenues for research in Web Assessment on how to build a successful online business. Companies such as Dell and Cisco create turnovers of billions of dollars on their Web sites.

The assessments suggest that the information phase is generally better implemented than the other phases (which is hardly a great surprise). The Internet is basically an information medium. Most companies, when undertaking the first steps in the new medium, try basically to leverage the advantage of the new medium. Only gradually, albeit quickly, the Web converts into a platform for buying and selling, finally maturing into an open electronic market. The initial euphoria about the friction-free economy has given way to a more reflected picture that recognizes the difficulties of implementing an online store that ultimately delivers a physical product to real people.

In order to identify general success factors it will be necessary to look at Web sites that are actually yielding profits. Profitable Web sites can offer best practice profiles. Providers of less successful EC applications can then be compared against the profitable ones. The comparison of profiles and the thus identified differences may suggest important aspects for improvement.

Further research and conclusions

The Web Assessment model proposes a comprehensive method for evaluating Web sites. This chapter presents some of the theoretical background of an empirical study, followed by a detailed description of the Web Assessment criteria, which especially consider the specific media characteristics of the Internet. The discussion of the results focuses on one special venue of online commerce, namely bookstores. These advanced retail sites in both segments make good use of media-inherent features. In particular, the information phase and the agreement phase are well covered by the offerings of the Web sites that were analysed. This comes as no surprise, since it reflects developments where companies typically started to transform their paper-based product catalogues into the new Internet medium and are now adding interactive elements.

However, although generally acknowledged to be important, the solutions implemented to cover the community component and, to a lesser extent, the settlement phase still leave much room for improvement. Generic service integration in the settlement phase and personalization features, as part of the community component, will require most attention of Web site developers in the near future. The Web sites in each respective category that best handle these issues will derive a substantial competitive advantage.

The chapter deliberately limits the analysis to business-to-consumer cases with a standpoint close to the customer. To further validate the proposed framework and to assess electronic commerce applications, the model needs to be applied to retail sites. But it needs even more to be applied to business-to-business cases, since Internet pundits expect this to be the major growth area in electronic commerce in the years to come. The ongoing project will produce a set of reference cases allowing the build-up of a benchmarking database in order to derive best business practices. Furthermore, the model will be extended to accommodate the company's internal perspective and its cross-company information systems links (intranets, extranets). A continuously updated documentation of this project can be found in the Web Assessment section of the NetAcademy on Business Media (http://www.businessmedia.org/businessmedia/businessmedia.nsf/ages/wa_main.html).

References

Armstrong, A. and Hagel, J. (1996). The real value of online communities. *Harvard Business Review*, May–June, 134–41.

Belz, C., Bircher, B., Büsser, M. *et al.* (1991). *Erfolgreiche Leistungssysteme, Schäffer*. Verlag.

Dutta, S., Kwan, S. and Segev, A. (1997). Strategic marketing and customer relationship in electronic commerce. *Proceedings of the Fourth Conference of the International Society for Decision Support Systems*, Lausanne, Switzerland.

Economist (1997). In search of the perfect market – a survey of electronic commerce. *The Economist*, 10 May, survey section.

Economist (1999). When the bubble bursts. *The Economist*, 30 January, pp. 21–23.

Elofson, G. and Robinson, W. (1998). Creating a custom mass-production channel on the Internet. *Communications of the ACM*, **41**, 56–62.

Erickson, T. (1997). Social interaction on the Net: virtual community as participatory genre. *Proceedings of the Thirtieth Annual Hawaii International Conference on System Sciences*, Maui, Hawaii.

Figallo, C. (1998). *Hosting Web Communities: building relationships, increasing customer loyalty, and maintaining a competitive edge*. Wiley Computer Publishing.

Hagel, J. and Armstrong, A. (1997). *Net Gain: expanding markets through virtual communities*. Harvard Business School Press.

Iacono, S. and Weisband, S. (1997). Developing trust in virtual teams. *Proceedings of the Thirtieth Annual Hawaii International Conference on System Sciences*, Maui, Hawaii.

Kotha, S. (1998). Competing on the Internet: how Amazon.com is rewriting the rules of competition. In J. Baum, ed., *Advances in Strategic Management*. Jai Press, pp. 239–65.

Kromrey, H. (1998). *Empirische Sozialforschung: modelle und methoden der datenerhebung und datenauswertung*. UTB.

Kuttner, R. (1998). The Net: a market too perfect for profits. *Business Week*, 11 May, p. 20.

Lee, H. G. (1997). Electronic market intermediary: transforming technical feasibility into institutional reality. *Proceedings of the Thirtieth Annual Hawaii International Conference on System Sciences*, Maui, Hawaii.

Lincke, D. M., Schmid, B., Schubert, P. and Selz, D. (1998). The NetAcademy – a novel approach to domain-specific scientific knowledge accumulation, dissemination and review. *Proceedings of the Thirty-First Annual Hawaii International Conference on System Sciences*, Maui, Hawaii.

Malone, T. W., Yates, J. and Benjamin, R. I. (1987). Electronic markets and electronic hierarchies. *Communications of the ACM*, **30**, 390–402.

Möhrle, M. G. (1997). Ein computerunterstützter dialogfragebogen (CUDiF) in praktischer erprobung. *Wirtschaftsinformatik*, **39**, 461–67.

Nault, B. R. and Dexter, A. S. (1995). Added value and pricing with information technology. *MIS Quarterly*, **19**, 449–64.

Palmer, J. W. and Griffith, D. A. (1998). An emerging model of Web site design for marketing. *Communications of the ACM*, **41**, 45–51.

Parks, M. and Floyd, K. (1995). Making friends in cyberspace. *Journal of Computer Mediated Communication*, **1**.
    Available online: http://jcmc.huji.ac.il/vol1/issue4/parks.html

Porter, M. and Millar, V. (1985). How information gives you a competitive advantage. *Harvard Business Review*, July–August, 149–60.

Rockart, J. and Scott, M. S. (1993). Networked forms of organization. In M. S. Morton, ed., *The Corporation of the 1990s – information technology and organization transformation*. Oxford University Press.

Sarkar, M., Butler, B. and Steinfield, C. (1995). Intermediaries and cybermediaries: a continuing role for mediating players in the Electronic Market. *Journal of Computer Mediated Communication*, **1**.

Schmid, B. (1993). Elektronische märkte. *Wirtschaftsinformatik*, **35**, 465–80. http://jcmc.huji.ac.il/vol1/issue3/sarkar.html

Schmid, B. (1995). *Electronic Mall: banking und shopping in globalen Netzen*, B.G. Teubner.

Schubert, P. (1999). *Virtuelle transaktionsgemeinschaften im electronic commerce – management, marketing und soziale umwelt*. Josef Eul Verlag.

Schubert, P. and Selz, D. (1999). Web assessment – measuring the effectiveness of electronic commerce sites going beyond traditional marketing paradigms. *Proceedings of the Thirty-Second Hawaii International Conference on Systems Sciences*, Maui, Hawaii.

Schubert, P., Lincke, D. M. and Schmid, B. (1998). A global knowledge medium as a virtual community: the NetAcademy concept. *Proceedings of the Fourth Conference of the Association for Information Systems*, Baltimore, USA.

Schuler, D. (1996). *New Community Networks: wired for change*. Addison-Wesley.

Spar, D. and Bussgang, J. (1996). Ruling the Net. *Harvard Business Review*, May–June, 125–33.

Williamson, O. E. (1983). *Markets and Hierarchies, analysis and antitrust implications*. Macmillan.

Zbornik, S. (1996). *Elektronische Märkte, elektronische hierarchien und elektronische netzwerke*. Universitätsverlag Konstanz.

Appendix: list of Web sites

A list of Web site addresses of all organizations mentioned in this chapter follows:

Amazon	www.amazon.com
Barnes and Noble	www.barnesandnoble.com
Borders	www.borders.com
Business Media	www.businessmedia.org
Charles Schwab	www.schwab.com
eBay	www.ebay.com
Fnac	www.fnac.fr
Lotus Domino	www.notes.com
MCM Institute	www.mcm.unisg.ch
NetAcademy	www.netacademy.org
Yahoo	www.yahoo.com

6
Business impacts of the Internet for small and medium-sized enterprises

Amelia Baldwin, Andrew Lymer and R. Johnson

Introduction

Commercial use of the Internet and the Web is expanding at an astounding rate. As we move into the twenty-first century, the number of people online worldwide now exceeds 275 million (Nua, 1999), whilst the number of Web hosts approaches 50 million (Internet Software Consortium, 1999). From a business perspective, approximately 90 per cent of all corporations now maintain a Web presence (Booz·Allen and Hamilton, 1999). Indeed, the Web has gained media attention for the better part of a decade. Hundreds of thousands of companies have begun exploiting the commercial potential of the Web and the market has evolved into a multi-billion-dollar economy. The Web has proven to be the catalyst that has permanently launched the Internet into commerce.

Evidence shows that in many areas the Internet is having a positive impact on business competitiveness and profitability. Much attention is being paid to how the Internet is changing big business, corporate relations, education and work. However, and critically, much less attention has been given to smaller businesses using Internet technology. Small and medium-sized enterprises (SMEs) play a central role in the global economy. A typical SME employs fewer than 250 people – the common definition adopted by the European Commission. Nevertheless, as a group, SMEs are a significant provider of employment and a major source of commerce's important innovations.

As a significant contributor to national economies, the SME sector generally provides the majority of jobs. In the USA, for example, where there are more than 23 million SMEs, this sector generates more than one-half of all employment (Small Business Administration, 1999). Further, these SMEs not only create more than one-half of the gross national product of the USA (totalling US$6.9 trillion in 1999; Central Intelligence Agency (CIA), 1999), they are also the principal source for new jobs and generate 96 per cent of all US exports (Small Business Administration, 1999). In Europe, companies with fewer than 500 employees comprise 99.9 per cent of businesses and generate 70 per cent of all jobs (*Certified Accountant*, 1994).

The significant economic force represented by SMEs has long been a user of traditional IT, such as accounting software (Evans and Nesary, 1991; Chen and Williams, 1993). Further, the growth of the Internet and Web-based technologies is creating a unique and immense opportunity for these SMEs (Venkatraman, 1994; Poon and Swatman, 1995).

This chapter describes the developing state of Internet use by small and medium-sized business enterprises. The following section describes current demographics of Internet use by SMEs, and this is accompanied by a discussion of the technological evolution of such organizations. Subsequently, the focus turns to an analytical framework for examining the various impacts of the Internet on SMEs, and this is then applied to several cases of real small and medium-sized business enterprises, providing a useful evaluation tool.

SMEs and the Internet

In order to examine the impact of the Internet on SMEs, we must consider various levels of use ranging from Internet access, to Web presence, to full-blown electronic commerce.

While estimates vary widely, we can confidently assert that in the more technologically advanced economies, such as France, Germany, the UK and the USA, the majority of SMEs have Internet access or could easily gain Internet access (Nando Times, 1999). In less developed nations the percentages are much lower but, in Slovenia for example, approximately 50 per cent of small businesses have Internet access (RIS, 1998). Thus, Internet access is becoming accepted and is likely soon to become universal for global small businesses.

While there are fewer SMEs with Web sites than with Internet access, more than half of SMEs in countries such as France, Germany, the UK and the USA have a Web presence (Nando Times, 1999). In Australia, the percentages are slightly smaller but growing. In less developed nations – particularly those where technology infrastructure has been lacking – the percentage of SMEs with Web sites is markedly lower, but still significant. For comparison, consider that in Slovenia, one-third of medium-sized companies and one-fifth of small enterprises have Web sites (RIS, 1998).

Nearly 500 000 small businesses went online to sell products and services in 1998. In the USA, nearly 60 per cent of small businesses now report that the Internet is essential to their success (Cyber Dialogue, 1999), whereas in 1998 only 30 per cent considered the Internet important. In the UK, about 35 per cent of SMEs expected to engage in electronic commerce by early 1999 (Durlacher Research, 1998).

Barriers to the use of Internet technology by SMEs typically include lack of time and lack of specialized technical expertise (Business Information and the Internet, 1998). However, the lack of in-house expertise has not prevented many SMEs from creating successful electronic commerce Web sites. The Web sites of SMEs that show the greatest return are those designed by Web consultants and marketing companies (Lyons, 1998). Other concerns include security and perceived cost, and internal knowledge and skills (IBM Australia, 1998). Often, entrepreneurs in SMEs just have not yet learned how affordable Internet access, Web hosting and EC activities have become.

While the principal reason that most SMEs move toward electronic commerce is cost savings (IBM Australia, 1998), SMEs have always been known for their relative quality of service, something that large corporations cannot generally match. This comparative advantage can serve SMEs well in the electronic world, as Internet technology allows SMEs in geographically disparate locations to reach customers they have never reached before. In fact, so many new users are coming online and purchasing goods and services over the Internet that 50 per cent of online sales are to new customers (Cyber Dialogue, 1999). SMEs may build new customer constituencies that were not previously available.

In the middle of 1999, online orders at small-business Web sites of companies located in the USA were worth US$19 billion, a growth of almost 100 per cent over 1998 (Cyber Dialogue, 1999). This market will continue to grow at an impressive rate. Even in countries with little Internet presence, electronic commerce can be significant. For example, online shoppers in Arab countries, which have very low rates of Internet access (and in come cases, low rates of telephone availability), spent approximately US$1 billion in 1998 (Jarrah, 1999).

In many countries, governments are helping small businesses move toward electronic commerce. The British government has invested in plans to help 1 million SMEs use electronic commerce by 2002 (BBC, 1999). The Irish government has heavily invested in that country's Internet infrastructure (Reuters, 1999). The US government also has programmes to encourage SMEs to use electronic commerce (Seminario, 1999).

In fact, the potential of electronic commerce is not even being fully realized by the SMEs that are currently using it. Many small businesses that were already online in 1998 report that they do not feel they get the most out of their Web sites (Lyons, 1998).

Small businesses and technological evolution

To some, the growth of the Internet is just another step in the continuing technological evolution of society. Others assert that the Internet simply provides SMEs with one more way of doing the same old things they have been doing for decades. However, business use of telecommunications technology has evolved through many stages, not necessarily in an even progression but including post, telegraph, telephone, radio, television and fax. Therefore one may ask how the Internet fits into this evolutionary trend. Internet technology, including the World Wide Web, represents a relatively low-cost technology with the potential for high returns to small and medium-sized businesses. Internet technology offers a combination of the affordability and interactivity of the telephone, ease and passivity of the television, efficiency of the fax and the potential for multifaceted interactivity that can possibly mimic live in-person communication when it is not otherwise available. Clearly, the Internet is more than just another step in the progression of business technology.

It is interesting to note how quickly the Internet is becoming a normal form of communication for small businesses. One answer lies in the nature of technology diffusion. For small and medium-sized businesses to be likely to use a new technology, the technology must become widely available to ordinary people. The speed with which the Internet's World Wide Web is becoming an accepted part of life can be illustrated by comparing the rate of its spread with previously well-accepted technology innovations. The radio reached 50 million users within 38 years. Broadcast television required about 13 years to reach 50 million people. Cable TV reached 50 million people after approximately 10 years. The World Wide Web was created in the early 1990s and reached 50 million people in about 5 years (Morgan Stanley, 1997; Greenstein and Feinman, 1999). Clearly, the Internet and Web have been rapidly absorbed into society and smaller businesses can now easily and affordably reach a wider audience than ever before.

The potential returns from using Internet technology for electronic commerce are not just financial, but span a wide range. The truly entrepreneurial small or medium-sized enterprise can possibly create improvements in virtually all areas of the business, such as:

- increased sales
- easier product returns
- easier order tracking
- improved communication with customers, vendors and employees
- faster response to customer inquiry.

However, the Internet and the World Wide Web are not the panacea for the technological ills of every small and medium-sized enterprise. Internet technology and electronic commerce bring their own potential problems.

To succeed at using Internet technology, SMEs must be prepared to alter their business processes. They must learn to deal with a greatly increased level of interactivity and the changed nature of communication with and among customers, suppliers and also within the organization itself.

Successful SMEs of the future must have a number of key characteristics. These include export generation, niche marketing, information technology utilization and strong partnerships and strategic alliances (*Certified Accountant*, 1994). For many SMEs, exports have not previously been a major element of the usual business plan. However, the Internet allows communication with customers in far-flung locales, thus creating a global market that is, in fact, reachable for smaller enterprises. With this rapid expansion of easy global communication, niche markets can grow to meet the needs of customers not just in local or regional markets but also in the worldwide business arena. Information technology is truly pivotal as it is likely to be the mechanism through which other key characteristics or processes are developed and delivered. Networked computers are increasingly used by SMEs to extend their reach (Baker, 1994; Fuller and Jenkins, 1995), enabling them to tap into the global information superhighway. The Web allows SMEs to expand from local and regional activities to global trade, thus supporting *smaller* businesses on a truly *global* scale.

For SMEs, the Web can enhance three major business processes. Clearly, the potential of marketing and advertising to attract new customers is apparent to anyone even moderately knowledgeable about Internet technology. Further, additional and improved communication channels can enhance the service and support of existing customers in both quantity and quality. Finally, new market and distribution channels can be created for existing products (Kalakota and Whinston, 1997).

The Internet affects the way a SME communicates with its business contacts and partners, the way it manages its data and how it projects its image. The introduction of the Internet into business activities results in changes to fundamental business processes and operations. In order to assess these impacts and to compare changes within an organization and between other businesses, a structured approach is useful. The following section of this chapter describes a matrix model of the impacts of the Internet on SMEs.

Business impacts of the Internet

The following section details the construction of an impact framework. This is accompanied by the application of the model in three real, but very different, businesses: a confectionery retailer, a public relations company and a wholesale importer of cut flowers. Such examples help to illustrate and assist understanding of the use of the model. This framework draws on general IT impact models, as well as on other models from areas such as expert systems, artificial intelligence, systems theory and some prior research done on the commercial use of the Internet (in particular, Perrow, 1967; Baker, 1994; Fuller and Jenkins, 1995). The most methodological, intuitive and comprehensive approach to assessing impacts in this domain was identified as the two-dimensional matrix model (Baldwin-Morgan and Stone, 1995).

General IT impacts

A review of existing IT impact literature supports the proposition that inferences relating to the likely impacts of Internet technology can be gained from a broad spectrum of IT applications. A number of papers note education as being an area subject to impact (Huber, 1990; Winston, 1990; Duchessi and O'Keefe, 1992; Baker, 1994; Baldwin-Morgan and Stone, 1995). Managerial roles (HM Treasury, 1984; Winston, 1990; Duchessi and O'Keefe, 1992; Duchessi et al., 1993), organizational culture (HM Treasury, 1984; Kwon and Zmud, 1987; Huber, 1990; Duchessi and O'Keefe, 1992; Duchessi et al., 1993; Baldwin-Morgan and Stone, 1995) and decision-making streams (Huber, 1990, Duchessi et al., 1993) are also likely to be affected.

These areas are also likely to be impacted by Internet use, particularly organizational culture and education (Perrow, 1967; Baker, 1994). Changes may also occur in costs (Perrow, 1967; HM Treasury, 1984; Huber, 1990; Duchessi et al., 1993), personnel shifts and downsizing (Duchessi et al., 1993), the workforce (HM Treasury, 1984; Kwon and Zmud, 1987; Huber, 1990; Duchessi et al., 1993), the environment (Perrow, 1967; HM Treasury, 1984; Winston, 1990; Duchessi et al., 1993), decentralization (Huber, 1990), informal networking (Perrow, 1967; Kwon and Zmud, 1987) and relative advantage (Perrow, 1967; Kwon and Zmud, 1987; Fuller and Jenkins, 1995). Of these items, education, efficiency and business environment are repeatedly cited as being of particular importance.

Developing the framework

Table 6.1 shows the matrix framework. To begin, let us focus only on the structure of the matrix rather than on the contents of the cells. The vertical axis of the matrix indicates categories of impact, and is composed of communication, information retrieval, knowledge management, productivity and environment. These categories are grouped to reflect impacts focused on inputs to the business activity of the SME (communication and information retrieval) and outputs of the business activity (knowledge management and productivity/use of knowledge). A description of the context of impact is also included as the environment category. The model can be used to consider each area specifically in isolation from and combined with levels of impact as given on the horizontal axis. These levels consider the company's business contacts, the organization as an entire enterprise and individual tasks or processes that are undertaken by the enterprise. In addition to these controllable

Table 6.1 Matrix model of Internet impacts

Categories of impact	Levels of impact			
	Contacts	*Industry*	*Organization*	*Task*

Productivity	Quality of service
	Costs
	Timeliness
		Market size
		Market share
			Costs
			Performance
			Management
			  involvement
			Market
			Organizational
			  structure
			Employee
			  impression
				Performance
				Autonomy
				Change in tasks
				Inducement of
				  initiative
				Lateral thinking

Information retrieval	System stability Perception Effectiveness	Property and intellectual rights Best practice advice	Performance Structure Management support	Performance

Communication	Performance
	Support
	Timeliness
	Frequency
	Security
	System stability
		Wider market
		Worker unification
		Timely dissemination
		  of information
		Effective
		  dissemination of
		  information
			Law
			Performance
			Truthfulness
			Worker unity
			Company image
			Security
			System stability
			Communication
			  frequency
				Performance
				Truthfulness
				Communication
				  frequency
				System stability

Knowledge	Efficiency Effectiveness Interactivity Increased interest Costs	Efficiency Effectiveness Co-ordination Feedback	Timeliness Efficiency Effectiveness Costs Expertise Productivity Feedback	Efficiency Effectiveness Timeliness

Environment	Hardware/software
	Staff usage
		Hardware/software
		Environmental
		  instability
			Business resources
			Office space
			Office culture
			Security/ethics
			Labour market
			Structure
				Business resources
				Technical
				  orientation
				Work at home
				Human interaction

aspects of business impact brought about by the introduction of Internet technology, there may be other issues such as cross-industry influence. These important contextual elements are integrated into the model.

The model given in this chapter is a refinement of previous versions of a model developed for the same purposes. For further information on the model development see Lymer *et al.* (1996a, b).

Justification of the levels of impacts

The Internet impact model facilitates the examination of impacts at numerous levels within an organization, as well as considering external factors. These areas of impact move from external areas on the left of the matrix to internal locations on the right. Focusing only on the controllable aspects of the model (i.e., not including industry-level impacts), these are:

- *Business contacts.* This class of impact describes all of the external individuals and organizations with which a company communicates. These include customers, suppliers, governmental agencies, competitors, banks and so on. The Internet potentially impacts all such relationships. For example, if customers have access to the Internet, they may interact with the company via e-mail, view information about the company or its products via the Web, purchase commodities online, pay with their debit/credit cards or some other form of electronic payments card. The Internet therefore enables companies to extend their geographical reach and enables customers to purchase products from organizations with which it would otherwise be impractical to trade (Baker, 1994).
- *Organization.* Organizational impacts are those that affect the organization as a whole. These impacts are internal to the organization, in contrast to the external impacts between the firm and its commercial environment. The organization will be impacted upon in many different ways. Labour changes might arise (Kwon and Zmud, 1987; Huber, 1990), management operations and roles could be altered (Duchessi and O'Keefe, 1992), communication flows might change (Huber, 1990) and the physical work environment may be changed (HM Treasury, 1984). Organizational changes are likely to be significant impacts.
- *Task.* Task refers to individual processes that are carried out within the organization. This has long been a topic of research (Kwon and Zmud, 1987; Huber, 1990; Venkatraman, 1994; Baldwin-Morgan and Stone, 1995; Lymer *et al.*, 1996b). This element involves assessing the day-to-day impacts affecting employees and the ways in which they work. New technology has a significant effect on many employees and their ability to undertake their job-specific tasks. It has empowered workers to undertake new tasks that previously would have been considered impractical and even, perhaps, impossible. The Web may continue this trend through re-engineering the activities employees undertake (Baker, 1994; Fuller and Jenkins, 1995; Poon and Swatman, 1995).

The categories of impacts

Five categories of impacts are included in the two-dimensional matrix model. These categories are communication, information retrieval, knowledge management, productivity and environment:

- *Productivity.* To sustain productivity gains and remain competitive in a global marketplace, companies are increasingly reliant on information technology. The major impact of IT on these gains relates to improvements in the use of business knowledge and expertise. Therefore, the Internet impact model incorporates productivity-impacts as an output variable. Productivity includes efficiency and effectiveness impacts. Companies might find that the Internet enables them to undertake some activities more quickly, more easily and less expensively (HM Treasury, 1984; Duchessi *et al.*, 1993; Fuller and Jenkins, 1995).
- *Information retrieval.* The Internet provides technology that enables businesses to retrieve considerable amounts of information on a multitude of subjects. Corporate information is the most vital resource a company owns, so any improvements obtaining useful knowledge as an input to the business will add significant value to the company as a whole (Perrow, 1967; Galbraith, 1973; Baker, 1994).
- *Communication.* Communication is one business activity that will undoubtedly be impacted by the Internet, which includes a multitude of communication facilities. Many of these facilities are cheaper and more efficient than other forms of communication and hence companies are likely to notice real impacts in this area of business. Huber (1990) draws particular attention to communication, noting when mediated by a computer, it can impact upon organization design, intelligence and decision-making.
- *Knowledge management.* A company's ability to manage corporate knowledge is increasingly important for commercial success (Baker, 1994; Poon and Swatman, 1995). In satisfying this need, the Internet can be used as a mechanism to develop expertise, as well as to provide an environment conducive to education and learning. The valuable role IT can play generally in education is well documented. If managed correctly, the presence of the Internet will potentially extend the usefulness of IT for this purpose.
- *Environment.* Both the external environment and the office environment have shown IT impacts (Perrow, 1967; HM Treasury, 1984; Duchessi and O'Keefe, 1992; Duchessi *et al.*, 1993; Venkatraman, 1994). Factors such as the physical office and the office culture, business strategy, technical orientation and human relationships are susceptible to change. Environmental issues are often difficult to quantify, but they will be ever present when changing business processes using Internet technology.

Industry-level impacts

As given, the model concentrates on controllable impacts. In order to understand these impacts on a case-by-case basis, it will be necessary to consider the context in which each business operates. One of the contextual factors that will affect the business impact of the Internet, for example, will be the *industry* within which the business operates. As Internet technologies are adopted at the industry level, there may be significant changes in industry structure and operation.

For example, regulatory bodies and professional institutes may be able to communicate, disseminate and retrieve information from members of the industry that are online. Closer electronic links between business partners may be developed. Indeed, Internet technology may even be used as a mechanism to facilitate an industry-wide set of objectives. Developments in the UK accounting profession are a good example of this. More incentives may be created to encourage joint ventures with competitors, developing mutual strategies as opposed to engaging in competition. However, on the other side of the coin, the market positions of some players may be strengthened – leading to improved market share – whilst others are weakened, especially as new and developing markets begin to grow.

As well as these more explicit impacts, the Internet may also impact on the industry through a series of more subtle effects. Industries that use the Internet may be perceived – by a range of stakeholders including customers, competitors, employees, shareholders and government – as more forward-looking and innovative. Segregating industry-level impacts from other external and internal impacts allows a much more accurate impression of how each element of the business environment is impacted. It is important to bear in mind these contextual factors when assessing the decisions of individual businesses.

Validation and use of the Internet impact model

This section details the application of the matrix model to three companies. Each of these was examined using a case-study methodology and intensive interview-based research (Yin, 1994). Further details of the methodology and other cases that formed part of the research undertaken are given in Lymer *et al.* (1996c). As we shall see, these short cases are quite different in both their characteristics and impacts.

Case 1: Hosa, Inc.

Hosa, Inc. is a fresh cut-flower importer located in the USA. Annual sales are currently US$17 million and the 8-year-old, privately owned company employs thirty-two people. The price of fresh cut flowers changes up to several times per day for each type of flower. This is a unique agricultural product subject to anti-dumping duties and customs from the US Department of Justice.

The company acquires flowers from farms by standing order, open market order or consignment. A standing order establishes a negotiated price with a farmer for a specific period of time. An open market order creates a fixed negotiated price as a one-off or for a short period of time. Consignment sales require the company to sell the items and provide a specified return to the consignee.

The company's customers are wholesalers and supermarkets. These customers have special orders that change routinely. The company began exploring ways to improve time-sensitive and information-rich processes, particularly the information flows between distant sales people and the company organization. In the process of improvement, the company has created its own extranet for the remote sales force. Thus, Hosa has improved connectivity and communication with both sales people and vendor farms, and between customers and sales staff.

In 1997, the company had no Web presence. At that time, remote sales staff used a limited telnet system. Now, sales people can telnet to a dedicated Unix server to use facilities such as a printer, bar coding and many others. The sales force can now do remotely almost anything that is needed.

In step-up costs, the company spent less than US$10 000, most of which was used to purchase a NT server. The company also purchased two PCs and a leased (T1) line. In many cases the company saw no need to buy new equipment; many other hardware items were literally scavenged from within the company. The financial controller stated: 'I'm big on opening old boxes and sticking in old parts'.

Significant savings in both office supplies and long-distance telephone costs have resulted. In March 1997 the cost of office supplies was US$6700/month; by March 1998 this figure had dropped to US$1785/month.

With reference to the model of Internet impacts, the following findings can be drawn from this case study:

- *Communication.* Customers can now contact sales staff by pager, phone or e-mail. This high level of availability and accessibility has resulted in outstanding service to the customer. For example, the farm inspector in Latin America now uses e-mail to communicate with the central organization in the USA. When inspecting a farm, he now has more information at his disposal. He knows whether a particular farm has had prior notices of quality problems, the nature of the problems and whether the quality of the product arriving in the USA has since improved. A system is presently being developed which will enable major customers to report product quality problems. Clearly, with a perishable product, actually returning poor quality items for credit is not a sensible proposition. Therefore, with the new system, customers will take digital photographs of products with quality problems. Company personnel will use the photographs to determine the amount of return credit for the customer.
- *Information retrieval.* Cut flower prices change up to several times per day. Daily commodity prices for various flowers are gathered electronically on the Web site. In the past, this had been done by traditional mail, resulting in reports with relatively useless information such as 'last month's price for X was Y'.

- *Knowledge management.* Every day each truck driver e-mails a report that includes every box picked up for delivery, customer destination, number of boxes, weight and so on. This report documents specific delivery responsibility. In the past, only the number of boxes (not even by individual customer) was recorded and tracked. Now, pallets are also tracked, including which boxes are on each pallet.
- *Productivity.* In the old system, the salesperson – on receiving a telephoned order – needed to research product availability and the commodity listing of current prices (which, of course, changed several times per day). The salesperson then worked out the product mix in each order and forwarded this to the sales manager. The sales manager checked the order and then forwarded this to the purchasing manager, who then enquired with the farms (some company-owned and some not) to determine where the order would be assembled (at the company or at the farm). Once everything was settled, the specific order was then approved. If a change had to be made at any point in the process, this process began anew. The new system streamlines the old. In the new system, the salesperson posts the special order on the company's extranet Web site using an order entry form. The average selling price for that day is calculated online using the company's database of commodity prices. This estimate gives the salesperson a basis to design the mix for the order. The sales manager accesses this online and forwards approved mixes to the purchasing agent. The purchasing agent analyses pending orders, selects farms as vendors and then approves the order. The successful mixes are reserved for the salesperson. An analysis of successful mixes is also provided as a planning tool for salespersons to view when creating future mixes. The company is reluctant to allow direct order by customers, which may circumvent the existing sales structure. Fresh cut flowers are a volatile perishable commodity that require knowledgeable human intervention and a sensitive interface between customers and the order fulfilment process. Before products can be delivered to customers, the company must receive invoices from the farms. Hence, a very fast turnaround for the invoices is required. In the past, the supplier farms always faxed the invoices, resulting in long, often illegible, faxes. Now, most farms use e-mail and communications have been considerably improved with vendors. The company is also working on plans to format invoice communications so the data can be manipulated and analysed. Similarly, the order fulfilment process has advanced through the use of Internet technology to some extent. To fulfil orders, each farm can access information online via a password. However, supplier farms are all located in Latin America and because, at present, Internet reliability is still low in that region, output for order fulfilment is still often faxed to most farms. Once the system was in place, sales began growing steadily. Sales in March 1998 increased by some 16 per cent over March 1997.
- *Environment.* There have been some notable changes in the organizational structure, employees and tasks. Nine new employees have been added in twelve months, most of these to the new products division.

The company environment is also becoming a more solid team culture. Now, everyone is more focused on improving customer service. The company has even created a new job role to evaluate quality control – an independent function reporting directly to the president. Importantly, the company is changing the way it assesses data – a fundamental change to the internal environment. In the past, data was received in whatever form (often by fax) and then manually input to spreadsheets for analysis. Now, data and processes are seen as dynamic, and automated processes mean minimal data entry is used.

Case 2: Sweet Seductions

Sweet Seductions is a high-quality confectionery shop in Leamington Spa – situated in the West Midlands area of the UK. The owner manages the shop and seasonally employs between three and fifteen staff. Sweet Seductions has been retailing chocolate and other confectionery both directly to the public and via mail order since 1993.

Sweet Seductions' Web pages (http://www.sweet-seductions.co.uk), which enable trade over the Internet through secure payments technology and electronic mail, were released live on the Internet in December 1995. The company runs the Web-based trade in parallel with its mail-order activities.

In terms of the categories of impacts, the case facilitates the following:

- *Communication.* The Web allows users to view pictures of products available via the business and to read descriptions of the products. It also allows customers to fill a 'virtual shopping basket' with goods as they browse, which they can order using a credit card for payment. The orders are communicated to Sweet Seductions via secure e-mail link. Once a customer has placed an e-mail order with Sweet Seductions, the company undertakes a standard set of procedures. The company finds that e-mail is efficient, timely and convenient for communication with Web-based customers and the Web site provider. The owner/manager of the shop is able to use e-mail to communicate directly with his customers to enhance the quality of the service provided and to encourage repeat orders.
- *Information retrieval.* Sweet Seductions' customers can use the Web to retrieve company history and product information. The company has its own mailing list and participates in chocolate-related newsgroups. These distribution channels help create repeat visits.
- *Knowledge management.* Via the Web, Sweet Seductions provides a number of knowledge-based documents for customer business contacts and mailing lists. The industry is likely to be impacted through improved communication with competitors, suppliers and customers, enabling the company to keep in touch with what is going on both within the UK, as well as the rest of the world.
- *Productivity/use of knowledge.* The company believes that it offers customers a better quality of service by providing them with an alternative purchasing channel. However, many of the sales via the Web

are to new clients. During 1996, Sweet Seductions has seen its market grow, both in monetary and geographic terms. Shop staff now spend an increased amount of time in front of a computer terminal for some tasks. However, once electronic orders have been collected and printed, these join the mail-order system for processing and delivery. Therefore, no additional task impacts are created through Web-based orders.

- *Environment.* The initial costs of creating the Web site were relatively low. The shop already had much of the hardware to enable online transactions to be processed.

Case 3: CPR Works

CPR Works is an owner-managed public relations company based in Birmingham, UK. It was formed as a limited company in December 1994 and currently has a turnover of just under £200 000 per annum. CPR Works provides a public relations service to the heating and energy industries. The company currently employs three full-time staff members, subcontracting out any additional work to freelancers.

The company uses two PCs in its office premises, and the managing director uses a third PC at his home. The company has used PCs since its inception; computers were introduced originally for word processing, spreadsheet applications and other basic office-based activities. In May 1995 the company was given the opportunity to have a leased line connecting it to the Internet.

CPR Works has e-mail, FTP, Web and Usenet Facilities. The Internet service provider (ISP) charges a management fee, which involves preparing and maintaining the company's Web pages (http://www.custard.co.uk/prguide), while also dealing with any queries or technical problems. The ISP has recently provided a dedicated one-to-one dial-up facility so that the managing director and other staff can connect to the Internet and work from home.

In terms of the model of Internet impacts, CPR Works demonstrates the following important developments:

- *Communication.* The benefits of networking communications – with and on behalf of clients – have been significant. In an industry where timing is critical, and effective time management is vital to commercial success, any improvements in ability to communicate bring significant benefits. This has, however, resulted in a change to the nature of communication management, requiring faster responses than were the case before the use of the Internet.
- *Information retrieval.* As a PR agency concerned with the activities of clients' rivals and partners, CPR Works is better able to monitor their activities through the Web than was previously the case. This results in more timely responses to rivals' campaigns and better co-ordination with partner activities. However, staff say they often have difficulty, on a regular basis, in finding sufficient time at the computer to carry out this discovery task.

- *Knowledge management.* It has been possible to digitize key business information to enhance access to and management of data. This includes better tracking of client PR materials.
- *Productivity.* In terms of productivity, the availability of client information in digital form makes it possible to manipulate and circulate information more efficiently than was previously the case, improving the response time of campaigns.
- *Environment.* CPR Works had already made the technology purchases necessary to create the entry-level environment for this technology. Employees did, however, report that the increased use of the Internet has made them more reliant on this technology, which creates new business risks for their operation. They are also beginning to make use of the teleworking potential of the new tools they now have for mobile working.

Discussion

In each of our case studies, the Internet has had significant impact on the organization's business contacts. Field research supports the suppositions that clients, suppliers and customers all experience at least some favourable impact from Internet technology. The Internet provides a new medium for interacting with business contacts and supplies an added-value mechanism for conducting trade. It enables companies to reach a wide market area and hence is capable of empowering an organization with enhanced market reach. Thus far, the dominant business impact of the Internet has been on communication with business contacts of all types.

Organization-level Internet-related impacts are common. In almost all instances, the impacts on the organizations have been favourable. Since many organizations have used IT previously, company organization environments often show the lowest levels of change. However, most cases exhibit major organizational changes driven by the introduction of the Internet into their operations.

For some SMEs, the Internet does not yet generate or eliminate many task activities. Instead, it is merely an alternative mechanism for performing existing specific tasks. The Internet does, however, require more of these tasks to be undertaken at a computer and hence will make organizations increasingly reliant on their IT infrastructures.

Summary

This chapter has given a brief review of the past and current state of use of the Internet by small and medium-sized businesses. The evolution of Internet technology use and diffusion in SMEs was also outlined briefly. Readers will now have a basic knowledge of the relationship between SMEs and Internet technology, including key success factors, benefits and some possible problems.

In order to provide some comparison possibilities between businesses of a diverse nature, an impacts model was developed that supported focused analysis. This tool has been used in a number of real business situations to help users understand the implications of the use of the Internet for their businesses. The results of using the framework on three very different case studies are rather interesting. Clearly, the Internet is having quite different impacts on different SMEs. Nevertheless, and perhaps as one might expect, the main focus has been on productivity, information retrieval and communication. Clearly, and similarly to the large organizations discussed in the last chapter, SMEs have a long way to go towards exploiting the full potential of the Internet.

References

Baker, N. (1994). The Internet as a Reach Generator for the Small Business. MBA Thesis, Durham University.

Baldwin-Morgan, A. and Stone, M. (1995). A matrix model of expert system impacts. *Expert Systems with Applications*, **9**, 599–608.

BBC (1999). £1.7 billion investment in computers. *BBC Online*, 9 March. http://news.bbc.co.uk/hi/english/events/budget_99/news/newsid_293000/293720.stm

Booz·Allen and Hamilton (1999). *Senior Executives Say the Internet Is Transforming Global Business – Regardless of Industry or Geography.* Economist Intelligence Unit.
http://www.bah.com/press/internet_survey.html

Business Information and the Internet (1998). British SMEs face barriers online. *Nua Online*, 29 May.
http://www.nua.ie/surveys/?f=VS&art_id=896438559&rel=true

Central Intelligence Agency (1999). *The World Factbook*. CIA. http://www.odci.gov/cia/publications/factbook/us.html econ

Certified Accountant (1994). How Europe can help the small firms, **86**, 21.

Chen, J.-C. and Williams, B. (1993). The impact of microcomputer systems on small businesses: England, 10 years later. *Journal of Small Business Management*, July, 96–102.

Cyber Dialogue (1999). Online Orders from Small Businesses Up More than 95 per cent. *Cyber Dialogue Online*, June.
http://www.cyberdialogue.com/press/releases/small_biz3.html

Duchessi, P. and O'Keefe, R. (1992). Contrasting successful and unsuccessful expert systems. *European Journal of Operational Research*, **61**, 122–34.

Duchessi, P., O'Keefe, R. and O'Leary, D. (1993). A research perspective: artificial intelligence, management and organizations. *Intelligent Systems in Accounting, Finance and Management*, **2**, 151–59.

Durlacher Research (1998). Fifty-four percent of SMEs online in the UK. *Nua Online*, 18 August.
http://www.nua.ie/surveys/?f=VS&art_id=903460563&rel=true

Evans, G. and Nesary, M. (1991). Computerizing small business. *Montana Business Quarterly*, Autumn, 2–7.

Fuller, E. and Jenkins, A. (1995). Public intervention in entrepreneurial innovation and opportunism. *Proceedings of the Babson Entrepreneurial International Conference*, London.

Galbraith, J. (1973). *Designing Complex Organizations*. Addison-Wesley.

Greenstein, M. and Feinman, T. M. (1999). *Electronic Commerce*. Irwin McGraw-Hill.

HM Treasury (1984). *Information Technology in the Civil Service: method for evaluating the impact of office technology systems*. HMSO.

Huber, G. (1990). A theory of the effects of advanced information technologies on organizational design, intelligence and decision making. *Academy of Management Review*, **15**, 47–71.

IBM Australia (1998). Aussie e-business drive is high but companies urged to strategise. *IBM Online*, 26 November. http://www-7.ibm.com/au/news/ausebus.html

Internet Software Consortium (1999). Internet domain survey. *ISC Online*, 10 February. http://www.isc.org/dsview.cgi?domainsurvey/index.html

Jarrah, F. (1999). Internet shoppers in Arab world spend US$95 million. *DIT Net Online*, 13 June. http://www.ditnet.co.ae/itnews/newsjune99/newsjune22.html

Kalakota, R. and Whinston, A. (1997). *Electronic Commerce*. Addison-Wesley.

Kwon, T. A. and Zmud, R. W. (1987). Unifying the fragmented models of information systems implementation. In R. Boland and R. Hirscheim, eds, *Critical Issues in Information Systems Research*. John Wiley and Sons, pp. 227–51.

Lymer, A., Johnson, R. and Baldwin-Morgan, A. (1996a). The impacts of the Internet on the business enterprise: the development and validation of an evaluation model. *Proceedings of the 3rd European Conference on Evaluation of Information Technology*, Bath.

Lymer, A., Johnson, R. and Baldwin-Morgan, A. (1996b). The Internet and the small business: a study of impacts. *Proceedings of the 5th European Conference on Information Systems*, Cork.

Lymer, A., Johnson, R. and Nayak, A. (1996c). The Internet and the small business: case studies in business development through technology. *Proceedings of the ISBA National Small Firms Policy and Research Conference*, Birmingham.

Lyons, M. (1998). Third of firms say Net not vital to business. *Irish Times*, 16 October. http://www.ireland.com/newspaper/finance/1998/1016/tech5.htm

Morgan Stanley (1997). *The Internet Retailing Report*. Morgan Stanley Investment Research. http://www.ms.com/main/link21.html

Nando Times (1999). Half of small French companies connected to the Internet. *Nando Times Online*, June. http://www.techserver.com/noframes/story/0,2294,14884-24827-181335-0,00.html

Nua (1999). How many online? *Nua Internet Surveys*, 1 February. http://www.nua.ie/surveys/how_many_online/index.html

Perrow, C. (1967). A framework for the comparative analysis of organizations. *American Sociological Review*, **32**, 194–208.

Poon, S. and Swatman, P. (1995). The Internet for small businesses: opportunities, government policies and implications. *Proceedings of the 5th Internet Society Conference*, Hawaii.

Reuters (1999). Ireland accelerates Internet development. *Nua Online*, 6 July. http://www.nua.ie/surveys/?f=VS&art_id=905355008&rel=true

RIS (1998). *Research on the Internet in Slovenia – company survey*. University of Ljubljana. http://www.ris.org/news/ncompanies.html

Seminario, M. (1999). New electronic commerce Tsar named. *Zdnet*, 1 December.
http://www.zdnet.com/zdnn/stories/news/0,4586,2170580,00.html

Small Business Administration (1999). Learn about SBA. *SBA Online*, 23 February. http://www.sba.gov/aboutsba/

Venkatraman, N. (1994). IT-enabled business transformation: from automation to business scope redefinition. *Sloan Management Review*, December, 73–87.

Winston, W. (1990). Avoiding administrative arthritis. *Executive Speeches*, February, 1–5.

Yin, R. K. (1994). *Case Study Research: design and methods*. Sage.

7

Industry transformation in e-commerce: Web diffusion in travel agencies

Craig Standing and
Thandarayan Vasudavan

Introduction

Traditionally, retail travel agencies have acted as intermediaries between airline companies and wholesale travel companies and the consumer. The Internet and the World Wide Web bring a whole new set of challenges and opportunities for this business sector. The major threat stems from airlines and wholesale travel companies who can now offer their products and services directly to the customer and thus bypass travel agencies. Large online travel agencies have gained significant attention and provide some evidence of a radical restructuring of the travel industry sector.

Retail travel agencies rely primarily on commission from ticket sales as their source of income. For many international airlines, expenditure on commissions paid to travel agencies ranks high (possibly, the third or fourth largest item of expenditure). Not surprisingly, airlines are keen to impose commission caps and develop alternative channels of reaching customers.

For some time, retail travel agents generally have been equipped with computerized reservations systems (CRS). However, recently a flurry of activities worldwide indicates moves to transform the distribution of travel products and services through new technologies using the Internet. Over recent years, airfares have been becoming cheaper in real terms and this triggers knock-on effects for reduced yields and ever-increasing operating costs. The Internet is therefore another challenge to retail travel agents' profitability and, in the next three to five years, may well be a source of their survival or demise.

Electronic commerce via the WWW has the potential to have a disintermediation effect on travel agencies as customers increasingly use the Web to source and reserve their own flights directly from airline companies. How are Australian travel agencies as intermediaries responding to this changing technological challenge?

Two phenomena have the potential radically to change the nature of the travel industry: the opportunities provided by the WWW, coupled with business process reengineering. Figure 7.1 shows that the major link in the travel distribution chain is between the retail travel agent and the consumer. Figure 7.2 shows that the WWW has the potential to open up the travel distribution network by creating an electronic marketplace.

Airline companies have already started to use the WWW to market their products directly to consumers. Some airlines are allowing auction bids to be made for unsold seats. Some people believe that as many as 20 per cent of travel agents will go out of business within the next 3–4 years. This will be due to growth of large online travel agents (Reinders and Baker, 1997) and customers' newfound ability to transact directly with airlines, hotels and the larger tour operators. Given the potential of the WWW for travel agencies, it is proposed that they should take an enterprise-wide approach in their utilization of Web technology by focusing on the potential of business process re-engineering.

Virtual travel agencies such as Microsoft's Expedia, Yahoo Travel and Travelocity have the potential to pass economies of scale on to the consumer. Reduced fares coupled with the convenience of making reservations from home are further challenges for the traditional retail travel agency that is operating on a small profit margin.

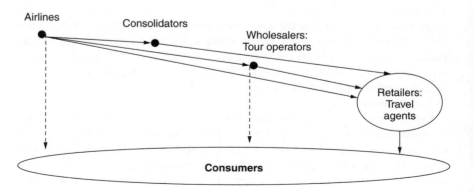

Figure 7.1
Participants in the travel distribution network (Raymond and Bergeron, 1997)

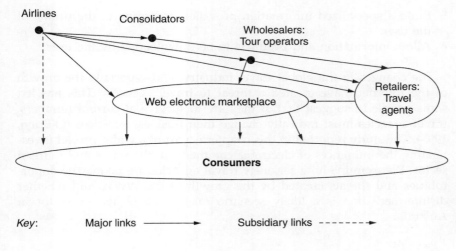

Airlines

Consolidators

Wholesalers:
Tour operators

Web electronic marketplace

Retailers:
Travel
agents

Consumers

Key: Major links ⟶ Subsidiary links ----→

Figure 7.2
The influence of the
WWW on travel
distribution chains

Travel agencies are no strangers to using information technology – they are highly dependent on up-to-date, accurate information. Information technology is widely used within travel agencies for reservations, accounting and inventory management functions. Raymond and Bergeron (1997) refer to the types of systems used by travel agents as:

1 global distribution systems (GDS) such as GALILEO, SABRE and AMADEUS, which are used for reservations, information search, client management and reporting;
2 organizational information systems (OIS), which are used for accounting, reporting, record management and billing.

Information technology (IT) has helped in reducing costs and improving service to customers.

For travel agencies in Australia, the Internet has brought both opportunities and threats. A report by Datamonitor predicts that travel will be the largest online product by 2002 (Nua Internet Surveys, 1998). By the same date, Datamonitor also expect that the travel industry will account for 35 per cent of all online sales. If this is correct then the WWW has huge potential for travel agencies to increase their business.

Various aspects of electronic commerce can be exploited by travel agents. Some of these include:

1 Use the Internet to build customer relationships – by having customers interact directly with the Web site.
2 Gather information from customers and potential customers to create customer profiles that can be used in marketing and product development.
3 Build information partnerships – co-operation between organizations to provide better service to the customer.
4 Transactions – selling products and services.

5 Build a specialized information provision according to the profile of
   the user.
6 Allow information and products to be downloaded by the user.

The changes in the global travel industry, and especially the growth
of the Internet, have created a threat to travel agencies. This has led
some people to suggest that, if they are to survive at current numbers,
travel agencies must radically change their business practices (O'Brien,
1998). The study reported in this chapter is part of a wider project investigating the influences of electronic commerce in the travel and tourism
sector. We examine how seriously travel agencies are taking the opportunities and threats created by the growth of the WWW and whether
disintermediation is a likely scenario for the travel agency sector in
Australia.

IT in small business

Travel agents are typically classified as small businesses. In Western
Australia, two-thirds of small businesses use a computer in their day-
to-day operations and 30 per cent of these businesses are connected to
the Internet (Institute for Small Business Research (ISBR), 1997). In their
survey the ISBR noted that the uses of the Internet were: e-mail 81 per
cent, accessing information 79 per cent and marketing 32 per cent. Dutta
et al. (1997) found that while many small businesses had an Internet
presence, few took full advantage of the various forms of electronic
commerce. For example, few organizations customized information
according to the type of user, performed online tracking of customer
behaviour and provided online forums for customers. It seems as though
even many of those businesses that have implemented Web technology
are not making the most of it.

The influences on executive decisions related to technology adoption
in small businesses have been studied by Harrison *et al.* (1997). They
found that an executive's decision to adopt IT to help his/her firm
compete is a function of attitude (perceived positive and negative consequences for the firm), subjective norm (social expectations) and perceived
control (resources to overcome obstacles). Additional variables such as
firm and individual executive characteristics had no unique effect on
adoption decisions.

Although there is general consensus that top management support is
important in IT adoption and implementation in small businesses
(Ginzberg, 1981; Cerveny and Sanders, 1986; DeLone, 1988), Thong *et al.*
(1996) found that it may not be so critical as external information systems
(IS) expertise. While top management support is essential for IS effectiveness, high quality external IS expertise, in the form of consultants and
vendors, is even more critical for small businesses operating in an environment of resource paucity. In our study of travel agents, we examine
whether the owner-manager of the travel agency is the driving force behind
the adoption of the WWW and whether external IT/IS support is sought.

Diffusion of Web technology

The research into the diffusion of Web technologies within organizations is still in its early stages. Jarvenpaa and Ives (1996) put forward five propositions as a result of their studies of Web diffusion in two organizations in the USA. The five propositions are:

1 The introduction of Web technology is likely to occur with only peripheral involvement of the information technology function.
2 The introduction of Web technology is likely to occur with minimal, if any, involvement by top management.
3 The introduction of Web technology is likely to be accomplished by an ad-hoc, cross-functional group that has no formal organizational responsibility (informal champions of Web technology).
4 A performance crisis can be used to stimulate the introduction of Web technologies to an organization, but it is not essential for this change to occur.
5 The introduction of Web technologies to an organization can be triggered or supported by staged events, some of which could be deliberately manufactured.

These five propositions were used and tested as part of a research project in an Australian university IT division into the diffusion of Web technology (Romm and Wong, 1998). The results presented are in stark contrast to the earlier American study (Jarvenpaa and Ives, 1996).

Romm and Wong's study (1998) of an Australian university found that the Web technologies project was strongly led by the information technology unit, with a high degree of involvement by top management. They also found that the introduction of Web technology was not triggered by a performance crisis, nor was it driven by event-based crises manufactured by the project team.

The differences in the findings of the two research projects are explained by two main factors (Romm and Wong, 1998). First, the American study examined two private computing companies whilst the Australian study examined a public university. Hence, industry sector was suggested as one of the reasons for the differences. The second reason suggested was differences in national culture: the suggestion being that, compared with American organizations, Australian organizations are more likely to be risk-averse and more inclined to value participative decision-making.

The need for planning

Business process re-engineering (BPR) looks at enterprise processes, particularly those that cut across business units. Information systems built for specific functions or units have often become outdated because new processes transcend what was often seen as a compartmentalized set of functions. BPR is about identifying and modelling business processes and changing existing systems, where needed, to support those processes. Re-engineering has many facets, although one trend is towards using newer technologies to support new ways of working (Hawryszkiewycz, 1997; Sia *et al.*, 1997).

The need for business process redesign comes about because of the following (Davenport, 1993):

- rapidly changing technologies
- shorter product life cycles
- increased competitive pressures and the increased demand for quality products and services
- inefficient use of organizational resources owing to organizational change or lack of change.

For travel agents, changing technology, increased business pressures and demand for quality service appear especially apposite.

Despite the potential of BPR, some people are rather wary about it as an organizational strategy. Martinsons and Revenaugh (1997), for example, suggest that whilst BPR has been an important concept in the 1990s, it is commonly associated with negative connotations such as corporate downsizing and inflated consultancy fees. They also suggest that BPR has commonly been associated with slashing staff numbers. They suggest that, while this may be a short-term fix, it is not a long-term strategy for success.

Details of the study

Following on from the above, an Australian-wide study has been under-taken to investigate some of the key issues. In particular, the study summarized in this chapter sought to discover the following:

1 the take-up rates of Web technology within travel agencies
2 the perception of travel agents of the significance of the WWW on the industry
3 the levels of planning and strategies used by travel agencies when investigating use of the WWW
4 the perceptions of the key obstacles and barriers to adopting the WWW
5 the key issues in the process of implementing the technology in travel agencies.

A questionnaire was developed and sent to almost 2000 travel agencies, randomly selected within each state. A total of 247 questionnaires were returned and the number of invalid responses was very low.

Questionnaire

The questionnaire was structured with several sections to reflect the objectives of the survey.

1 Company information (questions about the company such as number of employees, company turnover, type of agency and percentage of business for the leisure or corporate sector).
2 Adoption rates and perceptions of significance (questions related to the various forms of Web technology adopted by the agents. Those employing Web technology were asked to provide information on the functions it fulfils).
3 Strategy (questions related to general planning and strategy in the organization, as well as the form of planning and strategies used in relation to the adoption of Web technology).
4 Barriers and key factors for successful implementation.

Industry profile of respondents

Travel agencies are small businesses typically employing fewer than ten people (see Table 7.1). Three quarters of respondents had a turnover less than A$5 million (see Table 7.2).

Results of the study

Here we provide some summary tables of the data drawn from the study, with some brief discussion and analysis. Much of the data is presented 'as is' for the benefit of the reader. The implications of this are discussed in the next section.

Internet usage

The data in Table 7.3 show that the majority of travel agencies have access to e-mail, file transfer and the WWW. Currently, just over one-third have a Web site but 28 per cent expect to have one within the next

Table 7.1 Number of employees at travel agencies

Number of employees	1–2	3–4	5–6	7–10	>10
Percentage	14	37	19	13	17

Table 7.2 Travel agency turnover

Turnover (A$ millions)	<1	1–2	2–5	6–10	11–20	>20
Percentage	16	25	34	10	8.5	6.5

Table 7.3   Use of e-mail and Web technology

	Electronic mail (as part of a WWW browser or separate e-mail package) (%)	Electronic file transfer (e.g., by ftp or e-mail attachments) (%)	WWW browser (to search for and read documents) (%)	WWW server (to make information available) (%)
Now	66	47	64	37
Soon (within 6 months)	10	12	14	28
Within 7–12 months	5	7	7	6
Long term (within 12–24 months)	15	5	7	9
No plans at present	4	29	9	20

six months. Overall, it would appear that travel agencies have been active in becoming connected to the Internet. A small percentage has no plans at present to connect to the WWW or to develop a Web site. This latter point is in contrast to an earlier study (conducted in April 1998) of travel agencies in Western Australia that found a much larger percentage of recalcitrant agencies (Standing *et al.*, 1998). A likely explanation for this discrepancy in the two sets of findings is that the most recent survey may include a high proportion of Internet users (which are motivated and enthusiastic in relation to Web technology use). It is suggested that the non-respondent corpus contains a higher proportion of businesses that are not on the Internet. This point is further substantiated by recent efforts by the authors to search for travel agents' Web sites. Our searches produced only a few links to Web sites.

Uses of the Internet

When accessing other sites the top three uses of the Internet are:

- accessing tourist attraction information
- fare information
- package tour information.

The most common functions provided by travel agents' Web sites include fare and holiday package information, timetable information and airline and hotel reservations. Less than half of the Web sites allowed for payment by credit card.

Budget

Over 72 per cent of travel agencies with a Web site had spent less than A$2000 on its development (see Table 7.4). Considering the turnover of

Table 7.4   Amount spent on developing a travel agency Web site

Amount (A$)	0– 500	501– 1000	1001– 1500	1501– 2000	2001– 2500	2501– 3000	3001– 3500	3501– 4000	4001– 5000	5001– 10 000	10 101– 15 000	15 001– 40 000
Percentage	19	23	4	24	4	4	0	4	8	4	2	4

the businesses this is a very small amount and suggests that sites may have been developed by non-professionals or by small businesses, with minimum time spent on strategic planning and requirements analysis. It would cost considerably more than the average amount spent to develop a system that had full transaction capabilities. Some travel agencies have developed Web front ends that connect to Web Computer Reservation Systems (CRS) such as SABRE.

Strategy

From the data (see Tables 7.5, 7.6 and 7.7) it can be seen that a significant number of travel agencies have undertaken some strategic planning but most have not attempted to quantify the benefits in the form of a cost–benefit analysis. Depth and breadth of planning also appear to be limited, since many view Web technology as an add-on to current operations. Use of the Web is regarded as low risk, not radical and not involving an examination of its impact on the business on an enterprise-wide basis. However, most see top management support to be important in successful adoption of the technology. This would be especially true for a small business where the owner-manager has great control over the business.

Table 7.5   Planning approach for use of WWW (%)

No planning	Have done a little	Have planned in relation to certain functions	Enterprise-wide (a thorough plan of how WWW will influence business)
17	31	41	11

Table 7.6   Use of strategic plans and feasibility studies

	Has any feasibility study (CBA) been conducted for use exploitation of WWW?	Is there a strategic plan for the organization?	Has WWW electronic commerce been identified as part of this?
No	73	28	44
Yes	27	72	56

Table 7.7   Travel agents' perception about WWW adoption

Perceptions of travel agents	Yes	No
Do you perceive adopting the WWW in your business to be high risk?	9	91
Do you see the WWW as an add-on to current operations?	95	5
Do you see the planning involved in adopting the WWW as requiring a clean-slate approach? (A complete rethink of the business)	30	70
Do you believe an organization has to review its entire operation when considering adopting the WWW as part of its business?	37	63
Do you think that implementing the use of the WWW takes a long time?	28	72
Do you believe adopting the WWW requires a cultural (attitude) change in your business?	55	45
Do you perceive adopting the WWW in your business to be a radical level of change?	31	69
Do you think that adopting the WWW involves a structural change in your business?	34	66
Do you think that top management participation in adoption of Web technology is essential for success?	88	12

Perception of significance

Travel agents perceive that the WWW will have a profound influence on their own business but also on the travel agency sector as a whole (Tables 7.8 and 7.9). These perceptions are interesting when considered together with the low levels of planning undertaken and the relatively small amount of money invested in Web site development.

Barriers

The most significant barriers to the adoption of Web technology are implementation costs, operating costs, the lack of expertise and difficulties in providing adequate training (Table 7.10). It appears that travel

Table 7.8   Perceived benefits of using the WWW in agent's own business over next 5 years (%)

No benefits	Very little	Moderate	Significant	Very significant
13	9	28	29	31

Table 7.9   Perceived influence of the WWW on the travel agency sector over next 5 years (%)

No benefits	Very little	Moderate	Significant	Very significant
2	8	27	28	35

agencies are very concerned about cost issues and feel that they lack expertise to make informed judgements. Training and education is therefore an important issue but travel agencies have to be prepared to invest in this area.

Factors for successful implementation

The key factors for successful implementation of Web technology in travel agencies are ranked in Table 7.11. Customer support is seen as the most important factor.

Table 7.10 Barriers to adopting WWW

Barriers	Ranking (1 = most important; 19 = least important)
Start-up costs (implementation)	1
Lack of staff expertise	2
Operating costs	3
Providing adequate training	4
WWW service provider products and services	5
Integration of WWW with internal applications	6
Time-consuming to adopt the WWW	7
WWW service provider performance	8
Not enough perceived benefits	9
Application software package WWW capability	10
Security problems associated with using WWW	11
Staff resistance	12
Lack of business partners who are WWW-capable	13
Need for re-engineering of business processes	14
Inter-connection among WWW service providers	15
Customer resistance	16
Other: (specify)	17
Difficulties with WWW document standards	18
Lack of space for computer	19

Table 7.11 Factors for successful implementation of Web technology

Factor	Rank (1 = most important; 5 = least important)
Customer support	1
Top management support	2
Quality of vendor support	3
Effective consultants	4
Employee support	5

Discussion

Following on from these results, it is useful to take a number of lessons that can be learnt from this industry case study. These are discussed with respect to both travel agents and other business sectors.

Travel agencies would appear to have a number of characteristics that act as barriers to employing information technology, in this case the WWW, for radical business transformation. They are commonly owner-manager led, have few employees, operate on a low profit margin and have poorly paid staff.

Travels agents see the impact of the WWW as being significant on their industry but, as yet, they have not utilized it as a major catalyst for change. From the results of this study, a large percentage of travel agencies are using the WWW but, as mentioned previously, the results could be biased towards those that are enthusiastic about this technology. Travel agents see the WWW as an add-on to current business operations. This add-on mentality is further substantiated by the lack of detailed planning and enterprise-wide perspective. The low-budget approach suggests that travel agents do not see adopting the WWW as a strategic initiative with transformational capabilities. The Web sites' functions are perceived mainly as providing information and e-mail reservations. Many fewer Web sites allow credit card transactions to be performed. Neither does a cultural transformation appear to be taking place. Only one travel agency recruited a new member of staff to help in the new initiative. In general, travel agencies rarely give employees training in the use of the Internet.

For information technology to be optimally effective in business organizations there needs to be planning in relation to its integration with other business processes (Talwar, 1996). In most cases, travel agents are not doing this. Disintermediation seems a likely scenario for many traditional travel agencies who are slow to respond to the opportunities provided by electronic commerce.

Travel agency managers should become aware of the transformational capabilities of the Internet. Too many managers spend too much time on day-to-day business operations. Managers need to take time out to think about or be educated in business strategy via the Internet. Managers also need to provide training for their staff on the capabilities of the World Wide Web. Far too many travel consultants were ignorant of the potential of the Web within the travel industry sector. Finally, individual travel agencies should investigate the option of forming consortiums jointly to explore the potential of electronic commerce.

Travel agencies need to have a business strategy and their Web site should be an implementation of that strategy. It is clear from the study that travel agencies are using the Internet as a means of promoting awareness of their business rather than as a transformation agent for their business. Given the competition they face, this limited utilization of the Internet will not be enough to make a significant business impact.

With the threat of disintermediation looming large in their industry, travel agencies may find that they need to adopt a range of strategies to offset this threat. Effective strategies could include business specialization, information specialization and innovation. Travel and tourism is becoming increasingly specialized. Travel agencies could, for example, focus on the markets for senior citizens, backpackers or, alternatively, specialize in certain tourist destinations or activities. For example, for an agency trying to attract windsurfing enthusiasts it would be helpful for their Web site to show information about the sport as well as links to other windsurfing-related sites such as weather reports of resorts, sport equipment stores and windsurfing clubs. Windsurfing chat, comments from top windsurfers, video downloads could also be used to good effect. In this case, the aim should be to build a Web site that caters for the windsurfing community. Unfortunately, most travel agents examined in the study were trying to appeal to a broad general market and hence face great competition from other travel agencies and virtual travel agencies.

Currently most travel agencies focus resources on providing their customers with a transaction and reservation service. Instead they could try shifting the emphasis to providing an information service. Providing a wealth of information via a Web site with relevant links to other sites could do this. Information draws potential customers to the site. There is also the question of whether, in the future, travel agents can charge customers for that information or for packaging travel itineraries which have involved a great deal of research.

It would appear that most travel agencies lack innovative ideas and imagination. Often their Web sites are unmemorable. An exception is www.travel.com.au – this travel agency is effectively operating by using the Web to provide information, facilitate transactions and send e-mails (Figure 7.3). This company aggressively promotes its travel products on the Web. It also sends weekly e-mails to a large number of potential customers. The ideas used within e-mail headers and the ways in which the e-mail is designed to be eye-catching all revolve around the regular flow of new ideas to market and to promote the business. In May 1999, when travel.com.au entered the Australian Stock Market, the initial stock was oversubscribed ten times.

Let us turn our attention to industries in general. Small businesses are typically concerned with day-to-day issues. Many small businesses lack a long-term outlook. In today's rapidly changing environment all businesses need to expend time and effort to explore new opportunities for growth (Thompson and Strickland, 1995). Leaders in adopting new technologies can secure a competitive advantage. Therefore, being one of the leaders is vital for success (McKeown and Watson, 1996). The Internet provides opportunities for cyber intermediation. That is, a company can start up without stock but can take cash orders and source goods from suppliers. The profit on stock and the fact that money is banked *before* goods are paid for (or even dispatched to the customer) means that this type of business can be very profitable.

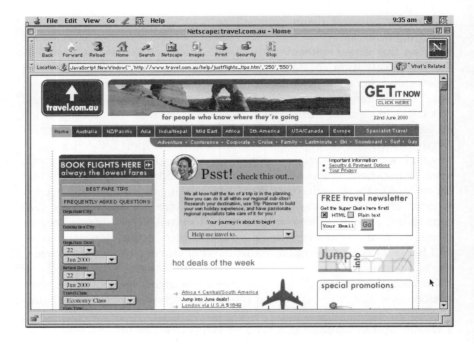

Figure 7.3
The travel.com.au
Web site

However, there are dangers for organizations when new developments, such as Web technology, are driven by information technology without due consideration of the strategic directions of the business. These types of projects can result in systems that:

1 take too much time and money to develop because they do not have the full backing of senior people;
2 do not provide a significant return to the organization because they are peripheral to core business needs;
3 consume organizational resources thus displacing other, perhaps more worthy, projects from being developed;
4 are not maintained effectively and eventually become a problem for the business. The Web developments may be badly perceived by the customers and/or employees.

Some organizations have rushed too quickly into developing an Internet presence without due consideration given to aligning new initiatives with sound business strategy. In some cases Web site development projects have been abandoned because they are not perceived as providing a sufficient return to the business. In other cases, Web sites have undergone radical changes. For example when Gibson music (www.gibson.com) offered 10 per cent discount on guitars bought through their Web site, the company received so many complaints from retail dealers that, within a month, Gibson had discontinued this offer (Kalin, 1998).

Diffusion of Web technology in travel agencies

It is interesting to compare this industry analysis to other prominent studies of Web diffusion. In particular, when the five propositions by Jarvenpaa and Ives (1996) are applied to our study of travel agents we find some quite contrasting results. In particular:

1 *The introduction of Web technology is likely to occur with only peripheral involvement of the information technology function.*

This proposition is not really applicable to travel agencies as they typically do not have a dedicated IT function or people responsible for IT.

2 *The introduction of Web technology is likely to occur with minimal if any involvement by top management.*

This is not true for travel agents, as all cases involved a great deal of support from top managers.

3 *The introduction of Web technology is likely to be accomplished by an ad hoc, cross-functional group that has no formal organizational responsibility (informal champions of Web technology).*

This is not true for travel agents. The introduction of Web technology was not led by informal champions.

4 *A performance crisis can be used to stimulate the introduction of Web technologies to an organization, but it is not essential for this change to occur.*

Travel agents on the whole were not stimulated into adopting Web technology because of crises within the organization. The technology was seen more of an enhancement to the business rather than a tool or strategy to fight off a crisis.

5 *The introduction of Web technologies to an organization can be triggered or supported by staged events, some of which could be deliberately manufactured.*

There was no evidence from our survey to suggest that this strategy was used.

It can be seen that the results of our study are closer to Romm and Wong's (1998) than Jarvenpaa and Ives' (1996). We suggest that national culture may be significant in explaining some of these similarities and differences, although we have not specifically compared our results with travel agencies from other countries. However, our findings indicate that industry sector (whether private or public) is not significant since the travel agencies were all privately owned. Another factor that is perhaps significant in its impact on these results, but not mentioned in previous studies, is the size of the business, (i.e., whether small, medium or large). A small business typically relies greatly on the owner-manager for ideas and drive. Many small businesses do not have a dedicated IT section. Because of the small number of employees in each travel agency there may not be scope for political groups to develop on the same scale as in large organizations.

Conclusions

The results from our study of the Internet and travel agencies indicate that this business sector is not coping well with the rapidly changing environment. Many travel agencies lack strategic business planning and have a poor understanding of the potential of Internet commerce. This may mean that these travel agencies are likely to face decline over the next few years.

The growth of cybermediaries (virtual travel agents) is a challenge both to developed and developing economies. The key for governments is to put investments in information technology, communications infrastructure and IT education and training at the top of the national agenda.

References

Cerveny, R. P. and Sanders, G. L. (1986). Implementation and structural variables. *Information and Management*, **11**, 191–98.

Davenport, T. H. (1993). *Process Innovation: re-engineering work through information technology*. Harvard Business School Press.

DeLone, W. H. (1988). Determinants of success for computer usage in small business. *MIS Quarterly*, **12**, 51–61.

Dutta, S., Kwan, S. and Segev, A. (1997). Strategic marketing and customer relationships in electronic commerce. *Proceedings of the Fourth Conference of the International Society for Decision Support Systems*, Lausanne, Switzerland.

Ginzberg, M. J. (1981). Key recurrent issues in the MIS implementation process. *MIS Quarterly*, **5**, 47–59.

Harrison, D. A., Mykytun, P. P. and Riemenschneider, C. K. (1997). Executive decisions about adoption of information technology in small business theory and empirical tests. *Information Systems Research*, **8**, 171–95.

Hawryszkiewycz, I. (1997). *Systems Analysis and Design*. Prentice Hall.

Institute for Small Business Research (1997). *The Small Business Opinion Survey*. ISBR.

Jarvenpaa, S. L. and Ives, B. (1996). Introducing transformational information technologies: the case of the World Wide Web. *International Journal of Electronic Commerce*, **1**, 95–126.

Kalin, S. (1998). Conflict resolution. *CIO WebBusiness Magazine*, 1 February. http://www.cio.com/archive/webBusiness/020198_Sales_content.html

Martinsons, M. G. and Revenaugh, D. L. (1997). Reengineering is dead; long live reengineering. *International Journal of Information Management*, **17**, 79–82.

McKeown, P. and Watson, R. (1996). *Metamorphosis – a guide to the World Wide Web and electronic commerce*. John Wiley and Sons.

Nua Internet Surveys (1998). Datamonitor: travel will be largest online product by 2002. http://www.nua.net/surveys/

O'Brien, P. (1998). Electronic commerce, the Internet and travel cyber-mediaries. *Proceedings of the Australian conference on Information Systems*, Sydney, Australia.

Raymond, L. and Bergeron, F. (1997). Global distribution systems: a field study of their use and advantages in travel agencies. *Journal of Global Information Management*, **5**, 23–32.

Reinders, J. and Baker, M. (1997). The future for direct retailing of travel and tourism products: the influence of information technology. *Proceedings of the International Conference on Information and Communication Technologies in Tourism*, Edinburgh, UK.

Romm, C. T. and Wong, J. (1998). The dynamics of establishing organizational Web sites: some puzzling findings. *The Australian Journal of Information Systems*, **5**, 60–8.

Sia, C., Tan, B., Teo, H. and Wei, K. (1997). Applying total quality concepts to continuous process redesign. *International Journal of Information Management*, **17**, 83–93.

Standing, C., Vasudavan, T. and Borbely, S. (1998). *A study of the Web, BPR and travel agents*. Proceedings of the Australian Conference on Information Systems, Sydney, Australia.

Talwar, R. (1996). Re-engineering – a wonder drug for the 90s. In C. Coulson-Thomas, ed., *Business Process Re-engineering*. Kogan Page.

Thompson, A. A. and Strickland, A. J. (1995). *Strategic Management: concepts and cases*. Irwin.

Thong, J. Y., Sap, C. and Raman, K. S. (1996). Top management support, external expertise and information systems implementation in small business. *Information Systems Research*, **7**, 248–67.

Section Two
Shaping the virtual organization

In contemporary business environments, organizations are faced with tremendous competitive pressures. The global economy, combined with issues of rapid technological change and the increased power of consumers, places huge demands on firms to remain responsive and adaptable (Drucker, 1995). Globally, common influences include rapid political changes, regional trade agreements, low labour costs in some countries and frequent and significant changes in markets. In addition, there are trends towards the changing nature of the workforce (older, better educated and more independent), government deregulation and reduction of subsidies and ethical, legal and social responsibility of organizations (Naisbitt, 1994). Furthermore, technology is playing an increasingly important role in business in this environment; increased innovation and new technologies are providing vast improvements in cost-performance and an important impetus to strategy, rendering existing technologies and infrastructures obsolete.

In the past, a variety of techniques have been developed to enhance a firm's ability to react to and cope with such pressures, including business process re-engineering (Hammer and Champy, 1993)), total quality management (Edwards Deming, 1986), downsizing (Trimmer, 1993), outsourcing (Bettis *et al.*, 1991) and empowerment (Lipnack and Stamps, 1997). However, the power of such methods often appeared limited and transient.

Recent technological developments promise to facilitate a new approach to this perennial problem. Some of the same technologies that have enabled developments in electronic commerce have the potential to change forever the relationships between stakeholders in the business-to-business arena. One on hand, the proposed solution absorbs and refines earlier ideas; on the other, it espouses a fundamental rethink of the nature of business and organization. The 'virtual organization' may provide the much sought after flexible and synergistic business model for this Millennium.

As we shall see, the virtual organization can take on many forms and definitions. Nevertheless, the rationale for this business model is clear – co-operate to compete; the virtual organization advocates collaboration, partnerships, alliance and similar ideas. At the heart of the concept is the notion that individual organizations cannot excel at everything. Therefore, there may be some logic in combining forces with other players (even competitors), either temporarily or on a long-term basis; by sharing resources, costs and goals with highly competent partners, the sum may be much greater than the parts. This, in turn, may afford significant benefits in terms of flexibility and opportunism in seizing new market possibilities, better utilization of resources and excellence in terms of the collection of core competencies (Grenier and Metes, 1995). As such, high levels of customer service can often be achieved.

The concept of the virtual organization is obviously a complex undertaking for any set of partners (Chesbrough and Teece, 1996). If successful, it could reap rich rewards – productivity, revenues, profits, market share and so on (Friedman, 1998). However, there are many important issues to consider. A shared purpose or vision is critical. Similarly, and related to this, there must be high levels of trust in the virtual organization and sharing of not just benefits, but risks and costs; a company needs to gain more benefit inside than outside the partnership. Information and knowledge flows are obviously an important part of communication and collaboration, as are innovations and transfer of benefits. Again, this is a challenge, and requires a considerable amount of intellectual and cultural change to achieve; some information, knowledge and innovations may be easier to share than others (Chesbrough and Teece, 1996).

The idea of using technology to interact in this way is not new by any means; electronic data interchange (EDI), for example, has been used for decades. However, the technologies now available can extend teamworking possibilities and business-to-business relationships to new levels of sophistication. The Internet and related standards provide the core platform for many of these technologies, including e-mail and intranets/extranets (smaller Internet-type networks focused on an organization/value chain; see Bernard, 1997). Such new technologies afford high degrees of flexibility, eroding traditional geographical, physical or even time barriers. Some technologies, including videoconferencing and some groupware, even allow working in real-time (Coleman, 1996). Modern database technologies and networking facilitate access to business partner's databases. Lotus Notes and similar integrated groupware tools enable diverse groups of people in different organizations to collaborate (Krantz, 1998). The advancement of mobile computing technologies, including the creation of wireless application protocol (WAP) and other standards, is likely to bring yet further flexibility for virtual working practices (*Financial Times*, 2000).

Marshall Industries, a large USA-based electronic components distributor, is a classic example of a company that has used such technologies to virtualize its operations. Once a classic intermediary, it has recently moved all its business to the Web and redefined its old supply chain as an information-based value chain, linking with suppliers, customers and system integrators. On the supplier side, the system records point-of-sale (POS) data, enables 24-hour access by suppliers and assists them in running sophisticated marketing campaigns. The system also lets Marshall offer real-time inventory access and 'just-in-time' (JIT) stock management. The Web pages give the company's 40 000 customers access to a number of applications, including tracking the status of their orders, technical data sheets, interactive training sessions and product seminars. Such business transformation and investment has been very productive and, although the firm has cut staff levels, it has been able to double sales and profits (Symonds, 1999).

The new organizational forms afforded by improvements in technology and changing paradigms of corporate culture promise to bring significant benefits to firms. However, many of the true implications of the virtual organization are not well understood. This section examines the above issues in some detail, drawing attention to the possibilities, limitations and real-world application of the virtual organization.

Section Two begins with an exploration of the nature of the virtual organization in Chapter 8. This helps to set the scene and provide a basic framework for the other definitions and forms of virtual organization that are explored in the remainder of the section. Similarly, Chapter 9 also provides some foundations. It shows that the idea of collaborating using electronic means is a long-standing one; using empirical survey and case evidence, it examines the key issues regarding strategic collaboration using EDI. This helps to put the complexity of the issue in perspective. It is also useful for later comparison to the improved capabilities of recent technologies.

Chapters 10 to 14 explore the notion of the virtual organization in some depth; using theory and a variety of original case studies they demonstrate some of the possibilities and issues in creating and managing IT-facilitated virtual organizational forms. Chapter 10 extends the thinking from Chapter 8, exploring what virtual organizations are, what they need to thrive and some of the possible forms that they can take in practice. The well-explained cases provided a useful insight into the variety of possible strategies and structures available. Further, Chapter 11 explores how the virtual organization can be managed and supported, using a modular framework. The framework has considerable practical relevance and has been applied successfully in the case study used – KLM Distribution.

Chapter 12 delves into one particular facet of the virtual organization – team working. In particular, it examines the roles of knowledge and human factors in the virtual workplace. Using evidence from case studies in construction, manufacture and engineering environments, it demonstrates some of the important factors necessary for virtual teamwork operations.

Chapters 13 and 14 provide insight into the development and implications of virtual organization for two quite different industries – grocery retailing and information technology. The first of these chapters examines how Internet-based EDI applications can facilitate major strategic transformation in the supply chain. Using a prominent case of Australia's leading supermarket chain, Coles Myer, it demonstrates the major e-procurement benefits of using these new technologies to link to small suppliers. Chapter 14 examines how the principles of virtual organization are being applied in the IT industry. Via theory and three case studies, it analyses in detail the extent of virtual operations, the subsequent benefits and the roles of information and communication technologies.

Finally, Chapter 15 takes a critical perspective on the virtual organization: will it really solve the problems of organizations in the way it promises? Although it clearly has an important role, the reality is perhaps more limited than proponents suggest; certain parts of the organization are eminently more suitable than others for virtual operations.

References

Bernard, R. (1997). *The Corporate Intranet*. John Wiley and Sons.

Bettis, R. A., Bradley, S. P. and Hamel, G. (1991). Outsourcing and industrial decline. *Academy of Management Executive*, **6**, 7–16.

Chesbrough, H. W. and Teece, D. J. (1996). When is virtual virtuous? Organizing for innovation. *Harvard Business Review*, January–February, 65–71.

Coleman, D. (1996). *Collaborative Strategies for Corporate LANs and Intranets*. Prentice Hall.

Drucker, P. F. (1995). *Managing in a Time of Great Change*. Truman Tally.

Edwards Deming, W. (1986). *Out of Crisis*. Cambridge University Press.

Financial Times (2000). Information technology survey: mobile computing and the Internet. 1 March, 1–6.

Friedman, L. G. (1998). The elusive strategic alliance. In P. Lloyd and P. Boyle, eds, *Web-Weaving: intranets, extranets and strategic alliances*. Butterworth-Heinemann, pp. 109–16.

Grenier, R. and Metes, G. (1995). *Going Virtual: moving your organization into the twenty-first century*. Prentice Hall.

Hammer, M. and Champy, J. (1993). *Re-engineering the Corporation*. Harper Business.

Krantz, S. (1998). *Building Intranets with Lotus Notes and Domino*. Maximum Press.

Lipnack, J. and Stamps, J. (1997). *Virtual Teams*. John Wiley and Sons.

Naisbitt, J. (1994). *Global Paradox*. Breadly.

Symonds, M. (1999). Business and the Internet: survey. *Economist*, 26 June, 1–44.

Trimmer, D. (1993). *Downsizing*. Addison-Wesley.

8
Defining the virtual organization

Lucas Introna

Introduction

> ... the only constant in today's world is exponentially increasing change. (Huey, 1994).

Never before in the history of business have organizations been subjected to as much change – or so some argue. The drivers of this change are both complex and various. Stewart (1993) suggests that there are four large, unruly forces of revolution: the globalization of markets; the spread of information technology (IT); the birth of the information economy; and the dismantling of hierarchy. These forces are simultaneous and inter-reactive. Not only have these forces threatened the very survival of many great corporations such as IBM (Chesbrough and Teece, 1996) and General Motors (Drucker, 1994), but they have also caused the disintegration of traditional organizations and their once untroubled environment:

> Global competition wrecked stable markets and whole industries. Information technology created ad hoc networks of power within corporations. Lightning-fast, innovative entrepreneurs blew past snoozing corporate giants. Middle managers disappeared, along with corporate loyalty. (Huey, 1994)

In response to this challenge, a wide range of management approaches and techniques have emerged. Outsourcing, business process re-engineering (BPR), downsizing, employee empowerment, total quality management (TQM), core competence and decentralization have all been used – with varying degrees of success – to reshape and redefine organizations (Drucker, 1994; Ashkenas, 1995). Each approach – some might use the word 'fad' – became a powerful metaphor that fired the imaginations of large numbers of academics, futurists, consultants and managers. Nevertheless, it is argued that they all seem to capture only part of the picture. Even when successfully implemented, these techniques for driving organizational change seem to bring only marginal or short-term returns. In a business environment that is increasingly volatile such techniques seem incapable of sustaining organizational survival – let alone longevity.

From this bleak picture emerged the concept of the *virtual organization*. Davidow and Malone (1992) – in their book *The Virtual Corporation* – are credited as the first to explicitly and coherently articulate this idea. The virtual organization now seems to represent a new corporate model to structure and revitalize organizations for the twenty-first century. Grenier and Metes (1995) argue that unlike earlier management change metaphors, which were conceived as means of resolving specific ends, the virtual organization is now perceived as the *end* in itself. Davidow and Malone (1992) support this view with the bold claim that the virtual organization can 'for the first time tie all of these diverse innovations together into a single cohesive vision of the corporation in the twenty-first century'. If true, then this must be a concept in need of serious consideration. If false, then it needs to be made explicit why the promise of the virtual organization may remain 'virtual'.

Towards a definition

For its many proponents, the concept of the virtual organization seems to emerge as a logical answer for today's fast-moving business environment where markets are global, competition is fierce and market opportunities are transitory. Hence, the evolving virtual organization ought to contain the characteristics of *speed*, *flexibility* and *fluidity* (Byrne, 1993b; Coates, 1993). Nevertheless, these are perceived in different forms by different authors, defining the virtual organization as:

- '. . .an *enterprise* that uses *collaborations* both inside and outside its boundary to marshal more resources than it currently has on its own.' (Byrne, 1993a)
- the use of *technology* to execute a wide array of temporary alliances in order to seize specific market opportunities.' (Byrne, 1993a)
- 'a collection of *management theories* ranging from JIT (just-in-time) production, lean manufacturing, and trust.' (Davidow and Malone, 1992)
- 'a *network* or loose coalition of manufacturing and administrative services uniting for a specific *business purpose*, disassembling when the purpose has been met.' (Anonymous, 1994)

For some, the virtual organization is essentially the creative use of technology. For others, it is a framework of one or more alliances. The salient literature is diverse, and there is evidently a lack of a harmonious definition of the virtual organization. This is arguably because the concept of the virtual organization is still rather immature and because of the fact that the idea is also surrounded by a fair degree of 'hype'. The following definition is perhaps the most representative of what may be implied by a virtual organization:

> A virtual corporation is a temporary network of independent companies – suppliers, customers, even erstwhile rivals – linked by information technology to share skills, costs, and access to one another's markets. It will have neither central office nor an organization chart. It will have no hierarchy and no vertical integration. (Byrne, 1993b)

Byrne's definition suggests that a virtual organization is a coalition between different – essentially independent – groups of people or organizations. But, for Byrne, the term 'virtual organization' also seems to indicate that it is an organization that 'draws' on information technology in some way. The reasons for this link with IT may be related to the way in which the term 'virtual' evolved in computing technology.

Virtual and virtuality

According to the Cambridge Dictionary, the word 'virtual' is defined as 'almost, even if not exactly or in every way'. In recent years, 'virtual' has successfully become the metaphor for technology. The computer industry has popularized such neologisms as 'virtual memory', 'virtual computer', 'virtual reality' and 'virtual space' (i.e., the space provided by the Internet). In each of these instances, the word 'virtual' connotes the IT which possess the ability to: (1) provide a way of making a computer act as if it holds more (storage capacity) than it really possesses (Bryne, 1993a); or (2) give users the illusion to exist at any time and any place needed (Davidow and Malone, 1992).

The term 'virtual organization' has caused the technology-inspired idea of virtuality to enter the domain of organizations. This may not solely imply technology but rather the ability to summon vast capabilities as a result of various collaborations assembled *only as required* (Bryne, 1993a). Unlike the earlier examples of 'virtual', the existence of a virtual organization is not wholly dependent on IT – though some IT is still required. Many proponents argue that IT now plays a secondary role; IT is merely an enabler or a messenger, with the task of disseminating the timely information that is critical to a virtual organization (Grenier and Metes, 1995). This brings us onto another important facet of our definition – the nature of 'organization' in virtual organizations.

The nature of organizations

An organization can be defined as 'a group of people who work together in a structured way for a shared purpose'. Here, 'together' does not necessarily mean that an organization must be in the form of a physical entity (bound in the unity of time/space) such as the traditional company. Conversely, Scott Morton (1991) has advocated that an organization comprises 'five sets of forces in dynamic equilibrium among themselves even as the organization is subjected to influences from an external environment'. These forces are structure, strategy, technology, roles (individual) and a management process. By advocating such a view, Scott Morton recognizes that the organization, being made up of the five forces, must be able to maintain its coherence as it *moves through time* in order to accomplish its objectives.

Framing the organization in this way has prompted business managers to realize the importance for the organization to transform itself to meet the needs of the time. More importantly, underneath a successful transformation are two conditions that must be met. These are: (1) the creation of a vision which must be clearly understood and supported by everyone in the organization; and (2) the need to align infrastructures (such as IT, work structures and processes) with the organization's business goals. These conditions must remain true no matter what form or structures the organization takes – even for the virtual organization.

To put this in perspective, the virtual organization can be conceptualized as an essential part of the on-going process of organizational transformation (Scott Morton, 1991). Hence, the virtual organization is postulated as a mutable – almost protean – organization in which resource allocation remains flexible to meet the changing business environment and customer needs (Coates, 1993; Ashkenas, 1995). A virtual organization must challenge formerly well-delineated structures so as to regenerate continually its configuration. As Davidow and Malone (1992) suggest:

> To the outside observer, the virtual corporation will appear almost edgeless, with permeable and continuously changing interfaces between company, supplier, and customers. From inside the firm the view will be no less amorphous, with traditional offices, departments, and operating divisions constantly reforming according to need. Job responsibilities will regularly shift, as will lines of authority – even the very definition of employee will change, as some customers and suppliers begin to spend more time in the company than will some of the firm's own workers.

Elements of the virtual organization

From the above, it seems evident that the virtual organization is almost the perfect antithesis of the traditional bureaucratic organization whose efficiency is built on principles of a clear division of labour, well-defined structures and so on (Weber, 1947). However, what does this mean? How will this entity (if we can call it this) operate? To answer these questions we need to examine some important details.

Strategic alliance

John Sculley, the Chairman of Apple Computer Inc., is quoted as saying:

> When we talk about virtual corporations today, we're mainly talking about alliances and outsourcing agreements. Ten or twenty years from now, you'll see an explosion of entrepreneurial industries and companies that will essentially form the real virtual corporations. Ten or thousands of virtual organizations may come out of this. (Ogilvie, 1994)

For most authors the key attribute of a virtual organization is strategic alliances or partnering (Byrne, 1993b; Ogilvie, 1994). This is a strategy frequently used by companies to command speed and flexibility so as to: (1) gain access into new markets or technologies; and (2) break down market barriers to new products by rallying the required skills and expertise from groups, individuals and even rivals from outside their organizational boundaries. The characteristics of being highly adaptable and opportunistic (Byrne, 1993b) suggest that a strategic alliance is – almost by definition – short-term or temporary. In turn, this means that once the original goal has been reached, the companies that made up the virtual organization will disband and then proceed to create new partnerships with other companies and people.

Strategic alliances have long characterized industries such as movie making and construction – where expert teams collaborate for the duration of a specific project. In the computer industry, the first instance of a successful strategic alliance was in 1981, when IBM partnered with Microsoft and Intel to launch the first-ever personal computers (Anonymous, 1993; Byrne, 1993b; Chesbrough and Teece, 1996). It is often argued that the virtual organization will mix and match the finest skills and expertise from partners to create a new organization – the virtual organization – that brings together the 'best-of-everything'.

Notwithstanding, the setting up of a network of strategic alliances between partners in a virtual organization is not without ramifications. For one, a strategic alliance implies a certain mutual dependency between partners to achieve a specific goal – that is, the launch of the *virtual product*. This means that all partners share a destiny tied towards the creation of that product. In many ways the relationship is like a house of cards; when one partner falls, the others may be seriously affected. Should this happen, it could jeopardize the integrity of the virtual organization as a whole. Consequently, it is in the combined interests of all parties to create win–win deals and remain mutually supportive; in this way organizations can ensure optimum benefit from the strategic partnership. James R. Houghton, Chairman of Corning Inc, suggests:

> More companies are waking up to the fact that alliances are critical to the future. [This is because] technologies are changing so fast that nobody can do it all alone anymore. (Byrne, 1993b)

Core competence

In 1990, Prahalad and Hamel popularized the idea of core competencies in their article 'The core competence of the corporation'. In this article, the authors advocate that a company should focus on its key activities or processes and thereby be fully equipped to face any challenges presented by the business environment. Core competencies, the theory suggests, are activities (such as marketing or design) that a company does well; via these core activities the company can gain a competitive edge over rivals. Ogilvie (1994) describes core competencies as those things in an organization that are difficult for competitors to replicate. Embodied in core products, core competencies form the roots of a company, which will remain more or less stable over time.

In effect, the focus on core competencies has led organizations – such as the UK British Home Stores (BHS) and Continental Bank – to dispose of those activities (in the form of outsourcing) that are considered incapable of giving competitive advantage (Fitzgerald, 1994). Firms such as these argue that their goal is a *lean* organization with a world-class operation.

Taken to a higher level, the concept of core competencies furnishes the creation of a virtual organization. This is seen in the form of a partnership essentially made up of associates who have, in their turn, 'concentrated only on their core competencies, the things that give them their competitive edge' (Ogilvie, 1994). By transforming their own core competencies into the required end products, partners thus contribute towards the construction of the final product.

Thus, it is appropriate to say that value is created when the virtual organization seizes the advantage of acquiring the best efforts of world-class partners to, for example, bring products to market faster (Anonymous, 1993; Byrne, 1993b). This is, surely, a prime reason for creating a virtual organization in the first place.

Trust

In recent years, the notion of trust has gained popularity in the management literature. A survey of management journals shows that an increasing number of authors – such as Handy (1995) and Baillie (1995) – now argue that trust is an essential element in managing people. In the face of delayering, decentralization and empowerment, trust is a valuable asset and a source of competitive edge. This is particularly the case when combined with the ability of technology to distribute knowledge, information and people.

Handy (1995) argues that the increasing 'virtualization' of organizations has prompted management to address the issue of trust more directly. Handy perceives the virtual organization to be made up of people who 'need not be in one place in order to deliver their service' and 'communicate electronically and telephonically rather than face to face in a room'. Handy believes that trust will be the only way for managers to manage a group of people whom they seldom see, if ever. Similarly, Byrne (1993b) suggests that virtual relationships 'make partners more reliant on each other and require far more trust than ever before'.

Deeper examination of this issue uncovers some important implications. In particular, this relationship of trust may involve the following:

1 That the partners of virtual organization exhibit 'unprecedented levels of trust and commitment in placing the fate of the company in the hands of people who are not even employees of the company' (Davidow and Malone, 1992).
2 That this popularity of alliances and tightening of links between customers and suppliers may mean that firms will have to co-operate with potential competitors without the security of legal ties (Baillie, 1995).
3 That the partners in the strategic alliance will have to trust each other in carrying out their designated roles and responsibilities, and supplying the correct information critical for creating value in the final product.
4 That the individual workers, when trusted, will be forthcoming with their ideas and information.

Organization restructuring

The final aspect of the virtual organization is that of organizational restructuring. Like conventional corporations, the virtual organization is also greatly dependent on its structure for successful execution of identified work tasks. Grenier and Metes (1995) point out that this entails meticulous planning of all inherent activities and processes to take advantage of the information infrastructures owned by the collaborating partners. Conversely, it also requires the tailoring of information infrastructures around those designated operations.

Herein lies a problem: restructuring an operation for a virtual organization is not a one-time job. The virtual organization is composed of a disparate combination of companies, people and infrastructures. Such a configuration will require a unique virtual operation to be designed and implemented every time a new alliance is formed – if an alliance is to be meaningful. From here, it is a small step to suggest that one prerequisite for an alliance partner of a virtual organization lies in a willingness and dedication to periodic restructuring. Only by so doing can the virtual organization create value out of an *integrated* operation, which is built in a unique virtual environment that allows all partners to work together effectively *apart*.

Virtual operations

So far, we have discussed the idea that a virtual organization can generate value through the achievement of virtual teams. This would not be possible without the careful design of the virtual operation – that must be aligned with the business objective – which lies at the heart of a virtual organization. Essentially, the virtual operation is the adhesive that binds together all partners and activities into an intrinsic whole.

Virtual work tasks can be defined as work assignments designed for simultaneous electronic information access (Grenier and Metes, 1995). Using the computerized network as the main means of communication, the work tasks underpin the sharing of online electronic information between partners who may be scattered in diverse locations. Developing work tasks on top of the partner's existing information infrastructure means that partners can not only keep up to date with each other's work, they can also monitor progress of the whole work process and carry out their work simultaneously and in a complementary manner. For those involved in the process, the contribution of virtual work tasks is seen in reducing the time needed to bring a product to market.

For a virtual organization to be effective, it is suggested that virtual teams (created from strategic alliance partners) should design and establish certain beliefs, skills, culture and understanding. In an environment where partners rarely meet it is vital to establish trust. Virtual teams must not only develop capabilities to work (often in stressful situations) with electronic information and evolving communication technologies, but they must also work with a variety of partners who have their own competence and who are leaders in their own right. As a result, the competencies needed by virtual teams require 'a variety of personal and collective changes in attitudes and behaviours, not to mention knowledge and skills' (Grenier and Metes, 1995).

According to the proponents, learning in a virtual organization is a deliberate process. As such, learning must be designed in a collaborative, continuous manner for individuals, teams and organizations. Through this learning process the knowledge, skills, perspectives and experience are acquired to: build a team culture; sustain organizational and cross-organizational operations; and to develop the higher levels of speciality and virtual operations capabilities needed to meet the increasing work demands of the virtual future.

The last component of virtual operations is virtual communication. As the name implies, this involves the building, exchange, access, use, distribution, recording, change and sharing of information and knowledge, to support all work and learning processes. Owing to the importance of communication in a virtual environment such as the virtual organization, communication is thus regarded as work, not as an adjunct or support function for work. Further, since it plays a complex and vital role in virtual operations, communication is too critical to be allowed to just happen, it must be designed specifically to take advantage of the information infrastructures that exist between all participants.

Conclusions

In recent years, the concept of the virtual organization has gained much popularity. The idea itself has enormous appeal in both academic and popular circles. However, as yet, there is no generally accepted consensus on what actually constitutes a virtual organization. In an attempt to clarify matters, this chapter has explored in some detail the concept of the virtual organization. This chapter has represented the notion of a virtual organization through the discourse (and rhetoric) of its proponents. We now have a baseline picture of what a virtual organization is or may be. Thus, this chapter lays the foundation for the chapters to follow, each of which examines a particular case or aspect of the virtual organization.

Notwithstanding, it is worth bearing in mind that although the notion of virtual organization has many proponents, the idea itself is not without its problems. The final chapter in this section of the book develops a critique of the virtual organization that uses the articulation of this chapter as its basis. The purpose of the critique is to point out the contradictions and tensions that underlie current thinking. The ultimate aim of the critique is to develop a more critical appraisal of what has become a highly regarded discourse on organizational development.

Note

Bee Leng Tiow, a former M.Sc. student at the London School of Economics, made a considerable contribution to an earlier version of this chapter.

References

Anonymous (1993). Virtual corporations: fast and focused. *Business Week*, 8 February, p. 134.

Anonymous (1994). Make way for the virtual enterprise. *Purchasing*, 15 December, pp. 18–19.

Ashkenas, R. (1995). Capability: strategic tool for a competitive edge. *Journal of Business Strategy*, **16**, 6.

Baillie, J. (1995). Trust: a new concept in the management of people? *People Management*, **1**, 53.

Byrne, J. A. (1993a). The futurists who fathered the ideas. *Business Week*, 8 February, p. 103.

Byrne, J. A. (1993b). The virtual corporation. *Business Week*, 8 February, pp. 98–102.

Chesbrough, H. W. and Teece, D. J. (1996) When is virtual virtuous? Organizing for innovation. *Harvard Business Review*, **74**, 65–71.

Coates, J. F. (1993). An edgeless future. *Across the Board*, **30**, 58–60.

Davidow, W. H. and Malone, M. S. (1992). *The Virtual Corporation*. Harper Business.

Drucker, P. F. (1994). The theory of business. *Harvard Business Review*, **72**, 95–104.

Fitzgerald, G. (1994). *The Outsourcing of Information Technology: revenge of the business manager or legitimate strategic option*. Technical Report No. 9408. Birkbeck College, University of London.

Grenier, R. and Metes, G. (1995). *Going Virtual: moving your organization into the 21st century*. Prentice Hall.

Handy, C. (1995). Trust and the virtual corporation. *Harvard Business Review*, **73**, 40–50.

Huey, J. F. (1994). The new post-heroic leadership. *Fortune*, **129**, 42–50.

Ogilvie, H. (1994). At the core, it's the virtual organization. *Journal of Business Strategy*, **15**, 26–34.

Prahalad, C.K. and Hamel, G. (1990). The core competence of the corporation. *Harvard Business Review*, May–June, 79–91.

Scott Morton, M. (1991). *The Corporation of the 1990s*. Oxford University Press.

Stewart, T. A. (1993). Welcome to the revolution. *Fortune*, **28**, 32–38.

Weber, M. (1947). *The Theory of Social and Economic Organization*. Oxford University Press.

9

Interorganizational systems to support strategic collaboration between firms

Feng Li and Howard Williams

Introduction

Over the past two decades collaboration has been in fashion in the business community across the world. In many cases, interorganizational systems (IOS) have been said to play an important enabling role. By facilitating the cost-effective diffusion of information between firms, such systems can reduce the co-ordination costs associated with the marketplace and permit increased collaboration between firms (Borman and Williams, 1996; Butler *et al.*, 1997). Further, the continuous rapid development and diffusion of computers and telecommunications infrastructure and services have further increased business and academic interests in this area.

It has been widely publicized that along the value chain in certain sectors (such as retailing and car manufacturing), IOS have been set up for the exchange of product information, orders and invoices (Li, 1995). Similarly, competing firms in certain sectors have also collaborated to provide common communications infrastructures for essential services. Examples include: the LINK network of cash dispensing machines among the main UK banks and building societies (Li, 1995); the online seat reservation and ticket reservation network among major airlines in the USA (Rotemberg and Saloner, 1991); and smaller, less well-known cases such as Demepool in France – an information exchange network created by a group of independent transportation firms for the exchange of jobs and for avoiding the running of empty vehicles on return delivery trips (Bloch, 1987). Such cases have demonstrated that IOS can serve to stabilize and strengthen existing relations between firms and raise the entry barriers for potential competitors (e.g., Emmelhainz, 1987; Large, 1987; Sharpe, 1987; Rochie, 1993).

The work described in this chapter has not only confirmed these findings from previous studies, it has also revealed that IOS can facilitate new inter-firm collaborations in strategic business areas – collaborations that did not (or could not) exist without the support of IOS. The main barriers to the success of inter-firm collaborations based on IOS are also identified, and will be conceptualized as a three-layered model. The empirical evidence has been drawn from six intensive case studies from the car manufacturing and retailing sectors and a survey of seventy-four electronics firms in Scotland. More details about the empirical work will be given in the latter part of the chapter.

In the next section, previous studies in this area are briefly reviewed. Following this, a framework is outlined to classify IOS into three categories. The chapter then uses recent evidence to: (a) illustrate the emergence of new collaborations between firms in a number of sectors; (b) assess the role of such systems in inter-firm collaborations; and (c) identify the main barriers to the success of such applications. Some key lessons emerging from the study are highlighted. Finally, the chapter rounds off with a number of conclusions and an agenda for further thought.

The nature of interorganizational systems

The origin of IOS can be traced back to the 1970s. At that time, some large firms placed computer terminals in their customers' offices and offered these customers direct access to certain information (such as stock availability and price) held on their central computers (Large, 1987; Rochie, 1993). However, until the late 1980s, the development of IOS had been slow and fragmented both in terms of the sectoral coverage and in the range of applications they supported (Rotemberg and Saloner, 1991; Rochie, 1993). Only since the late 1980s has IOS began to diffuse rapidly into an increasing number of sectors (Cunningham and Tynan, 1993; Rochie, 1993; Bensau, 1994; Teo *et al.*, 1995).

IOS refer to the computer and telecommunications infrastructure developed, operated and/or used by two or more firms for the purpose of exchanging information that supports a business application or process. These firms can be suppliers and customers in the same value chain, strategic partners or even competitors in the same or related markets (Forenego, 1988; Cunningham and Tynan, 1993; Rochie, 1993; Li, 1995). Such systems are sometimes called inter-firm networks or computer-mediated inter-firm information systems. In this chapter, these terms are used interchangeably. IOS can take many different forms, typically: (a) dedicated, closed group IOS; (b) semi-closed group networks based on value-added network services (VANS); and (c) completely open systems based on open mediums such as the Internet. In order to aid our understanding, let us examine each of these types of IOS in turn.

The first category of IOS are built with an interface proprietary to a particular group of firms. As such, firms wishing to join the network often need to invest in the special hardware and/or software for the system. The reasons for adopting this type of IOS are divergent. In some cases, they were intended by some firms to lock in customers and lock out competitors. In others, common standards were not available when these networks were first introduced or available open technical solutions could not provide the sophisticated technologies or the level of confidentiality required by the partners for particular applications. This type of network brings many advantages but problems have also been increasingly recognized. It is also interesting to note that some new strategic collaborations (e.g., the joint design and development of new products between firms) are often based on this type of IOS.

The second category of IOS, currently the most widely used form, is based on standard, common purpose computing facilities and communication protocols, very often, but not always, using VANS. VANS describe the electronic communication services provided – usually by a third party – to two or more trading partners that not only establish an information link between the participants but also assist and add value to the communication process in some way. One of the most widely used standards for VANS is Electronic Data Interchange (EDI). So far, EDI has primarily been used in the subcontracting area and has been proven most effective in supporting operational-level applications, mainly because of its limited technical capabilities and the existence of multiple technical standards. In order to support more complex and strategically more important applications and processes, some firms have preferred to maintain dedicated data links between their computer systems by themselves, using various interfaces and communication protocols capable of handling more sophisticated forms of information exchange, i.e., the first category IOS discussed earlier (Borman and Williams, 1996; Li, 1995). However, the rapid development of the Internet and related services may change this situation in the near future.

In both categories of IOS discussed above, all parties involved in the systems are predetermined and have agreed to trade or exchange other information electronically. These types of IOS are sometimes referred to as 'electronic alliance' (Kokuryo and Takeda, 1995). However, new developments such as the Internet have now opened up the possibility – in theory and, to a limited extent, in practice – for instant encounter and trade between unpredetermined members (Benjamin and Wigand, 1995; Steinfield *et al.*, 1995). By using the Web browser, any person on a networked computer can now access servers anywhere in the world. A firm wishing to offer its products and services can now simply store an electronic catalogue on its server for the world to look at. It is now also possible for any firm to establish electronic communications with any other firms at very low costs. This third category of IOS is sometimes referred to as an 'electronic market' (Kokuryo and Takeda, 1995; Steinfield *et al.*, 1995).

Clearly it takes more than just the technical possibility to make such open trading and communications work. On the one hand, some firms may prefer dedicated IOS using proprietary interfaces or even VANS-based IOS, particularly because such systems can serve to lock in customers and lock out competitors. On the other hand, most commercial transactions between firms are based on trust – currently lacking in the electronic market (Handy, 1995). Kokuryo and Takeda (1995) proposed the establishment of so-called 'platform businesses' – organizations similar to credit card companies in retail markets – to tackle this problem. However, the difficulties and uncertainties involved in the process are enormous. International, or at least regional, efforts are needed to overcome the extremely difficult barriers. Some recent, large-scale schemes, such as the United Nations-backed 'Global Trade Point Network' and the 'Tradecard' project set up by the World Trade Centres Associations, may overcome some of the barriers and provide the basis for global electronic commerce in the near future.

Interorganizational systems and changing inter-firm relations

The rapid development of IOS has had profound implications for inter-firm relations and for the future form of organizations. In recent years, an increasing number of studies on IOS have been published. Some studies illustrated how IOS can give firms (particularly large ones) multiple benefits – including lower costs, shorter lead-times, lower stock levels and improved cash flows (e.g., DTI, 1987, 1989; Large, 1987; Rochie, 1993; Li, 1995; Mukhopadhyay *et al.*, 1995; Rao *et al.*, 1995; Teo *et al.*, 1995). For small firms, the benefits and dangers of being locked in and locked out of such systems were also highlighted. However, many of the visions of inter-firm collaboration based on IOS were unsubstantiated by empirical evidence or were based on evidence from a handful of case studies whilst implying that their findings were widely applicable. Only since the early 1990s have some studies begun to systematically test hypotheses about, for example, the use of EDI and changes in buyer–supplier relations, often using quantitative survey data from particular sectors in particular geographical areas (Picot *et al.*, 1993; Howells and Wood, 1995; Nidumolu, 1995; Teo *et al.*, 1995).

In the last few years, a growing interest is also forming around concepts such as the virtual organization and electronic commerce – based on projections about the future development of the Internet (e.g., Normann and Ramirez, 1993; Barnatt, 1995; Benjamin and Wigand, 1995; Handy,

1995; Kokuryo and Takeda, 1995; Rayport and Sviokla, 1995; Chesbrough and Teece, 1996). Such interest – although largely speculative – represents a particularly broad perspective on computer networking within and between firms and implications for the nature and future form of firms and markets in the information economy (Butler *et al.*, 1997). However, despite the enormous potential of the Internet, we believe it is still too early to make any concrete conclusions on how the electronic market based on open mediums such as the Internet will evolve – let alone their organizational and market implications – because there are so many uncertainties. Some non-technological barriers are extremely difficult to overcome.

Following on from the above, it is therefore not surprising that, until recently, most substantive studies have focused on the role of closed and semi-closed IOS (i.e., electronic alliance) in inter-firm relations. Electronic alliance systems – that is, IOS with predetermined participants – have been particularly developed between firms along value chains. Such systems are sometimes referred to as centred (inter-firm) networks (Bloch, 1987; Forenego, 1988; Li, 1995), or electronic hierarchies (to distinguish from electronic markets; Steinfield *et al.*, 1995). The large firm at the centre of the trading network usually initiates these IOS in order to interact electronically with regular suppliers or/and buyers. The main purpose is typically to reduce transaction costs, stock levels and lead-times. In some cases, these systems have been developed through the natural extension of the centre firm's internal computer and communication systems. The development of such IOS often entails the extension of the centre firm's internal gains of computer networking to its suppliers or/and customers, in order to reduce the total cost of the final products and to improve the responsiveness of the value chain to market changes. Sometimes, such systems are imposed on trading partners by the large firm at the centre. The costs to each firm are normally recovered by productivity gains, increased sales or secured long-term contacts, and sometimes the development is directly subsidized by the centre firm (Bloch, 1987; Li, 1995).

Previous studies have found that electronic alliances can stabilize existing relations between suppliers and buyers, and raise the entry barriers for potential competitors (e.g., Emmelhainz, 1987; Large, 1987; Sharpe, 1987; Rochie, 1993). This is because setting up and maintaining IOS require close co-operation between participating firms which, in turn, helps them to foster a closer partnership and encourage the sharing of information. The use of such networks can also contribute to the removal of barriers to co-operation by reducing errors typical of paper-based communications. Should any errors happen, these networks can also facilitate problem resolution; problems can be more easily traced and be dealt with more quickly and effectively. In addition, introducing IOS requires both time and money, and their on-going maintenance often requires special skills. There are also security and reliability concerns. Switching partners (suppliers or buyers) would therefore, by definition, be costly and time-consuming. All these factors serve to stabilize existing inter-firm relations and improve inter-firm collaboration.

New evidence on inter-firm collaboration through IOS

Using evidence gathered from six case studies in the UK and the results of a survey in Scotland, this chapter focuses on the role of closed and semi-closed IOS (i.e., electronic alliance) in new inter-firm collaborations. The following six case studies have been drawn from the motor manufacturing and retailing sectors. Semi-structured interviews were conducted with both IT and non-IT senior managers in: (a) a large Japanese car manufacturer in the UK and two of its suppliers; and (b) a large British retail chain and two of its suppliers. Documents from various sources, including company annual reports, press releases, newspaper articles and published research notes, were also carefully studied. At least two interviews were conducted in each company, and each interview lasted for at least an hour (some considerably longer).

The car manufacturer selected for the study is among the top ten in the world. Interviews were conducted with its managing director, information systems director and operations manager in charge of logistics in the UK. Also studied are two of the car manufacturer's suppliers; one supplies car seats, the other supplies braking systems. The retail chain is one of the largest in the UK – with an annual turnover in excess of £7 billion in 1997. Its group information systems director and a store manager were interviewed. The two suppliers to this retail chain are also large companies: the first has over 3000 employees and fifteen factories in different parts of the UK, specializing in the design and manufacture of quality clothes; the second is a diversified multinational company with strong business interests in textiles. More background about these companies will be given later in the chapter. These case studies have revealed a number of important tendencies in new inter-firm collaborations based on IOS. Evidence gathered from a telephone-based survey of seventy-four firms – representing 15 per cent of the electronics and support firms in Scotland – will be used to reveal to what extent the tendencies identified from the case studies exist in this particular sector of the Scottish economy.

Our research has generally confirmed findings from previous studies but has also identified several new tendencies. Our case studies suggest that inter-firm collaborations based on IOS are progressing beyond electronic trading and routine transactions to strategically more important processes. In particular, once two firms have established a successful inter-firm system at the routine transaction level, they often develop new applications based on the same or more powerful links. A particularly interesting tendency is the development of new collaborations in strategic areas, such as the joint design and development of new products between suppliers and buyers. Although this tendency was not confirmed by our survey, the survey did suggest that whilst 32 per cent of the firms surveyed used some form of IOS, 18 per cent had two or more different types. This result perhaps indicates that some firms have begun to appreciate that a single class of inter-firm links can play only a limited role.

Another important issue emerged from the research; although IOS have played an important role, the most difficult barriers to inter-firm collaboration are often non-technological in nature. This finding has been confirmed both by the case studies and the surveys.

From routine transactions to strategic applications: case study evidence

The development of inter-firm collaboration in strategic areas is clearly reflected in the large retail chain and its regular suppliers of quality clothes in the UK. In the late 1980s, an IOS was developed between the retail chain and some large suppliers, using third-party EDI on *Tradanet* for electronic ordering and invoicing. The general benefits from the development included improved communication, reduced administration costs for all participants (less paperwork handling and less relaying), closer co-operation, increased business volume and improved quality of services to final customers. However, it is interesting to note that in some cases, after the electronic trading became operational, applications beyond basic transactions have been developed – either using the same inter-firm network or by installing new and more powerful links.

An interesting application was developed between this retailer and a regular clothes supplier. The EDI link between them was not only used for electronic trading but also for exchanging the supplier's latest designs. Using local software at both ends of the link, each design can be coded into a series of digital figures representing the particular patterns, materials and colours of the new design. These figures can be transmitted to the retailer via EDI and then decoded, so that the retailer can modify the design before issuing orders. This system is extremely important to both firms. Firstly, the supplier can frequently send its latest designs to the retailer. In turn, the retailer can respond to the supplier more frequently and quickly, inform the supplier of its latest demand and order more frequently. The business volume between them has since increased considerably and the network consolidates the buyer–supplier relationship.

In the case of the retailer and a very large supplier, some more interesting inter-firm collaborations have been developed after the EDI network became operational. Being a large firm, the supplier took the initiative to set up a more powerful communications network with the retailer in order to capture the latest market information (the latest customer preferences in terms of colour, materials and styles, for example) from the retailer's stores all over the UK. The information is then incorporated into the supplier's latest design and production activities. The network is also used for the exchange of colour pictures of the supplier's latest product designs (rather than the technical designs as used by the other supplier illustrated above), which the retailer's purchasing staff can view and modify before issuing orders. This network has served to strengthen the relationship between the two firms, giving this supplier a unique advantage over others.

Similar evidence has been found in the manufacturing sector. We examined the experience of a Japanese car manufacturer and its regular suppliers in the UK. The car manufacturer started production in the UK in the mid-1980s. By the early 1990s it employed a total of 4500 people in the UK, making well over 100 000 cars per year. In 1992, the manufacturer imposed electronic trading on all regular suppliers. The benefits to all suppliers included: early delivery requests from the car manufacturer, which can help suppliers to minimize inventory holding and achieve better production scheduling; and by interfacing EDI data with suppliers' internal IT systems, administration costs could also be reduced. Since investments in EDI by suppliers did not have to be dedicated, the car manufacturer only invested in the extensive facilities necessary to support the data transmissions and required all suppliers to fund their own link. Similar links with sub-suppliers were also made possible and actively encouraged by the car manufacturer.

The success of this electronic trading network opened up numerous opportunities for new application development. The first application is the implementation of so-called 'synchronous supply' with some local suppliers. Some components (e.g., car seats) are only delivered to the car assembly lines by the suppliers – with the right variants and specifications – twelve to fifteen minutes after the car manufacturer issues the order. Apart from the locational proximity between them and the convenience of electronic ordering based on EDI, one key to this application is that suppliers are granted direct access to production planning and forecasting information stored on the car manufacturer's mainframe computers. Suppliers can thereby plan their own production before receiving orders. For suppliers in other parts of the UK and in Europe, the lead-time from order to delivery has also been reduced dramatically. By the mid-1990s, the car manufacturer had shaved the average inventory and stock holding for European-originated parts to less than one day. Essential to the improvement is the sharing of business information between business partners via IOS.

The second application is in the area of interactive, joint development of new products. The car manufacturer is currently working with technically more competent suppliers for the development of the next car. So far, few suppliers have the technical capability to supply a complete product component unaided (as a 'black box'), but the car manufacturer is developing what was described as a 'grey box' solution. In this approach, the car manufacturer supplies CAD data on the space the component occupies and its technical specifications; the supplier will then begin to design the component, passing it back to the car manufacturer via IOS for feedback. Through interactive communications, any problems caused by the relative lack of sufficient engineering skills on the part of the suppliers can be resolved. Essential to this application is the support of broadband communication networks between their respective computers.

The third application is in the area of manufacturer–dealer relations. Whilst the in-bound material flows for the car manufacturer are of a world-class standard, its out-bound logistics are similar to most European car manufacturers. Inventory levels for finished cars are currently in the range of two-and-a-half to five months of production (even in Japan the best figure for leading companies is still as high as two months). The working capital tied to the finished car is huge and the potential for improvement is enormous. The key to improving the inventory level of finished cars is to progress the relation between dealers and manufacturers – thereby by-passing the distributors – so that the manufacturer can cut scheduling and delivery times. More importantly, it is essential to have the support of sophisticated IOS and the sharing of a wide range of business information, both between the car manufacturer and the dealers and between the dealers themselves. Dealers using the system need to be able to monitor stock movement of other dealers and to check production-in-progress in the factories. However, unsurprisingly, many firms are currently not prepared to share such information with competitors! The non-technical barriers to this application are extremely difficult to overcome and thus success of the application may take a very long time to achieve. The managing director himself suggested this could be 'a twenty-year job'. This application also suggested that non-technical barriers are probably the most difficult to overcome both in inter-firm networking and in developing strategically important applications based on such networks. In particular, before such strategic collaborations can become feasible, firms may have radically to change their basic assumptions about the nature of firms and markets.

These case studies indicate that the development of successful routine electronic transactions between firms is probably a necessary first step for them to develop strategic collaborations based on the same or more powerful IOS. Apart from the enormous technical difficulties involved, numerous non-technical barriers have to be overcome before the full potential of IOS can be exploited. Similar evidence was found in a number of other case studies.

A survey of inter-firm networking in the Scottish electronics industry

Although inter-firm collaboration in strategic areas was identified from several case studies, our survey of the Scottish electronics industry did not reveal widespread development of such applications. Nevertheless, the survey suggested that the primary objective of firms in developing IOS is not to improve the efficiency of existing information processing activities, and there is a recognition of the value-added that information can contribute to the business. For example, only 27 per cent of firms highlighted reduced costs as a very important consideration when installing an IOS, while 86 per cent were motivated by the potential to access a greater quantity of better quality information. Almost every firm considered the ability of IOS to supply more information or improve the quality of information already communicated to be a very important influence on their decision to introduce them.

However, despite such encouraging intentions, once one looks in more detail at how firms are using IOS, it becomes apparent that most firms are using the technology to support existing patterns of activities and organization, rather than facilitating new forms of collaboration or collaboration in new areas. Firms appear, thus far, to have focused considerable attention on improving access to information but insufficient attention on how to innovatively apply that information to improve their business. In particular, most firms still essentially associate a given piece of information with a particular task, and there is limited realization that (as well as such standard usage) the same information reanalysed or reformatted might be of value elsewhere in the organization. Interestingly, 69 per cent of the surveyed firms suggested that the introduction of IOS had facilitated closer working relations with trading partners, but trading patterns remained virtually the same for 71 per cent of the firms. Essentially, IOS were only being used to support established business rather than to help the firms to generate new business opportunities or to support new collaborations.

The majority of survey respondents were of the opinion that IOS are mainly suited to the communication of hard or factual information, stating that electronic communication is typically bereft of many of the contextual clues that attend more personal communications. However, nearly 50 per cent of firms have substantially reduced their use of traditional communications media (such as postal services and telephone) following the introduction of IOS. Thus, it can even be questioned whether the introduction of IOS is leading to enriched communications between firms.

Main issues stemming from the empirical work

The empirical work discussed above has highlighted a number of important issues. Some of the key issues include the following:

- contrasting results have been identified from the case studies and the survey
- different types of IOS are perhaps needed to support different inter-firm applications
- IOS may significantly reshape the internal activities and processes of the firm
- the successful collaboration between firms requires more than the exchange of information.

Let us discuss each of these issues in turn, drawing attention to some of the key findings.

First, whilst the case studies suggested that some firms are increasingly exploiting the potential of IOS by developing new collaboration in strategic areas, the survey revealed that most firms in the Scottish electronics industry are not using IOS to their full potential. The reasons for this finding can be very complex. For one, most firms are probably still experimenting with IOS and have not yet progressed beyond basic-level applications such as straightforward transactions. Indeed, even at this level, many firms experience serious technical problems, particularly in terms of system reliability and in managing incompatible standards and networks. Let us consider an example. A survey respondent pointed out that its suppliers were connected to different third-party EDI networks, and there was limited interconnection between different networks. In particular, issues relating to message audit trails and allocation of responsibility for lost messages remained unresolved. Reliability of EDI is also problematic, and there is insufficient trust by the firm to allow EDI data to be fed directly into production schedules or computer-controlled machines. In many cases, use of EDI was merely restricted to peripheral areas such as processing financial transactions, and messages were invariably pulled off the machine and manually checked. Such technical problems may have prevented some firms from developing new collaborations in strategic areas.

The second issue highlighted by the empirical material is that different applications may require the support of different types of IOS. Many firms have placed emphasis on providing a 'single solution' to all inter-firm communication needs and often fail to understand that they need to access a variety of communication capabilities so that the most appropriate can be used for a given task. A further problem is that firms are at different stages on the path to inter-firm networking. As each firm may want different things from the network, a common timetable for developing strategic collaborations based on such networks can prove problematic.

The third issue concerns the reshaping of internal organizational processes (e.g., decision-making processes, organizational structures and behavioural norms) by IOS. Problems of organizational and technical adaptation within the firm still represent considerable barriers to the effective use of even such simple services as EDI. This undoubtedly constrains the ability of the firms to use IOS for restructuring trading relations or developing strategic collaborations. EDI-based transactions often interface with a wide range of activities within the firm, including information networks and hierarchies within the firm responsible for processing data on: production components and specifications, production planning and scheduling, and pricing and accounting. More importantly, the use of IOS – even if via human interfaces – implies that the firms are essentially sharing information previously held back for internal use. Thus, questions about the nature of inter-firm relations, power, control and quasi-integration are raised. Many firms are reluctant to overly commit themselves to IOS because they do not fully understand the implications of such networks for them in the long run.

Finally, successful collaboration between firms appears to require more than the exchange of information (Handy, 1995; Huxham, 1995; Borman and Williams, 1996). It has been argued that economic activities need to be considered within an institutional context. The political, economic and judicial institutions of a society function as a web of interconnected formal rules and informal constraints that define the incentive structure within which organizations operate – the so-called 'rules of the game' (Borman and Williams, 1996; Li, 1997). Over time, an institutional framework evolves to support and promote particular production structures and inter-firm relations. However, radical innovations in ICTs and services may challenge the very basis of that structure and relationship, and the existing institutional framework may have to be fundamentally overhauled (Li, 1995, 1996; Butler *et al.*, 1997). In many cases, ICT-based innovations are changing the rules of the game, which may be particularly the case in the area of inter-firm relations. As yet, many firms may not be ready to accept such radical changes.

According to Drucker (1988), although the firm was only invented because it was perceived to be a useful 'tool' in the economy, it is now considered to have inherent values. The challenge is to change that perception – to recognize that too much emphasis is being placed on the importance of the individual firm. It is the norm for firms to see their future as being dependent on their own actions. The possibility that trading partners could help build that future is largely ignored by all but a small proportion of firms. Where firms claim that they are collaborating, the intention is often to make suppliers more responsive to their needs or to cut costs rather than to design more effective relationships.

Many firms are so preoccupied with supporting their individual businesses that they are failing to recognize a key opportunity – working together to increase the effectiveness of the entire value chain. Many firms simply want finished products from their suppliers, and they have little interest in tapping the suppliers' expertise to see if the effectiveness of that product could be improved. Equally, suppliers often simply respond to the demands of their customers, rather than helping to define them (Borman and Williams, 1996). As the survey results show, so long as the underlying basis of business is not questioned, the majority of firms appear willing to pay lip service to inter-firm collaboration. Thus, the development of inter-firm collaboration in strategic areas may to a large extent depend on changes in the institutional framework within which all firms operate and, indeed, on changes in people's basic assumptions about the nature of firms and markets in the information economy. A recent study by McKinsey concluded that owing to rapid development in ICTs and telecommunications services, transaction costs are going to decrease dramatically, which may force firms to reconsider fundamental issues about the nature and boundary of firms and markets (Butler *et al.*, 1997).

To sum up, innovative collaboration between firms based on IOS requires not only the development of an appropriate technical infrastructure, but also a recognition, understanding and acceptance that the role and structure of the firm and its boundaries require radical rethought. Information should not only be seen as a static, stand-alone asset typically associated with a pre-defined application. Firms need genuinely to recognize the contribution that information can make to their businesses. The changing nature of the economy, combining with the rapid development of ICTs, is radically changing the rules of the game (Kelly, 1997; Li, 1997). Many prevailing views and business visions existing in today's organizations may be the biggest barriers to the development of innovative collaboration between firms in strategic areas.

The main barriers to inter-firm collaboration through IOS: a three-layered model

The study has highlighted several barriers to the future development of IOS. There are not only serious technical barriers but also cultural and political barriers that are extremely difficult to overcome. These 'softer' barriers include: sharing sensitive business information with suppliers, customers and even competitors; the integration of business processes between firms; the control of one firm by another; the co-existence of competition and collaboration; and numerous other related issues. Many of these barriers have to be overcome *before* inter-firm collaboration in strategic areas can be developed. In fact, the full potential of IOS probably cannot be achieved without radical changes in the institutional framework in which most firms operate, and in the perception and assumptions of business leaders about the nature of firms and markets in the information economy.

The main barriers to the future development of IOS exist at three levels. At the bottom level, there are technical barriers that firms have to overcome – particularly in terms of system reliability and in managing incompatible standards and networks. Such technical problems – and the lack of trust of such systems – have prevented some firms from developing new collaborations in strategic areas. Although recent developments in technology, infrastructure and services have significantly relieved this problem, technical barriers will continue to constrain the development of IOS and new applications based on such systems.

A more difficult barrier exists at a second level, which requires radical changes in the understanding of the nature of firms and markets, and a firm grasp of the new rules of the game in the information economy. Issues such as sharing sensitive business information with suppliers, buyers and even rival companies still worry some business leaders (e.g., in areas such as stock availability, forecasting and production planning). However, if such issues are not resolved, many strategic inter-firm collaborations are simply impossible to develop and the full potential of IOS cannot be achieved.

Even when firms are prepared to share certain business information with each other, the success of inter-firm collaboration based on IOS is still not guaranteed. Successful collaborations between firms require more than the exchange of information. As has been argued earlier, differences between collaborating firms – in terms of aims, culture, structure, procedures, professional and natural languages, accountabilities and the sheer time required to manage the logistics of communication – often work against success. Of particular importance in effective collaboration between firms is the development of 'common knowledge' – an extremely difficult endeavour. As such, the success of inter-firm collaboration through IOS is much more difficult than many people have perceived. This explains – to some extent – why the enormous technical potential of IOS has so far not been fully exploited.

The main lessons from the study

What is evident from the empirical material discussed in this chapter is an evolutionary path for the development of IOS and inter-firm collaborations. Although, as the survey results suggested, most firms still used IOS primarily for routine transactions, the case studies clearly indicated that IOS can be used effectively to support new collaborations in strategic areas. In particular, the study has found that once two firms have established an inter-firm network for routine applications, new and more powerful applications are often developed between them. This evolutionary path, however, raises important questions about inter-firm networking. Among the questions raised are: uneven distribution of potential benefits between participants; the geographical conglomeration tendency associated with inter-firm networking and the long-term commitment implied by such locational adjustments; the existence of alternative channels of communications to inter-firm computer networks; and the danger of systems failure with inter-firm applications and the associated business implications.

This research highlights several important lessons. First, in order to develop inter-firm collaboration in strategic processes, a necessary first step is to develop routine applications with IOS. This can both provide important learning for the firms involved and nurture the development of trust between them. Only after firms have benefited from these routine transactions and learned to trust and work with each other via the electronic medium are some firms then prepared to explore the possibility for more complex and strategically more important applications.

Second, IOS can often serve to stabilize existing relations between suppliers and buyers, and raise entry barriers for potential competitors. Co-operation between participating firms involved in developing IOS can often help them to foster a closer partnership and encourage the sharing of information; switching partners can be both costly and time-consuming. However, although IOS are effective in reducing transaction costs, stock levels and lead-times, the overall benefits from inter-firm networking are often distributed unevenly among the firms involved and sometimes the benefit to one firm is achieved at the expense of others (such as pushing stock holding to suppliers). In the long term, such inequality may be detrimental to inter-firm relations. To a large extent, future development of IOS will depend on the degree to which people's perception of the nature and boundary of firms and markets changes. Further studies in this area – the 'new rules of the game' in particular – are clearly needed.

Third, although many firms have placed emphasis on providing a 'single solution' to all inter-firm communication needs, an increasing number of firms have realized that different applications may require the support of different types of IOS. It is also interesting to notice from the survey that the primary objective of firms in developing IOS is not to improve the efficiency of existing information processing activities and there is a recognition of the value-added that information can contribute to the business. Such positive signs clearly indicate that people's understanding of IOS are changing.

Future directions of IOS

Given that IOS are rapidly evolving, this is an area that must be monitored closely in the future. We believe that key development will occur in three main areas and thus three types of studies are particularly useful. First, continuous efforts are needed to identify new inter-firm applications based on IOS. Results from such research are important, because both the technical capacity of ICTs and our understanding of ICTs in the business contexts have been improving rapidly. Powerful innovations that can bring about radical and rapid improvements in the efficiency, effectiveness and flexibility of inter-firm relations are continuously being developed. It is important to identify and conceptualize such innovations as soon as they are developed, because many of them have the potential to diffuse into the wider economy. Business leaders need to understand the potential benefits and pitfalls of these innovations before introducing them. Subsequently, commercial interest in related studies is enormous. Such research can also inform policy makers at various levels of the government when formulating industrial and regional policies as well as policies and regulations governing the development of telecommunications infrastructure and information services. A particularly important focus is the Internet, which certainly has the potential to support radical changes in firms and markets, although realization of this potential depends on a wide range of technical and non-technical factors.

Second, there is a need to examine the diverse applications and development trajectories of IOS in order to formulate a more systematic analytical framework. Information systems are highly flexible, and one system often allows firms to undertake radically different actions for fundamentally different purposes, such as the contrasting use of IOS to strength inter-firm relations against increasing competitive positions in the market. The advantages of such studies will not lie in their discussion of isolated examples but in allowing researchers to reveal the general picture of the current transformation in specific contexts. The findings can also be used to test whether new tendencies identified in leading firms are being taken up in the wider economy.

Third, because of the rapid development and proliferation of ICTs and the radical change in the nature of the economy, IOS and changing inter-firm relations need to be examined in a much broader context – both inside and outside the firm. In fact, inter-firm innovations are often closely related to organizational innovations within the firm, such as corporate restructuring, business process re-engineering, lean production and just-in-time (JIT). The development of these inter- and intra-organizational innovations is often accompanied by the adoption of new business philosophies, missions, strategies and objectives, together with new requirements for new skills, new patterns of responsibilities, new management orientation, new methods of control and co-ordination and new organizational culture. These changes are happening in a rapidly altering business environment. As has been briefly discussed earlier, the rules of the game may be changing and understanding the emerging institutional framework is essential for developing strategic applications based on IOS.

References

Barnatt, C. (1995). Office space, cyberspace and virtual organization. *Journal of General Management*, **20**, 78–92.

Benjamin, R. and Wigand, R. (1995). Electronic markets and virtual value chains on the Information Superhighway. *Sloan Management Review*, Winter, 62–72.

Bensau, M. (1994). *Interorganizational Co-operation: the role of information technology*. Working Paper 94/68/TM/SM. INSEAD.

Bloch, A. (1987). *Telematics, Inter-organizations and Economic Performance*. Occasional Paper No.195. FAST.

Borman, M. and Williams, H. (1996). *Collaboration: more than the exchange of information*. Management Science Working Paper 96/4. Strathclyde Business School.

Butler, P., Hall, T. W., Hanna, A. M., Mendonca, L., Auguste, B., Manyika, J. and Sahay, A. (1997). A revolution in interaction. *The McKinsey Quarterly*, No.1, 4–23.

Chesbrough, H. W. and Teece, D. J. (1996). When virtual is virtuous? Organizing for innovation. *Harvard Business Review*, January–February, 65–73.

Cunningham, C. and Tynan, C. (1993). Electronic trading, inter-organizational systems and the nature of buyer and seller relations: the need for a network perspective. *International Journal of Information Management*, **13**, 3–28.

Department of Trade and Industry (DTI) (1987). *The Economic Effects of Value Added and Data Services*. HMSO.

Department of Trade and Industry (DTI) (1989). *Value Added and Data Services and the Small Firm*. HMSO.

Drucker, P. (1988). The coming of the new organization. *Harvard Business Review*, January–February, 45–53.

Emmelhainz, M. A. (1987). Electronic data interchange: does it change the purchasing process? *Journal of Purchasing and Materials Management*, **23**, 2–8.

Forenego, G. (1988). Interorganizational networks and market structures. In C. Antonelli, ed., *New Information Technology and Industrial Change: the Italian case*. Kluwer Academic Publishers.

Handy, C. (1995). Trust and the virtual organization. *Harvard Business Review*, May–June, 40–49.

Howells, J. and Wood, M. (1995). Diffusion and management of electronic data interchange: barriers and opportunities in the UK pharmaceutical and healthcare industries. *Technology Analysis and Strategic Management*, **7**, 371–86.

Huxham, C. (1995). Advantage or inertia: making collaboration work. In R. Paton, G. Clarke, G. Jones, J. Lewis and P. Quintas, eds, *The New Management Reader*. Routledge.

Kelly, K. (1997). New rules for the new economy: twelve dependable principles for thriving in a turbulent world. *Wired*, September, 140–97.

Kokuryo, J. and Takeda, Y. (1995). The role of 'platform businesses' as intermediaries of electronic commerce. *Proceedings of the Hititaubashi-Organization Science Conference on Asian Research in Organizations*, Tokyo.

Large, J. (1987). How networks net business. *Management Today*, February, 86–94.

Li, F. (1995). *The Geography of Business Information*. John Wiley and Sons.

Li, F. (1996). Structural innovations through information systems: some emerging tendencies in Europe. *Journal of Management Systems*, **7**, 53–66.

Li, F. (1997). From compromise to harmony: organizational redesign through ICTs. *International Journal of Information Management*, **17**, 451–64.

Mukhopadhyay, T., Kekre, S. and Kalathur, S. (1995). Business value of information technology: a study of electronic data exchange. *MIS Quarterly*, June, 137–55.

Nidumolu, S. R. (1995). Interorganizational information systems and the structure and climate of seller–buyer relationships. *Information and Management*, **28**, 89–105.

Normann, R. and Ramirez, R. (1993). From value chain to value constellation: designing interactive strategy. *Harvard Business Review*, July–August, 65–77.

Picot, A., Neuburger, R. and Niggl, J. (1993). Management perspectives of electronic data interchange systems. *International Journal of Information Management*, **13**, 243–48.

Rao, H. R., Pegels, C., Salam, A. F., Hwang, K. T. and Seth, V. (1995). The impact of EDI implementation commitment and implementation success on competitive advantage and firm performance. *Information Systems Journal*, **5**, 195–202.

Rayport, J. F. and Sviokla, J. J. (1995). Exploiting the virtual value chain. *Harvard Business Review*, November–December, 75–85.

Rochie, E. M. (1993). Measurement of telecommunications-based strategic linkages between firms and their customers, suppliers and business partners. *Communications and Strategies*, **9**, 97–115.

Rotemberg, J. and Saloner, G. (1991). Interfirm competition and collaboration. In M. Scott Morton, ed., *The Corporation of the 1990s*. Oxford University Press.

Sharpe, R. (1987). Renault's automatic transmission. *Data Management*, June, iii.

Steinfield, C., Kraut, R. and Plummer, A. (1995). The impact of interorganizational networks on buyer–seller relationships. *Journal of Computer Mediated Communications*, **1**, 1–17.

Teo, H. H., Tan, B. C. Y., Wei, K. K. and Woo, L. Y. (1995). Reaping EDI benefits through a pro-active approach. *Information and Management*, **28**, 185–95.

10

Structure, strategy and success factors for the virtual organization

Peter Marshall, Judy McKay and Janice Burn

Introduction

Of late, the notion of the virtual organization has attracted a great deal of attention. Indeed, in a comparatively short period of time, there has arisen an extensive literature on the subject and on the strategy of virtual organizing. However, for a number of reasons, this body of literature does not necessarily elucidate this topic. First, there is confusion in the literature on what is meant by 'virtual' and the 'virtual organization'. Arguably, while this semantic confusion exists, clarity in this field will not (indeed, cannot) be achieved. Second, there is a tendency to confuse 'virtual' with 'virtuous', 'virtuality' with 'virtuousness' (and hence goodness), and from this to draw comparisons with integrated structures or bureaucracies, which almost inevitably attract the 'bad' label from the other end of the continuum (Chesbrough and Teece, 1996). Third, there seems to be an issue of empirical evidence for many of the assertions made. While the discussion of virtual organizations remains at a largely conceptual and theoretical level, there would seem some justification to question the relevance and veracity of the debate to business practice. In light of these three issues, this chapter will represent a bold attempt to redress our concerns.

Overall, this chapter aims to provide a clear theoretical framework, evaluated against empirical evidence, to describe the notion of the virtual organization. The chapter will articulate our view of the virtual organization and, in particular, will attempt to identify its defining characteristics. A number of possible models of the virtual organization will be defined and illustrated by way of real-life case studies.

Characterizing the essence of the virtual organization

A careful examination of the literature on the virtual organization shows three approaches taken with respect to this particular concept. For some, a virtual organization is essentially an electronic one, an online organization. Proponents of this position offer Amazon.com and eBay.com as examples of organizations that have been created primarily to exist in and exploit the opportunities offered by the WWW and cyberspace. This so-called virtual (or electronic) organization is discussed in contradistinction to the traditional 'bricks and mortar' retail outlet (Czerniawska and Potter, 1998).

An alternative to this first definition presents the virtual organization as an organizational structure based primarily on the notion of collaborating entities. Here, firms come together to share competencies, skills, knowledge and other resources for the purpose of producing a particular service or good, or of taking advantage of a particular opportunity. While there is the clear expectation that IT and telecommunications play an important role in co-ordinating and controlling the activities of disparate components of the virtual organization, IT is merely a key component, as opposed to a distinguishing characteristic *per se* (see, for example, Marshall *et al.*, 1999; Turban *et al.*, 1999).

The third approach, with respect to the virtual organization, is perhaps the most confusing. This approach represents an amalgam of the previous two approaches. Here, authors move almost interchangeably between the virtual organization as an electronic or online organization, and the virtual organization as a somewhat transient network of people, ideas, competencies and resources that come together for a particular purpose (see, for example, Siebel and House, 1999).

The position we adopt in this chapter corresponds to the second approach. As a precursor to more detailed discussion, a virtual organization can be defined as:

> . . . composed of several business partners sharing costs and resources for the purpose of producing a product or service. [It] can be temporary . . . or it can be permanent. Each partner contributes complementary resources that reflect its strengths, and determines its role in the virtual corporation. (Turban *et al.*, 1999: 142)

This stance suggests a need to discuss more fully the essential and fundamental attributes of the virtual organization.

A key characteristic of the virtual organization is its adaptability and flexibility in the face of turbulent business environments, a condition sometimes described as 'agility' (Metes *et al.*, 1998). Virtual organizations are capable of rapid and adaptable responses to changing markets – whether these arise as a result of globalization, changing cost structures, changing customer needs and wants or other similar reasons (Goldman *et al.*, 1995). Virtual organizations use existing structures from one or more firms and combine these in creative ways to forge new capabilities and competencies. This strategy thus averts the need to recruit, train and forge new work teams, buy new equipment and buildings and work through a period of organizational learning (Magretts, 1998). Allied with its agility, an important attribute of the virtual organization is argued to be its more effective utilization of existing resources. This creates an important source of competitive advantage (Turban *et al.*, 1999).

The formation of business partnerships and alliances is pivotal to the concept of the virtual organization (Grenier and Metes, 1995; Henning, 1998). Acquiring and/or developing all the required resources and competencies in order to avail itself of windows of opportunity can be both too time consuming and too costly to be an appropriate response for an organization acting on its own. In other words, in the brief period of time available to exploit business opportunities, a single organization may not have the time or the financial resources available to obtain and/or develop the necessary skills, infrastructure or other resources. It may not even have the time to develop efficient business processes. However, access to the required knowledge, skills, resources and infrastructure may be available through entering into alliances or partnerships with all, or a part only, of other organizations. This notion is captured pictorially in Figure 10.1.

On its own, organization 1 may not have the capability to take advantage of a particular perceived business opportunity. Similarly, organizations 2 and 4 may be disadvantaged for different reasons. Organization 3 may possess the necessary knowledge and skills, but may

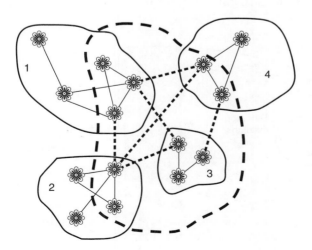

Figure 10.1
Formation of business alliances

lack other important resources, e.g., financial muscle. Nevertheless, by working co-operatively and synergistically with others, a virtual organization (depicted by the shaded area) may be formed to exploit the opportunity. By each contributing different knowledge, skills and resources, the virtual organization formed by the co-operative leveraging of assets and resources in organizations 1 to 4 may be highly successful in availing itself for a time of the original business opportunity.

Implicit in this description of the formation of business alliances is the notion that various components of the virtual organization may well be geographically dispersed. This gives rise to the challenge of communication and co-ordination across different time zones, locations, cultures and languages (IMPACT Programme, 1998). This is illustrated in Figure 10.2. Typically, this implies a need for excellent IT to support communication and co-ordination throughout the virtual organization.

Another key component of the agility ascribed to and required of virtual organizations is its human resources (HR) and its HR management practices (Pfeffer, 1998). The needs and requirements of virtual organizations demand that each employee has the skills to contribute directly to the value chain – contributing directly to the 'bottom line'. For example, this could be in the areas of product and service design, production, marketing or distribution. As each constituent member of the virtual organization contributes core competencies, the resultant collective HR effort would be geared appropriately and directly towards exploiting a particular opportunity. The collective output would thus be expected to surpass any of the individual contributing organizations (Turban *et al.*, 1999).

Ideally, employees must have a number of strong attributes. In addition to a capacity to learn new skills, employees must have a positive attitude towards the need for constant change, and tolerance of ambiguity and uncertainty in their working lives. They should also be sensitive to the possibly changing needs and wants of the organization's customers. For this to be achieved, a noteworthy characteristic of virtual organizations is employee empowerment, whereby decision making, responsibility and accountability are devolved to appropriate component parts of the structure and are readily accepted as such (IMPACT

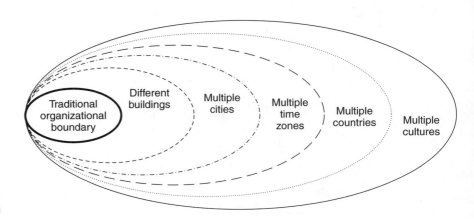

Figure 10.2
Characteristic dispersion of the virtual organization

Programme, 1998). Responsiveness and competitiveness in global markets implies a need for constancy and excellence in the development of appropriate skills and skill levels. It also requires employees to accommodate their work procedures, skills, skill levels, work times and even working lives to the demands of the organization's customers. However, the virtual organization offers high rewards to skilled and psychologically tough employees. Such rewards can be financial. In addition, many organizations try to give employees as much freedom as possible to structure their workplaces and working hours to fit their own needs and personalities. Outputs and results are carefully monitored and measured, but human inputs are left as much as possible to the individual (Coutu, 1998). Clearly implied is the need for the virtual organization to be rigorous and effective in the management and exploitation of its intellectual capital (i.e., knowledge) while providing a satisfying work experience for its employees (IMPACT Programme, 1998).

Agility and responsiveness also imply a need for administrative processes that are cost effective and lean. Heavy, clumsy bureaucratic practices have no place in the agile virtual organization. The needs of a centralized administration should impede as little as possible the work of those employees involved in creating value for the organization. Avoided at all costs should be the inertia, heaviness and clumsiness generally associated with the bureaucratic hierarchical organization of the late twentieth century. Unnecessary administrative activities should be minimized or abolished altogether. In the virtual organization, administrative work is done as efficiently as possible by as few staff as possible. Wherever possible, administrative overheads should be attributed to those staff directly involved in value-creating activities. This may be preferable since such staff will only engage in administration that is directly useful. When it becomes necessary to curtail certain administrative tasks that are no longer viable, the administrative activity winds down naturally without the difficulties of reducing a central administrative function or reassigning staff to other duties (Benjamin and Wigand, 1995; Goldman *et al.*, 1995). It is essential that the organization retain its ability to respond and adapt to changing conditions. High administrative overhead costs and/or slow, bureaucratic procedures may inhibit this essential characteristic.

Business opportunities are too often fleeting and transient – especially in contemporary business environments. Virtual organizations are opportunistic and avail themselves of profitable business circumstances even if the organization itself is apparently temporary. There is an acceptance of, even an enthusiasm for, change and uncertainty with respect to its products and services, its customer base, its structure and scope and in its very approach to doing business (IMPACT Programme, 1998). This characteristic means that virtual organizations are at ease with the notion of porous and changing organizational boundaries, and with the use of outsourcing and alliances as an effective means of changing and realigning the organization's skills and skill levels. In these ways virtual organizations incorporate the competencies of other organizations so as to adapt quickly to changing business situations. Virtual organizations can thus take advantage of emerging opportunities by changing their skills base to fit different circumstances. Such organizations are adept at co-ordinating and managing disparate resources and activities throughout the supply chain.

Virtual organizations are information intensive (Grenier and Metes, 1995) and hence may be heavily reliant on IT. Information and communications technologies underpin and enable their propensity for opportunistic behaviour. IT supports some of the new organizational alliances and forms necessary for designing and producing new goods and services quickly. IT also provides an organization with a fast and convenient channel through which to promote its products and services and to inform potential customers of organizational product and service developments. The same channel can also accept and process sales to customers (Benjamin and Wigand, 1995; Metes *et al.*, 1998). These new technologies provide the information and communication framework necessary for the 'anywhere anytime' work that takes place in virtual organizations (Upton and McAfee, 1996). However, it must be acknowledged that the virtual organization can exist without heavy reliance on IT (Sor, 1999), although it is generally acknowledged that in most contemporary cases IT will occupy an important position.

In the face of extreme turbulence and uncertainty in the business environment, the virtual organization is put forward as a low-cost, highly responsive and adaptable way to organize and compete. The essential characteristics of the virtual organization have been argued to be:

- adaptability, flexibility and responsiveness to changing requirements and conditions
- effectiveness in utilization of resources
- formation of business alliances of varying degrees of permanence
- dispersion of component parts
- empowerment of staff
- stewardship of expertise, know-how and knowledge (intellectual capital)
- low levels of bureaucracy
- opportunistic behaviours, embracing change and uncertainty
- high infusion of IT to support business processes and knowledge workers.

The practical implications for managers adopting the virtual organization structure and strategy need to be considered further. It is important to note in passing that as soon as one mentions managing in a virtual organization or of adopting virtual organizing as a deliberate strategy, then there is a sense in which one is almost inevitably talking about inter-organizational management. Thus, we refer to the co-ordinated and co-operative behaviours and endeavours of actors/ managers who originate in different organizations and who, after a period of time, may revert to different organizations.

Managing in the virtual organization: success factors

On paper, many of the defining characteristics of the virtual organization sound delightfully and seductively simple, indeed obvious. Yet, it would seem that if the virtual organization is to function effectively, a number of important managerial tasks must be accomplished. People in the virtual organization are drawn from diverse sources but, perhaps working in teams, need to find a shared purpose or vision in order to reach successful outcomes and results. A shared purpose or vision serves as the 'glue' of the virtual organization (Hedberg *et al.*, 1994; Wiesenfeld *et al.*, 1998). It also serves as the life cycle of the virtual organization. This is because the continued existence of the virtual organization depends on the existence of a *raison d'etre*: when the desired results have been achieved (and there is no longer glue to hold the structure together), then the virtual organization dissolves. For management and organizational members, therefore, a key function would seem to be quickly identifying and taking ownership of this shared purpose and vision.

However, in order that a purpose may be genuinely shared and for linkages to operate unimpeded, there must exist extraordinary levels of trust. Lipnack and Stamps (1998) suggest that in the virtual organization, trust must function to replace the usual rules, procedures and policies that dictate the behaviours of the more traditional hierarchical and bureaucratic organizations. With a trusting relationship in place amongst virtual organization members, there is also a requirement for the risk(s) associated with the joint initiative (i.e., inherent in the purpose of the virtual organization) to be shared.

Typically, in traditional organizational structures, risk is totally the preserve of a single organization, which alone tends to implement measures to manage exposure to risk. The more interdependent the nature of the virtual organization's activities, the more risk must be seen to be – and accepted as – shared. If risk is to be shared and high levels of trust maintained, then clearly the purpose of the virtual organization must be such that all members benefit in more ways from being within the virtual organization than they would from remaining outside the virtual relationship. Thus, the successful virtual organization relies on the ability of the alliance to offer benefits to individual members in terms of increased productivity, increased revenues, increased profitability, increased market share and so on (Friedman, 1998).

Fundamental critical success factors for the virtual organization can therefore be posited as: a shared purpose, a trusting relationship, a willingness to share risk and a mutual benefit being derived from the virtual organization's existence. This is illustrated in Figure 10.3.

It is thus argued that a successful virtual organization is based very much on the notion that mutual benefit for the parties involved is derived

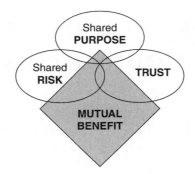

Figure 10.3
Critical success
factors for the
virtual organization
(Marshall *et al.*, 1999)

through the timely and appropriate initiation and formation of alliances to take advantage of possibly short-lived business opportunities. However, in order for the alliances to operate effectively and provide benefits to all collaborating parties, there is the very important assumption that management activity has achieved the requisite level of shared vision and purpose. Additionally, there needs to be a high degree of trust amongst virtual organization members and an acceptance and understanding that risk is to be somehow shared amongst those standing to benefit.

At this point, some caution needs to be exercised, for the virtual organization and virtual organizing should not be presented as *the* way of the future, almost akin to a business imperative for the successful enterprise in this internetworked era. Many of the characteristics, strategies and claims for the virtual organization are conceptually appealing. However, there seems to be a range of challenges for managers to nurture a successful business within the conceptual framework of virtual organizing. Some commentators would argue that many of the strengths and powerful characteristics of the virtual organization also tend to render it vulnerable. Hence, and paradoxically, its very strengths can be a source of weakness (Chesbrough and Teece, 1996). Chesbrough and Teece (1996) identify a number of such potential tensions in the virtual organization concept. Table 10.1 summarizes some of these.

Table 10.1 Inherent tensions in behaviours of the virtual organization (Chesbrough and Teece, 1996)

Strengths	How strengths become weaknesses
Opportunistic, entrepreneurial, risk taking	Personal incentives and rewards for risk taking increase, leading to self-interest in behaviours, etc., making co-ordination and co-operation amongst parties more difficult.
Mutual trust, shared risk, opportunistic	When conflicts or misunderstandings do arise, or unforeseen opportunities work to favour some of the parties more than others, there exist few established procedures for negotiation and conflict resolution.
Opportunistic	The spirit that drives parties to collaborate may also cause virtual organizations to fragment if one or more of the parties deliberately act to exploit more benefits for themselves than for the other parties.

The type of innovation involved – and the associated information flows and knowledge management strategies – can also enhance or moderate the likely success of the virtual organization. It is argued that, because of the information flows essential for innovation, autonomous innovations (i.e., stand-alone, independent innovations) are more suitable for the virtual organization than highly interconnected, systemic ones. Codified information (that which can be easily captured in industry standards and rules, for example) is argued to be as easy to transfer from one party to another in the virtual organization form as it is to transfer within a single organization. On the other hand, tacit knowledge (such as know-how, or ingrained perspectives) is not easily transferred or diffused, and is also subject to opportunism by individual parties who can control the extent to which they share it. Thus, autonomous innovation involving codified information and knowledge transfer may be more suitable for exploitation along virtual organizing principles than systemic innovation involving tacit information and knowledge (Chesbrough and Teece, 1996). These notions are captured in Figure 10.4. This framework is a useful predictor of likely success for the virtual organization.

Structure and strategic positioning of virtual organizations

We have so far discussed the fundamentals of virtual organizations and their managerial success factors. It now seems reasonable to conclude that virtual organizations are likely to differ from the structures and behaviours of more conventional organizations in two key areas: by the structures that they adopt and the manner in which they position

Figure 10.4
A framework for success in virtual organizing

themselves within their environment. A number of 'models of virtuality' have been articulated previously by Burn *et al.* (1999). Some of these will be further discussed in the remainder of this chapter. This discussion will be supplemented by original case studies to more fully articulate and illustrate the models. The case studies will also serve to further explicate the fundamentals and success factors of the virtual organization outlined above.

Co-alliance model

Co-alliance models are virtual organizations in which there are essentially shared partnerships (see Figure 10.5). Each partner makes approximately equal contributions of resources, competencies, skills and knowledge to the alliance, thus forming a consortium. Given the opportunistic nature of the virtual organization, it would be expected that the composition of the consortium might change to reflect market opportunities or the changing core competencies of each member (Preiss *et al.*, 1998).

Links between co-alliance partners are often premised by mutual convenience on a project-by-project basis. However, provided the co-alliance virtual organization functions effectively and beneficially from the perspective of all concerned, it would be expected to reconvene intermittently on an on-going basis when suitable opportunities present themselves. This is illustrated in Figure 10.6.

Case study: Perth Consulting Services (PCS)

Rachel Smith runs Perth Consulting Services (PCS). Rachel is skilled in facilitating strategic and strategic IS planning sessions. She guides and coaches groups of managers and professionals from public- and private-sector organizations in the formulation of corporate visions, missions, strategic plans and strategic IS plans. Rachel can offer very competitive prices for this consulting work since she works from home and has few of the infrastructure costs of the large consulting companies (such as the rent of expensive city office space). However, she cannot offer the broad skill set of the larger consulting companies.

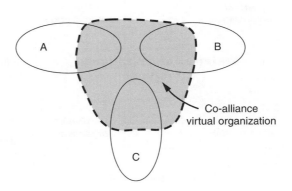

Figure 10.5
Co-alliance model

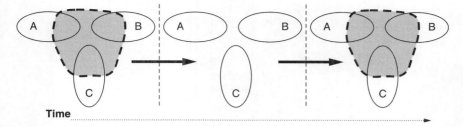

Figure 10.6
The on-going
operations of the
co-alliance model

Tony Jones has a very good technical knowledge of IT and offers an IT planning consulting service along with some analysis and programming skills. The analysis and programming services that he offers are limited and are usually restricted to specific small tasks that are identified during his IT planning work. If Tony requires substantial systems development work he contacts Tom and Stephanie More who run a systems development consultancy that offers systems analysis, design and programming services. Tom and Stephanie are skilled systems developers with a wide range of technical IT skills. They can also call on several other highly skilled systems developers to undertake analysis, design and programming tasks. They contract these systems developers on an 'as needed' project basis.

Together Rachel, Tony, Tom and Stephanie form an agile virtual organization able to respond effectively and inexpensively to a set of needs clustered about strategic planning, IS/IT planning and IS development. All the persons in this virtual organization work from their homes and utilize information technology to keep in contact with each other and with business and government in Australia and South East Asia. Request for tender documents and templates are downloaded from the Internet and shared between various members as necessary. Business responsiveness and agility is maximized while overhead costs are kept to a minimum.

The structure of this virtual organization is that of the co-alliance. Each of the partners brings approximately equal commitment and effort to this virtual organization. Partners collaborate on an 'as needed' basis and function as a group under the umbrella label of PCS, a consultancy with a reasonably broad set of skills to offer. Provided the parties feel that the co-alliance is operating effectively, Rachel, Tony, Tom and Stephanie reactivate PCS whenever they see business opportunities that require competencies that, individually, none of the partners can fully offer.

However, in the tasks undertaken by PCS, a high degree of collaboration and trust is required in order to carry out an assignment to the satisfaction of the client. In addition, trust has been nurtured over time as – knowing and respecting one another over a long period – none of the individual parties would act opportunistically to the disadvantage of the others. The structure of this virtual organization is shown in Figure 10.7.

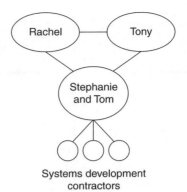

Figure 10.7
Co-alliance model
for business
planning and
systems development

Star-alliance model

Star-alliance models are co-ordinated networks of interconnected members reflecting a core surrounded by satellite organizations (see Figure 10.8). The core comprises the leader who is the dominant player in the market. The leader tends to dominate and has the power to direct and dictate the supply of competence, expertise, knowledge and resources to members. These alliances are commonly based around similar industry or company types. Typically in the star-alliance model, there would be an expectation for the fortunes of the entire virtual organization to be closely allied to the fortune of the dominant central partner.

The following case study explicates this model further.

Case study: Capital City Automobile Association (CCAA)

The Capital City Automobile Association (CCAA) began by offering members an automobile breakdown service in Australian state capital cities. If a member's car broke down, the CCAA would dispatch a qualified mechanic to the location of the breakdown. The CCAA guaranteed to rectify simple causes of vehicle 'breakdown' (such as a flat battery) and enable the motorist to get home or get the car to a garage or vehicle service centre. The CCAA owned a number of specially equipped vans

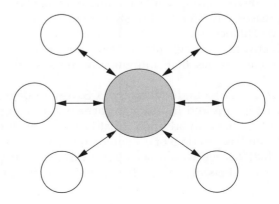

Figure 10.8
The star-alliance
model

driven by qualified mechanics, all employed by the CCAA, which would drive to the breakdown locations.

A very common reason for cars breaking down or not starting in the first place was a flat battery. Quite frequently, the motorist needed a new battery. This was not originally part of the charter of the CCAA, which was purely a breakdown service. The mechanics would attempt to recharge the battery to the point at which (at the very least) the motorist could drive home or, if necessary, drive to a garage and take more remedial action.

After some years, and at the suggestion of some of the mechanics, CCAA contracted certain individuals to provide a round-the-clock battery replacement service. CCAA carefully negotiated the contractor's hours of service availability, duties of service and pay. This ensured that contractors had as much freedom as possible regarding how they arranged their own business. Some of these contractors ran small enterprises such as garages or car repair/maintenance services, while others took on the battery replacement contract as their sole line of business. By having a number of battery replacement service contractors working for them, the CCAA was now able to offer members a 24/7 (24 hours a day/7 days a week) battery replacement service.

Over time, the CCAA examined the possible sources of supply for batteries. After examining prices and the reputations of battery distributors, the CCAA gave a contract to a distributor called Quality Batteries Australia (QBA), a company with substantial warehouses and stocks of batteries in two Australian state capital cities. QBA offered to supply a battery that was a good quality, well-known brand name. QBA undertook to work in concert with contractors to ensure that they had an appropriate stock of batteries available for battery replacement services. This meant some careful logistical planning with contractors in those capital cities without a QBA presence.

Cyber Logistics Australia (CLA) was contracted to transport batteries from QBA warehouses to battery service contractors' sites – as and when required. CLA has a well-known Web page and a good reputation for round-the-clock fetch and carry services for items of all sizes. It had a number of contractors working for the company in all Australian state capital cities. These contractors monitored e-mail requests received by CLA and responded on an internal CLA electronic bidding system. Requests came in on a 24/7 basis, since an 'anytime' service was part of CLA's offering to customers. Contractors would bid for fetch-and-carry business that was reasonably close to their own locations. The bids were for trips that they wished to do at CLA standard prices. If two or more CLA contractors offered to do the same trip the business would go to the first contractor that offered to do the trip within the time and other constraints/conditions set by the customer.

A manager in the CCAA breakdown service organization had noticed the Web site of Battery Disposals of America (BDA). BDA made money from stripping down dead or unwanted batteries and removing any valuable metals or useable acids. When contacted, BDA was willing to pay for dead batteries arising from CCAA's breakdown service provided these were sent in batches to the USA and that the CCAA arranged shipment. The CCAA contracted CLA to manage the logistics of transporting the batteries. For CLA this meant extending its business internationally. However, it had been planning a move to extend its operations to include Australia's major trading partners. E-mail, fax and telephone contact was established between CCAA, CLA and BDA.

Many CCAA specialist mechanics attending breakdowns had been reporting that, apart from the initial breakdown fault, many of the cars appeared to need various other services. Mechanics often advised clients to get a general service. They felt that it would be helpful (not to say, profitable) if they could service cars by CCAA-recommended mechanics. Hence the CCAA began to run a car servicing business. Again this was added to the CCAA list of services with very little additional capital being required. A set of highly competent mechanics was contracted to service CCAA members. Part of each of these mechanics' business became servicing CCAA members according to a CCAA specified service. CCAA and the service mechanics meet regularly to agree advertising campaigns, standards of car servicing, education and training needs for the contractors and their employees and profit sharing in the CCAA car servicing business.

A further set of contractors was organized to fit new windscreens to cars that had broken down or at clients' homes. These contractors were organized in a similar manner to the battery replacement and car service contractors. They increased the set of services that was offered to CCAA members on a 24/7 basis. The CCAA contracted with Best Windscreens of Australia (BWA) to supply windscreens to the CCAA windscreen replacement contractors. Each of the contractors kept a small stock of windscreens. CLA was contracted to help with the logistics of supplying windscreens to the contractors on a round-the-clock 'as needed' basis. A round-the-clock delivery service was particularly necessary since the stocks of windscreens kept by the contractors were small.

Now consider the structure of the virtual organization of the CCAA, its business partners and the various CCAA contractors. This is illustrated in Figure 10.9.

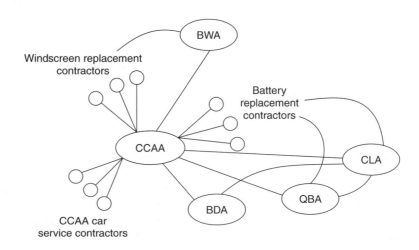

Figure 10.9
The CCAA virtual organization

The organization represented in Figure 10.9 offers more services and value added for clients or customers than can the CCAA alone. Indeed, it probably appears to customers that the CCAA has a larger 'presence' than it actually does. To offer this range of services to its customers the CCAA has had to add very little in terms of real capital structure. The virtual organization depicted can be created relatively quickly in response to perceived customer needs. This can be achieved without the problems of recruiting and training new staff, purchasing new machinery and equipment, or creating new working spaces (and hence possibly erecting new buildings). The role of IT in the CCAA case study is in enabling the necessary communications and hence assisting in the co-ordination of contractors and business partners.

The structure of the CCAA virtual organization is essentially star shaped, with the CCAA at the hub or centre of the star. Links to contractors are highly substitutable and cancelling and/or creating a contract is all that is needed to make or sever linkages with contractors. Links to CLA, QBA, BDA and BWA would require the establishment of more complex business relationships. For these four partners, it is more complex to replace and rearrange the services offered than are the car service and battery or windscreen replacement offerings. However, it would be easier to substitute out of the star structure each of these companies than it would the hub company CCAA. If the CCAA began to do badly or, even worse, failed, then so too would the virtual organization – and it would be difficult to replace the CCAA. Thus, the star structure does not permit the full flexibility and adaptivity that is possible in some virtual organizations.

The CCAA, its contractors and alliance partners bring together a range of value-added offerings to people whose cars have broken down. The value chain reworked by the CCAA comprises responding to motorists whose cars have broken down, analysing the breakdown problem and resolving this problem by enabling the motorist to get to help via repair and replacement services. Previously, if their car had broken down, motorists in Australia relied on the CCAA to get both them and their car to help. For serious breakdowns this is still the case. However, as we saw in the case study, alliance partners and contractors now allow the CCAA to provide a more complete on-the-road, round-the-clock repair and replacement service. The portion of the value chain previously serviced by repair garages is now, in part, offered to CCAA member in the form of an extra value and highly convenient on-the-road service. This is shown in Figure 10.10, where sub-chains E–F–G, K–L and M–N involve services to clients that would have previously occurred outside the boundary of CCAA breakdown services. These services would have involved arrangements of much less convenience to motorists whose cars had broken down. Hence, the virtual organization comprising the CCAA, its contractors and alliance partners offers a broader range of products and services that focus on parts of the value chain previously outside the narrow focus of the CCAA's basic breakdown service. Thus, the CCAA-based virtual organization has some of the characteristics of the value-alliance model.

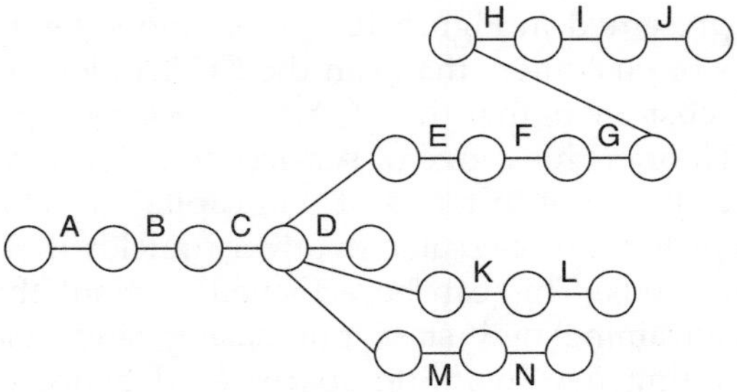

A: CCAA breakdown specialist contacted
B: Skilled person and equipment moved to breakdown
C: Identify and analyse cause of breakdown
D: Rectify faults
E: Obtain battery
F: Replace battery
G: Take away dead battery and give $ for battery

H: Transport battery to BRA
I: Dispose of batteries
J: Sell valuable extracts from dead batteries
K: Obtain windscreen
L: Replace windscreen
M: Recommend and schedule post-breakdown car service
N: Car service

Figure 10.10
The value chain of the CCAA star-alliance

Value-alliance model

Value-alliance models bring together a range of interrelated products, services and facilities that are based on an industry value or supply chain. The case study of Wildflowers of Australia explicates this model.

Case study: Wildflowers of Australia

Wildflowers of Australia (WFA) is a national firm that co-ordinates the ordering, transportation and delivery of flowers in Australia. WFA presents itself as the virtual face to the end consumer and retailer of a number of co-operating partners along an industry supply chain. In terms of actual operations, a number of essential parties are involved but, from the customers' perspective, WFA provides a service across the entire value chain. WFA directs and co-ordinates the orders from retailers and end consumers to growers of Australian wildflowers that can satisfy particular demands.

WFA has extensive information resources regarding the stocks of wildflowers of various types that are being grown and the best (or most appropriate) times for harvesting. Orders from retailers and end customers are accepted via standard electronic forms available on WFA's well-designed Web site. Orders are also accepted by telephone, fax or e-mail. Such orders are transmitted in total or in part to growers who can satisfy them by cutting the appropriate flowers. After cutting the correct flowers in the right quantities, growers call upon Cyber Logistics of Australia (CLA) to deliver the flowers, thus ensuring extra freshness for the end consumer. An overview of the operations of WFA is presented in Figure 10.11.

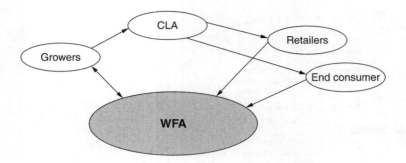

Figure 10.11
Value-alliance
model of WFA

WFA has arranged for Smart Cards of Australia (SCA) to deal with the recording and processing of transactions within the system of wildflower provision so that adequate records can be kept and appropriate payments made. Each business and contractor supplying flowers within the virtual organization has a smart card and a device for the input of transaction information. Transaction details are kept on the smart cards. Periodically, SCA downloads and processes the transaction information to give adequate financial accounting and payment details, and the subsequent disbursement of funds for the virtual organization's transactions.

Elements of the re-engineered value chain for WFA are shown in Figure 10.12. Within a number of the organizations shown in this new industry value chain, there are inbound and outbound logistics as well as some handling of the flowers. All these activities take time, which is all the more important given the perishable nature of the product. The value chain for the cut wildflower system co-ordinated by WFA has a reduced number of steps between grower and end consumer. This ensures less handling of the flowers before final display by the end consumer and, possibly more importantly, less time between when the flowers are cut and when they are displayed. Consequently, the product lasts longer at the point of consumption, giving increased customer satisfaction.

WFA and its partners have thus reinvented the cut flower value chain so as to permit an efficient, demand-pull operation that results in increased customer satisfaction. The firms involved in the virtual organization are all specialists, concentrating on their niche market specialisms or core competencies. Logistics has been plucked out of its many places in the traditional value chain and given to a specialist logistics company. The task of recording transaction details, drawing up accounts based on these and making appropriate payments has been taken out of the daily work of a number of players in the industry value chain and given to a specialist smart-card-based accounting firm. An essential element of the value-alliance model is that a single virtual organization is presented to the end consumer. In fact, the virtual organization is composed of a number of collaborating and interdependent firms operating along an industry value or supply chain.

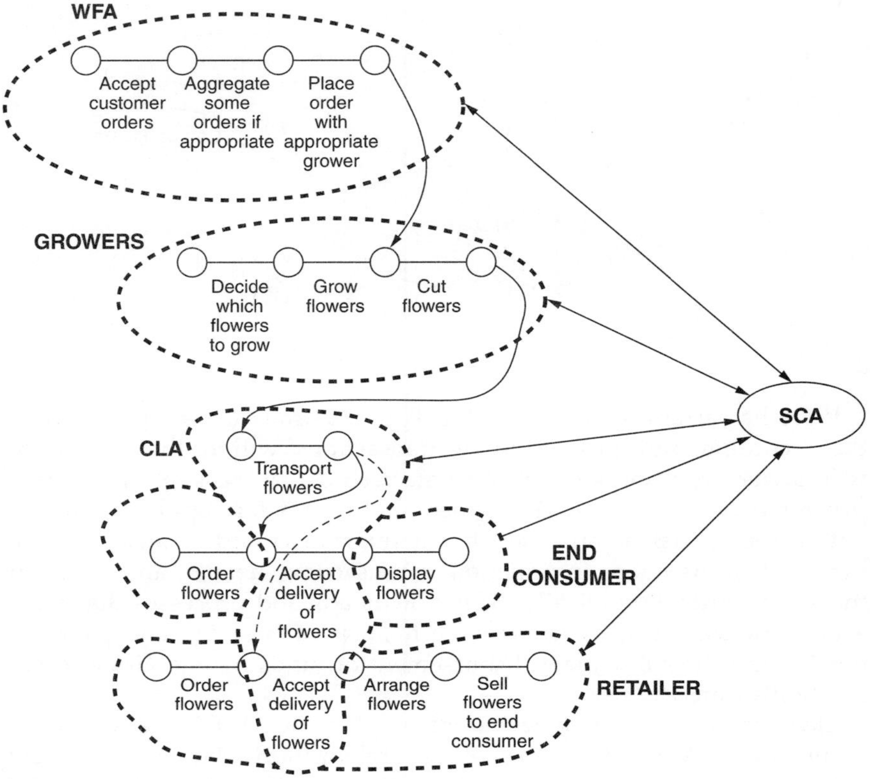

Figure 10.12
Value-alliance
of WFA

Market-alliance model

Organizations based on the market-alliance model come together to co-ordinate the manufacture, marketing, selling and distribution of a diverse but coherent set of products and services. The market-alliance model differs from the value-alliance model in the sense that several value chains are likely to be involved. From the end customer's perspective, the result is more akin to a marketplace or a community.

Case study: Australian E-Market

Australian E-Market (AEM) provides an online catalogue for consumer durables, including white goods, electrical and electronic goods and sporting goods. AEM acts as a virtual face to the customer, but serves only to co-ordinate the marketing, selling and distribution of a coherent set of consumer goods and services. It offers its marketing expertise to the market-alliance members and has contracted with a number of suitable manufacturers to provide an outlet for their goods and services. AEM also co-ordinates the logistics requirements for the sale and distribution of these goods with CLA. All payment and transaction processing is arranged in conjunction with SCA. AEM does not purchase the manufacturers' goods itself, but acts as a conduit for a range of goods and services to the end consumer, sharing the profits generated by so doing with the manufacturers and other parties in the market-alliance.

The online catalogue is accessible via the Internet, but is also available to AEM Shoppers' Club members via a CD-ROM and printed catalogue. AEM Shoppers Club members pay an annual membership fee of A$50 and a small charge if they wish to have the CD-ROM and/or paper-based catalogue. Over 100 000 products are available at very attractive discounts. After purchase, and for a small fee, products are delivered from the manufacturer to the customer by CLA. The smart card systems specialist, SCA, takes care of transaction records and payment systems for the AEM operation. The core of the AEM operation consists of its database and reputation for good deals. Its essence is the provision of information to consumers. The manufacturers who are members of the virtual organization provide the goods that are purchased, and CLA provides the logistics of getting the goods to customers. Thus, AEM has the characteristics of a market-alliance. Figure 10.13 shows the structure of this virtual organization.

Schwartz (1997) provides another example of a market-alliance. Cendant Corporation, the CUC-HFS market-alliance of Walter Forbes and Henry Silverman, is a similar virtual organization to AEM.

Conclusion

The virtual organization can obviously take on an infinite array of structures. This chapter has described a number of generic models (co-alliance, star-alliance, value-alliance and market-alliance) and illustrated each of these by way of an original case study. Each case study is an attempt to illustrate the major characteristics of the virtual organization as defined in the early sections of this chapter. The case studies are also an attempt to illustrate the criticality of the success factors for virtual organizing (as discussed earlier).

In the Perth Consulting Services (PCS) case study, success depends upon the shared purpose and shared goals of partners. They must trust

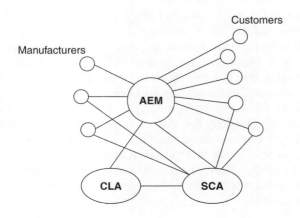

Figure 10.13
The market-alliance of AEM

each another implicitly. They must also recognize that, given their mutual interdependence, any benefit that is derived from their co-alliance virtual organization must be equal. Risk must be seen and accepted as shared amongst the players. Notwithstanding, they face further significant challenges. Arguably, the nature of their enterprise or innovation is essentially systemic and information and knowledge flows are primarily tacit. Mechanisms for resolving conflicts amongst the partners – entrepreneurial self-starters used to acting from motives of self-interest – are completely informal, and totally reliant on a trusting relationship. Not surprisingly, therefore, it can be concluded that the people involved, the relationships they construct and the strategies they adopt in operating as a virtual organization, are essential to the success of this enterprise (Stafford, 1998).

In the CCAA, it could be argued that the potential dominance of the central player means that, while a shared purpose is obviously vital, there may be a slightly lower requirement for high levels of trust than the PCS example. The enterprise or innovation in the CCAA case seems more autonomous than systemic, with information and knowledge flows involving more codified than tacit knowledge. The large established central player would be expected to have well-defined mechanisms for conflict resolution. Such mechanisms could possibly be offered throughout the virtual organization should any disruption occur. Notwithstanding, in some senses, disruption may be less likely to occur; the nature of the business operation may make it easier to specify contractually various outcomes and expectations.

The value-alliance model in the Wildflowers of Australia (WFA) case study stems from the clear mutual benefits derived from this partnering arrangement. Each of the players 'needs' the others in order to provide the requisite level of customer service. As in the CCAA example, the enterprise or innovation involved in WFA is essentially autonomous, involving the transfer of codified information and knowledge. While the partners in the WFA virtual organization may not have any well-defined arrangements for conflict resolution, in all other senses they meet the criteria for successful virtual organizing set down by Chesbrough and Teece (1996).

In the market-alliance model of AEM, as in the value-alliance case, there are clear benefits to be derived individually through enacting the shared vision and purpose. In much the same way as with WFA, it seems reasonable to conclude that there are sufficient indicators to suggest that their operation is suitably supported by a virtual organizing strategy.

Given the appropriate conditions and context, the virtual organization offers many attractive benefits as an organizing strategy for the modern enterprise. However, the strengths and potential benefits of virtual organizing need to be weighed against the potential risks and negative impacts. Notwithstanding, the virtual organization may prove to be a low-cost, highly responsive, adaptable and flexible way to organize and compete in modern business environments. New information technologies offer exciting possibilities for new organizational forms and structures into the next century. This chapter has attempted to characterize the essential features of the virtual organization, considering typical types of processes and activities. However, it has also clearly delineated some of the challenges of virtual organizing, and has argued that caution needs to be exercised in assessing a business opportunity as appropriate for a virtual organization. Certain conditions and criteria would seem to underpin a successful virtual organization venture.

References

Benjamin, R. and Wigand, R. (1995). Electronic markets and virtual value chains on the information superhighway. *Sloan Management Review*, Winter, 62–72.

Burn, J., Marshall, P. and Wild, M. (1999). Managing change in the virtual organization. *Proceedings of the 7th European Conference on Information Systems*, Copenhagen.

Chesbrough, H. W. and Teece, D. J. (1996). When is virtual virtuous? *Harvard Business Review*, January–February, 65–73.

Coutu, D. L. (1998). Organization: trust in virtual teams. *Harvard Business Review*, **76**, 20–21.

Czerniawska, F. and Potter, G. (1998). *Business in a Virtual World*. Macmillan.

Friedman, L. G. (1998). The elusive strategic alliance. In P. Lloyd and P. Boyle, eds, *Web-Weaving: intranets, extranets and strategic alliances*. Butterworth-Heinemann.

Goldman, S. L., Nagel, R. N. and Preiss, K. (1995). *Agile Competitors and Virtual Organizations: strategies for enriching the customer*. Van Nostrand Reinhold.

Grenier, R. and Metes, G. (1995). *Going Virtual: moving your organization into the 21st century*. Prentice Hall.

Hedberg, B., Dahlgren, G., Hansson, J. and Olve, N. (1994). *Virtual Organizations and Beyond: discover imaginary systems*. Wiley.

Henning, K. (1998) *The Digital Enterprise: how digitisation is redefining business*. Random House.

IMPACT Programme (1998). *Exploiting the Wired-Up World: best practice in managing virtual organizations*. IMPACT.

Lipnack, J. and Stamps, J. (1998). Why virtual teams? In P. Lloyd and P. Boyle, eds, *Web-Weaving: intranets, extranets and strategic alliances*. Butterworth-Heinemann.

Magretts, J. (1998). The power of virtual integration: an interview with Dell Computer's Michael Dell. *Harvard Business Review*, March–April, 73–84.

Marshall, P., Burn, J., Wild, M. and McKay, J. (1999). Virtual organizations: structure and strategic positioning. *Proceedings of the 7th European Conference on Information Systems*, Copenhagen.

Metes, G., Gundry, J. and Bradish, P. (1998). *Agile Networking: competing through the Internet and intranets*. Prentice Hall.

Pfeffer, J. (1998). *The Human Equation*. Harvard Business School Press.

Preiss, K., Goldman, S. L. and Nagel, R. N. (1998). *Co-operate to Compete*. Van Nostrand Reinhold.

Schwartz, E. I. (1997). Its! Not! Retail! *Wired Magazine Online*, 5 November. http://www.wired.com/wired/archive/5.11/cuc.html

Siebel, T. M. and House, P. (1999). *Cyber Rules: strategies for excelling at e-business*. Currency-Doubleday.

Sor, R. (1999). Virtual organizations: a case study of the housing construction industry in Western Australia. *Proceedings of the Australasian Conference on Information Systems*, Wellington.

Stafford, E. R. (1998). Using co-operative strategies to make alliances work. In V. Sethi and W. R. King, eds, *Organizational Transformation through Business Process Reengineering: applying the lessons learned*. Prentice Hall, pp. 315–29.

Turban, E., McLean, E. and Wetherbe, J. (1999). *Information Technology for Management*. Wiley.

Upton, D. M. and McAfee, A. (1996). The real virtual factory. *Harvard Business Review*, July–August, 123–33.

Wiesenfeld, B. M., Raghuram, S. and Garud, R. (1998). Communication patterns as determinants of organizational identification in a virtual organization. *Journal of Computer Mediated Communication*, **3**, 1–21.

11
Management support for the modular virtual organization: KLM Distribution

Matthijs Wolters and Martijn Hoogeweegen

Introduction

Today's managers are confronted with a continuously changing competitive environment. The reasons for this include rapid technological change, globalization of markets and trends such as the regained interest in the revitalization of customer service (Ives and Mason, 1990) and mass customization (Davis, 1987; Pine, 1993). The customization of customer preferences requires organizations to increase their product and service variety. In the quest for new organizational forms that incorporate appropriate levels of flexibility to offer a large variety of products and services – while keeping costs and lead times low – the *virtual organization* has emerged.

Many authors have tried to define the virtual organization (see e.g., Davidow and Malone, 1992; Byrne *et al.*, 1993; DeSanctis and Monge, 1998). The literature also discusses numerous case studies of virtual organizations (see e.g., Ogilvie, 1994; Davis and Darling, 1995). Although a universally accepted definition is lacking, two aspects of virtual organizations seem most noteworthy. First, there is a high level of managerial complexity of daily operations within the virtual organization

(Mowshowitz, 1997a, b). Second, information and communication technologies (ICT) are important both in the design and support of a virtual structure (Lucas and Baroudi, 1994).

In this chapter, the use of modularity is proposed as an additional means for the virtual organization to achieve standardized organizational structure and behaviour that allows for interchangeability and compatibility of the partners and business processes. Many authors – in diverging fields – consider modularity as an important means to increase a company's flexibility in product and process design (Sanchez and Mahoney, 1996; Baldwin and Clark, 1997). Virtual organizations are likely to benefit from the advantages of modularity for customizing their product or service and by organizing their complex processes efficiently through sourcing the right modules (Venkatraman and Henderson 1998).

By means of a management support tool called Modular Network Design (MND) (Hoogeweegen 1997), the complexity of managing a modular virtual organization is illustrated with a case study at KLM Distribution. This company is at the centre of a globally dispersed virtual organization with the task of co-ordinating the distribution of spare parts of airplanes around the world. MND supports managers of a modular virtual organization in four steps:

1 determination and analysis of customer requirements
2 tracking of possibilities to satisfy customer requirements
3 allocation of production tasks among network partners
4 ongoing assessment and redesign of activities and allocation procedures.

This chapter is organized as follows. The next section reviews the literature on virtual organizations, drawing particular attention to the complexities of managing virtual organizations and the role of modularity and ICTs. As part of this, supporting the management of the virtual organization is also briefly discussed. In the third and fourth sections the proposed analytical framework – Modular Network Design – is described and then applied using the case study of KLM Distribution. The final section draws some conclusions relating to the management of modular virtual organizations and how MND contributes to better order planning and process handling.

The virtual organization

Defining the virtual organization

As we have seen in earlier chapters, many authors have tried to define the virtual organization (see e.g., Alexander, 1997; Davidow and Malone, 1992; Byrne *et al.*, 1993; Englman, 1993; Wexler, 1993; Eicher, 1997; Hardwick and Bolton, 1997; DeSanctis and Monge, 1998). The diversity of these definitions illustrates the observation by Mowshowitz (1997b: 32) that the virtual organization '. . . lacks a universally accepted definition, lying as it does at the confluence of several intellectual streams fed by reflection on computers and their applications'. Also, many different terms have been given to similar emerging organizational forms, all designed 'to meet the imminent challenges of the information age' (Venkatraman and Henderson, 1998: 33). The differences in terms – demonstrated in Table 11.1 – illustrate the search for stressing the most important features or aspects of the new organizational form. Recurrent key features in the terms and definitions are: temporary alignments of a network of independent organizations; dynamic switching between network partners; end-customer requirements as a starting point; bringing together the core competencies of the partners; and intensive use of ICTs.

Many case studies – from a wide range of industries – describe and analyse the ways in which these virtual organizations operate, using ICTs to accomplish their goals. Ogilvie (1994) describes the cases of Apple Computer, McDonald's, Toyota and Marks & Spencer. Davis and Darling (1995) present an in-depth look at how one small company – Super Bakery Inc. – manages to operate as a virtual company. Loebbecke and Jelassi (1997) investigate how insurance company Gerling is moving towards a virtual organization. Voss (1996) suggests textile company Massimo Menichetti as one of the first virtual organizations (created in the early 1970s). Clemons *et al.* (1992) describe how a number of travel agents – the Rosenbluth International Alliance – combine their IS to form a virtual global corporation.

Remarkably, most of these studies indicate a difference in level of analysis compared with the definitions of the virtual organization provided in the literature. The definitions denote a *network* of organizations that form temporary alignments, while most of the case studies address the *single organization* at the core of the network that arranges and co-ordinates the various temporary alignments. Therefore, we distinguish two distinct roles that firms can play within the virtual organization: either a firm can be *co-ordinator* or it can be *subcontractor*. The co-ordinator is the core firm of the virtual organization, responsible for the (temporary) design of the virtual organization and the collection and fulfilment of customer orders. The co-ordinator contacts subcontractors to participate in temporary alignments for joint production and delivery. Subcontractors, for instance, take care of the manufacturing or delivery of a critical component. Baldwin and Clark (1997) use an

Table 11.1 Terms given to virtual organizational forms in the literature

Reference	Organizational form examined
Ashkenas *et al.* (1996)	'The boundaryless organization'
Benjamin and Wigand (1995)	'The virtual value chain'
Ciborra (1996)	'The platform organization'
Jarvenpaa and Ives (1994)	'The dynamic network'
Miles and Snow (1986)	'The dynamic network'
Normann and Ramirez (1993)	'Value constellation'
Rayport and Sviokla (1995)	'The virtual value chain'

analogous distinction in their discussion of possible roles within a modular cluster of hundreds of companies. They distinguish between an architect and a designer. An architect creates the design rules (or architecture) for the (virtual) organization. A designer produces the modules that conform to the architecture. Based on this distinction, and for our purposes, we define the virtual organization as:

> a temporary alignment of multiple organizations around a single core organization, combining the core competencies of its participants to produce and deliver customized demand at low cost and throughput times, which the participants cannot produce and deliver individually.

Managing the virtual organization

Management of the virtual organization is an important aspect in forming and co-ordinating temporary alignments. However, management of the virtual organization is also extremely complex. For example (see Alexander, 1997; Mowshowitz, 1997b):

- The different firms participating in the virtual organization may have conflicting goals. Nevertheless, they should trust each other and share information.
- The virtual organization should be very responsive. It should be able to deliver the required variety to meet customized demand.
- Resources within the virtual organization should be dynamically allocated to different customer orders.

Katzy (1998) states that the co-ordinator's recognized authority and management competence facilitates effective functioning of the virtual organization. The co-ordinator starts from a specific customer's requirement, searching for win–win situations for all partners and trying to integrate their different competencies.

To deal with these complexities, Mowshowitz (1997a) introduces *metamanagement* as a means to structure and manage goal-oriented activities. Metamanagement consists of four basic activities:

1 analysing abstract requirements
2 tracking the possibilities for satisfying requirements
3 developing and maintaining the procedure for assigning (or allocating) satisfiers to requirements
4 adjusting the optimality (or 'satisficing') criteria of the allocation procedure.

Requirements refer to the logically defined needs of a task. Making a product, for example, requires raw materials, tools and labour. Each of these requirements may be viewed as an abstract need, in the sense that it can be met in a variety of ways. The particular ways in which a requirement can be met constitute concrete satisfiers (Mowshowitz, 1997a: 374).

According to Mowshowitz, the essence of a virtual organization is dynamically to switch from one supplier to another, based on changing opportunities in the marketplace. Mowshowitz argues that new management activities are needed to organize virtual conduct, particularly to 'analyse abstract requirements and to track concrete satisfiers' (Mowshowitz, 1997a: 379).

Metamanagement requires standardized organizational structure and behaviour to achieve interchangeability and compatibility. One means to achieve this standardization and interchangeability is through modularity. A modular approach intentionally tries to create a product or process design that permits the 'substitution' of different versions of functional components. The purpose is to create product or process variations with different functionalities or performance levels (Sanchez and Mahoney, 1996). It provides standardized organizational structures, enabling constant change of the product or service design in response to customer requests. Modular design avoids creating strong interdependencies among specific component designs, preferring to create 'loosely coupled' component designs (Orton and Weick, 1990). The concept of modularity most often refers to manufacturing processes and how to offer a modularized product design (see e.g., Ulrich and Eppinger, 1995; Baldwin and Clark, 1997). Although manufacturing and service-oriented markets are considered fundamentally different (see e.g., Shostack, 1982; Morris and Johnston, 1987), Pine (1993) states that modularity may also be applicable in the latter. Overall, the key challenge in managing the operations of the modular virtual organization is to perfect the links between the different modules.

The use of ICTs, e.g., Electronic Data Interchange (EDI), could further support these standards and interfaces. Many authors stress ICTs as important enablers to design and manage the virtual organization and to achieve the desired levels of flexibility, responsiveness and cost effectiveness. Moreover, several authors claim that without the significant power of ICTs the establishment and operation of the virtual organization would become infeasible (e.g., Malone and Rockart, 1993, O'Leary *et al.*, 1997, Venkatraman and Henderson, 1998). Lucas and Baroudi (1994) mention a number of ICT design variables that characterize the virtual organization, including substitution of electronic for physical components, electronic linking and communications, electronic workflows and electronic customer/supplier links. Further, Venkatraman and Henderson (1998) distinguish three ICT-enabled vectors that constitute a strategy for virtual organizing: customer interaction (virtual encounter), asset configuration (virtual sourcing) and knowledge leverage (virtual expertise).

Supporting the management of the virtual organization

Previous discussions illustrate the difficulties and complexities of managing the virtual organization. The co-ordinator's role is especially difficult. To support the co-ordinator's role, qualitative methodologies such as soft systems analysis or systemic thinking may be useful (Checkland and Scholes, 1990). Quantitative techniques with objective performance criteria – such as time, cost and quality – are also very important (Katzy, 1998). Furthermore, '. . . as incentives become greater and risk taking increases, co-ordination among parties through the marketplace becomes more and more difficult' (Chesbrough and Teece, 1996: 66). In this respect, Alexander (1997) claims '. . . whether we talk about the lack of physical proximity or lack of ownership, in both cases effective tools and mechanisms are required to manage the ever-changing boundaries of the virtual firm'. The next section discusses such a tool. The proposed tool focuses on managerial support during the formation and operation of the ICT-enabled, modular virtual organization.

Modular Network Design

As mentioned above, the Modular Network Design (MND) approach is based on the concept of modularity (Hoogeweegen, 1997). Within MND, both the product and/or service range as well as organizational activities are described in modules; the product and/or service range is described in service elements, while the activities are described in process modules. The generic procedure of MND is depicted in Figure 11.1. It comprises four steps, analogous to the four stages of metamanagement (Mowshowitz, 1997a). The MND procedure operationalizes the four steps of metamanagement, making them more applicable for managing the virtual organization. The four MND steps are:

1 determination and analysis of customer requirements: service elements
2 tracking the possibilities to satisfy customer requirements: translation of service elements into production elements
3 allocation of production elements among network partners: translation of production elements into a process module network
4 ongoing assessment and redesign of activities and allocation procedures.

The four steps are supported with a quantitative analysis and visualization of the production activities, particularly to compare different chain designs or to evaluate opportunities for ICT use. Each of the steps is described in more detail below.

The first step of metamanagement concerns analysing abstract requirements. Within MND, abstract requirements are seen as specific features of the total product and/or service range offered by the virtual organization, called *service elements*. Either the customer specifies its requirements by selecting service elements from the available set or the co-ordinator of the virtual organization translates the incoming order into service elements. In different combinations, the service elements describe different types of orders. For instance, one could further distinguish between core and supplementary service elements (Lovelock, 1992; Anderson and Narus, 1995), where supplementary service elements

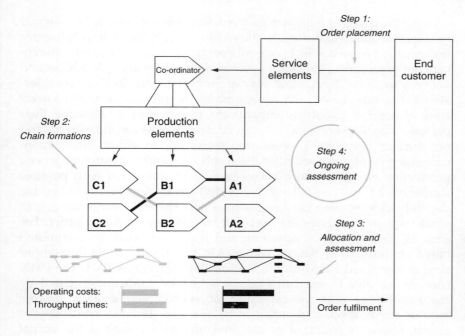

Figure 11.1
Managing the modular virtual organization with Modular Network Design

might provide added value to the core product or service. Whenever a customer requires a service element that is not available in the set, the co-ordinator could search for additional subcontractors able to fulfil this specific service element. Examples of service elements in manufacturing can be found in the computer and automotive industries, where customers can actually design their own PC or car by specifying numerous features of the product. Logistics, travel and transportation are good examples of service industries that use the service element concept (for an illustration of use of the service elements by Federal Express, see Lovelock, 1992).

The second step of metamanagement concerns tracking the possibilities for satisfying requirements. Within MND, this step is operationalized in the form of *production elements*. Production elements also describe specific features of the product and/or service range, but they are formulated in terms of production. Whereas service elements describe what customers see and may order, production elements describe what a specific organization is able to produce. The co-ordinator searches for ways to translate the selected service elements into production elements. It determines potential chain formations based on the production elements offered by the possible subcontractors of the virtual organization. Figure 11.1 illustrates two possible formations involving the organizations, C1–B2–A1 and C2–B1–A1. The number of feasible chain formations will depend on: (1) the number of available subcontractors; and (2) the degrees of freedom the co-ordinator has resulting from the customer's requirements and their restrictive influence on the design of the virtual organization. In general, the more specific a customer's requirements, the fewer degrees of freedom a co-ordinator has.

In the third step of metamanagement, the satisfiers need to be assigned to requirements. According to Mowshowitz (1997a), it is possible for management to switch from one subcontractor to another to take advantage of dynamically changing opportunities in the marketplace. Cost and delivery or throughput times play an important role in these considerations. For this reason, the *process module* is introduced as the lowest level of process activity to support the participants in assessing their performance. A process module can be described as a standardized (and not further divisible) process step, referring to either information-processing or physical activities. Each subcontractor translates its generic production elements into a set of process modules. For each possible formation, a *process module network* (PMN) can be designed based on the dependencies between the process modules. These networks indicate in what sequence modules are executed to fulfil the customer order. For each of these networks, operating and transaction costs are computed based on the Activity Based Costing (ABC) technique, while throughput time is computed based on the Critical Path Method (CPM). The PMN concept can also be used to evaluate allocation limitations, caused by the insufficient resource capacities of subcontractors. Each process module needs specific resources to be executed. Limited availability of certain resources could, of course, limit the co-ordinator of the virtual organization in choosing the best configuration. All of these calculations can be used for the definite allocation of the production elements among the subcontractors. The PMN concept thus allows for objective choice of contractors, instead of the use of more subjective criteria such as reputation, mutual trust or historic relationships.

The fourth step of metamanagement concerns the adjustment of optimality (or 'satisficing') criteria for the allocation procedure. According to Mowshowitz (1997a), examining criteria and goals explicitly injects self-reflection in organizational life and the habit of self-reflection should be a regular feature of management behaviour. Within MND, this step has been operationalized as an ongoing assessment and reflection of all previous steps. For instance, visualization of all business processes in PMNs could enable the detection of possible improvements and redesign options. The MND approach may be used to compare different PMNs that all refer to the fulfilment of the same set of service elements, but which use additional ICT applications (for example EDI or the Internet) or use ICT differently. Based on such a comparison, decisions about implementing specific ICT applications can be supported through an assessment of impacts on PMN design, costs and throughput time. Furthermore, MND allows the co-ordinator constantly to evaluate the composition of its set of service elements, the way in which service elements are translated into production elements and, last but not least, the composition of the network of subcontractors. It may also support management in defining the right modular architecture and the interfaces between modules.

Case study: KLM Distribution

The applicability of MND to support the management of the (modular) virtual organization – and the evaluation of ICT use within such a virtual organization – is illustrated with a case study at KLM Distribution. This business unit of KLM Royal Dutch Airlines is at the centre of a globally dispersed virtual organization, with the task of co-ordinating the global distribution of airplane spare parts. They offer door-to-door service to their customers, including reliable delivery, careful handling and tailor-made service concepts. To offer these customized logistic solutions to its clients KLM Distribution needs to subcontract to numerous other organizations all around the globe. For each (new) customer demanding worldwide distribution, KLM Distribution searches for possible sub-contractors willing to co-operate in the virtual organization. The case study illustrates how MND can be used by KLM Distribution for the planning and fulfilment of these customized transport orders. The results presented in this chapter focus on the modelling and analyses of five specific customer orders placed at KLM Distribution. For these orders, all four steps to manage virtual organizations described previously are taken to analyse the applicability and usability of MND as a management support tool.

Determination and analysis of customer requirements: service elements

KLM Distribution offers its customers (shippers) the set of service elements shown in Table 11.2. Our five orders under investigation differ in the service elements that have been selected by the customers (shippers). Order numbers 1 and 2 concern return flights from Amsterdam Airport (Schiphol, SPL) to different locations in the USA. Order 3 involves only the import part of such an order. Order 4 concerns the transport of goods within the Schiphol area itself. Order 5 is also an order without air transport and concerns only road transport within Europe. The orders not only differ with respect to their destinations, but also booking and payment procedures and the type of goods are different. Delivery method may also be different per order.

By offering a set of service elements of this kind, KLM Distribution allows customers to put together their own customized logistic orders by selecting the service elements they require. KLM Distribution – being the co-ordinator of the virtual organization – is not able to deliver all service elements itself. This set represents the services offered by the entire virtual organization. (In reality, this set is more detailed than shown above; for example, there is the possibility to choose more specific road and air transport routes and destinations.)

Table 11.2   Selected service elements

Category	Service element	1	2	3	4	5
S1 Booking and payment	S1.1 Telephone			■	■	
	S1.2 Facsimile	■				
	S1.3 EDI					■
	S1.4 Paper invoicing	■				
	S1.5 Electronic invoicing					■
S2 Type of goods	S2.1 Commodity	■				
	S2.2 Perishable					
	S2.3 Speciality			■		
S3 Method of delivery	S3.1 Loose	■				
	S3.2 Pallet					■
	S3.3 Unit load device		■			
S4 Regional Road Transport	S4.1 Within SPL	■				
	S4.2 Within NL	■				
	S4.3 Within EUR					■
	S4.4 Within USA		■			
S5 Customs	S5.1 Import NL	■				
	S5.2 Export NL	■				
	S5.3 Import USA			■		
	S5.4 Export USA	■				
S6 Air Transport	S6.1 SPL ⇒ EUR					
	S6.2 SPL ⇒ USA	■				
	S6.3 EUR ⇒ SPL					
	S6.4 USA ⇒ SPL	■				
S7 Documents	S7.1 Air Waybill		■			
	S7.2 Customs document					■
S8 Tracking and tracing	S8.1 Departure	■		■		
	S8.2 Arrival			■		
	S8.3 Delivery		■			

As an illustration, we will examine one specific service category of Table 11.2: tracking and tracing. The shipper chooses whether it wants to receive status messages and, if so, which type of status message. These messages are used to determine the location and status of the goods and documents – often a very useful or even essential service to the customer. Status messages may be sent by fax or electronically, depending on the availability of specific dedicated IS at the different locations. The most frequently used tracking and tracing points are departure and arrival of the plane and the delivery of the goods at the consignee. Obviously, more measurement points can be included when the required systems are available. Interestingly, looking at the first order in Table 11.2, we notice that only departure was selected; in this order, the shipper itself decided to take care of the road transport within the USA.

Tracking the possibilities to satisfy customer requirements: translation of service elements into production elements

The next step for the co-ordinator of the virtual organization is to track the possibilities for satisfying the customer's requirements. Within MND, this means searching for ways to translate service elements into production elements. In other words: what needs to be done to fulfil a specific combination of service elements? For this purpose, the co-ordinator can choose from a set of production elements at its disposal. Each member of the virtual organization offers to the co-ordinator a set of production elements indicating their production capabilities. Such sets could be stored in a central database, accessible and editable by all members of the virtual organization. Such a system did not exist at the time of this case study, although KLM Distribution had started developing a system that formalizes the translation of service elements into production elements. Therefore, in this case study, the authors carried out this translation (with the co-operation of KLM Distribution managers). The case-experiences with specifying the allocation procedures served as a starting point for the development of this system. Mowshowitz (1997a) indicates that not all of these procedures can be as formal as the techniques of, for instance, operations research. However, requiring managers to think about these couplings could already lead to improvements in efficiency and performance. MND in itself does not possess a formal allocation procedure – these procedures are often very case-specific. However, in the concluding section of this chapter we elaborate our findings and ideas about formalizing the service-production-element allocation procedure within MND.

To illustrate the diversity in allocation decisions within a virtual organization like KLM Distribution, we will describe two straightforward examples from our case. The first example concerns the exact choice of air transport route for order 1. The second deals with the preparation of various travel documents for orders 1 and 2.

Figure 11.2 shows the two different options available for the co-ordinator to arrange the air transport route for order 1. The first route goes via Los Angeles (LAX) and the second via New York (NY). Such a choice not only affects the air transport route but also the accompanying customs and cargo handling activities at the respective airports. For both options, KLM Distribution needs to subcontract other parties to execute these activities. Figure 11.2 illustrates the different (simplified) allocation patterns for the same choice of service elements by the shipper. The direct link between service and production elements is illustrated by synchronous colouring of these elements.

The second example concerns the preparation of the various travel documents for orders 1 and 2. These documents are the Air Waybill (AWB), an air cargo travel document, and the customs document, required for customs formalities. For the first order, the customer chooses to prepare all documents itself, without selecting any service elements from this category. KLM Distribution therefore does not have

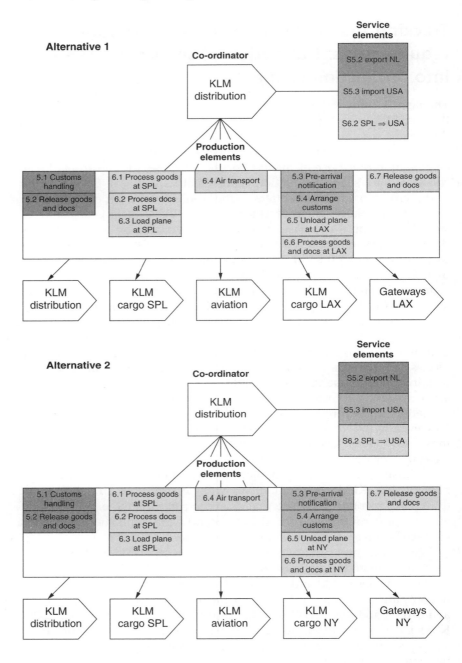

Figure 11.2
Two air transport alternatives for order 1

to organize this activity. However, for the second order the customer allows the co-ordinator to manage this activity by selecting service elements 7.1 and 7.2 (see Table 11.2). KLM Distribution, as co-ordinator, then requests the cargo department at Schiphol to execute this activity. Smaller shippers usually choose to have KLM Distribution organize these activities. The difference between these choices is illustrated in Figure 11.3. One can see that for the first order, production elements 7.1 and

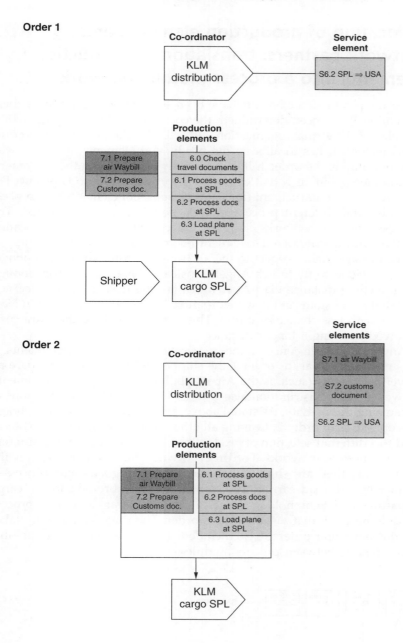

Figure 11.3
Preparation of travel documents for orders 1 and 2

7.2 are outside the scope of the co-ordinator. The shipper itself executes these production elements. The figure also includes service element S6.2 'SPLfiUSA', as the choice in type of document preparation affects the allocation of the first part of this element. Note that an extra production element is required for the first order (6.0), which consists of checking the travel documents delivered by the shipper. Such interdependencies obviously need to be signalled by the co-ordinator.

Allocation of production elements among network partners: translation of production elements into a process module network

After the production elements have been selected and all possible chain formations have been determined, the co-ordinator has to decide which member of the virtual organization will actually take care of each production element. It has to allocate the production elements in such a way that not only is the order fulfilled precisely according to the customer's requirements, but such that costs and lead times are also kept low. For this reason, each participant translates its subset of elements into process modules and different process module networks are constructed. The process module networks support the co-ordinator in its allocation choices with quantitative assessment on costs and throughput times.

For instance, with respect to the air transport route (discussed above) it was decided to fly to Los Angeles instead of New York, even though the travelling distance via LA was greater. The reason for this decision was that the customs at LA were organized more efficiently than in New York – with less chance of errors. This compensated for the extra costs involved in flying a longer distance.

Another example concerns the preparation of the travel documents. It was mentioned that for order 1 the shipper itself wanted to prepare all travel documents (such as the Air Waybill and the customs document). However, KLM Distribution also wanted to evaluate the implications of organizing this activity. As stated above, smaller shippers usually choose this option, as in order 2. Leaving all other factors the same, both choices lead to a different selection of production elements and, in turn, different process module networks. For order 1, when the shipper prepares the documents, they are shipped together with the goods and processed further by the road carrier, after which they are brought to the cargo department at Schiphol. Figure 11.4 depicts a fragment of a process module network that visualizes this order. The time each activity takes for this particular order is also included. The arrows indicate sequential dependencies between process modules.

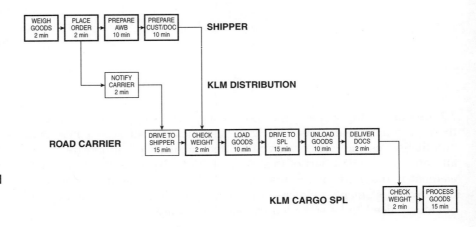

Figure 11.4
Process module network for order 1 – shipper prepares documents

The shipper places order 1 with Distribution by fax (service element S1.2 was selected in Table 11.2). Distribution then notifies the road carrier to pick up the goods from the shipper. At the same time, while waiting for the road carrier to pick up the goods, the shipper prepares the necessary documents. The road carrier then loads the goods and drives them to Schiphol where the documents are handed to KLM Cargo (SPL). After verifying whether the actual weight of the goods corresponds with that given in the documents, the goods can be processed further. Note that activities on the critical path have been drawn with a bold border.

Now consider the second order (see Figure 11.5). Here, the shipper places its order with Distribution, which then faxes the required data to Cargo. KLM Cargo (SPL) then prepares both required documents. The preparation activities are thus removed from the critical path, allowing this part of the order to take less time than the same part of order 1. Although this example is rather straightforward, it does illustrate the applicability of MND in a reasonable manner.

Ongoing assessment and redesign of activities and allocation procedures

Even when all planning and allocation decisions have been analysed for every order under investigation (using a detailed visualization of all production tasks), together with a calculation of costs and lead times, the virtual organization cannot just let things happen. It has to remain aware of possible process redesign options to improve the order fulfilment process and constantly evaluate and update the set of service elements. It also needs to assess the added value of current subcontractors and to search for other possible subcontractors who could join the virtual organization.

In our case, KLM Distribution tried to further improve the procedure of preparing travel documents. It was realized that a single EDI-message from shipper to Distribution could replace the facsimile order placement procedure. Distribution would then automatically forward the message to both the road carrier and KLM Cargo (SPL). This could obviate the

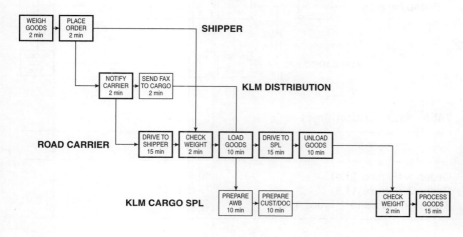

Figure 11.5
Process module network for order 2 – KLM Cargo SPL prepares documents

need to check the weight of the goods each time, because of the lower chance of errors and electronic preparation of the documents. This redesign scenario, which was based on the process module network of order 2 (Figure 11.5), is illustrated in Figure 11.6.

The critical times for the three different process module networks are shown in Table 11.3.

By connecting to a central IS for sending status messages the tracking and tracing capabilities of all partners could be improved. This resulted in a reduced total order processing time and improved customer service, turning tracking and tracing into a standard service usable by all customers. In addition, both redesign options also increased the co-ordinating capabilities of KLM Distribution.

Summary and conclusions

Virtual organizations emerge in the search for the appropriate level of flexibility to offer a high variety of products and services – while keeping costs and lead times low. Broad attention has been paid to this phenomenon in the literature, leading to many different descriptions and definitions. Numerous empirical examples of virtual organizations are provided and analysed from different perspectives. Remarkably, most of these empirical studies indicate a difference in level of analysis compared with the definitions of virtual organization provided in the

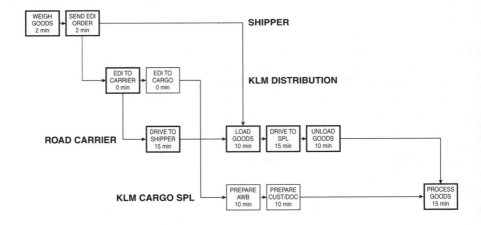

Figure 11.6
Use of EDI for document preparation (redesign scenario for order 2)

Table 11.3   Critical times

	Critical time
Order 1 (Figure 11.4)	80 min
Order 2 (Figure 11.5)	75 min
Redesign scenario (Figure 11.6)	69 min

literature. Therefore, two different roles within a virtual organization are distinguished: co-ordinator and subcontractor. Two key aspects of forming virtual organizations are most noteworthy: the managerial complexity of the daily operations within the virtual organization and the importance of ICTs to design and support a virtual structure.

This chapter has focused on supporting managerial aspects of the formation and operation of the ICT-enabled virtual organization. The virtual organization in action is difficult to manage. For example: the various firms that participate in the virtual organization may have conflicting goals, but should trust each other and share information; the virtual organization should be very responsive and yet able to deliver the required variety to meet customized demand; and resources within the virtual organization should be dynamically allocated to different customer orders. The use of modularity was proposed as a means to achieve standardized organizational structure and behaviour to allow for interchangeability and compatibility of the partners and business processes. This led to the introduction of the modular virtual organization.

Furthermore, a management support tool has been introduced – Modular Network Design (MND). MND's plan of approach is analogous to Mowshowitz's (1997a) four steps of metamanagement. It supports managers of a virtual organization by:

1 determination and analysis of customer requirements
2 tracking of possibilities to satisfy customer requirements
3 allocation of production elements among network partners
4 ongoing assessment and redesign of activities and allocation procedures.

The complexity of managing a virtual organization and the applicability of MND has been illustrated with a case study at KLM Distribution. This firm is at the centre of a virtual organization, with the task of co-ordinating the global distribution of airplane spare parts. The KLM Distribution case study shows how MND can contribute to better order planning and process handling. Moreover, it also demonstrates how the concepts of MND can be used in practice.

The service and production element concepts proved to be very useful and applicable for KLM Distribution. By making them explicit, the modular approach increased the firm's insight into their own and their partners' product and service portfolios and the coupling between these portfolios and back-office processes. With respect to formalization of the allocation procedure, i.e., translating service elements into production elements, there are some interesting findings. As Mowshowitz (1997a) has already indicated, designing a formalized procedure for allocating production elements to service elements is not possible. The couplings often are very case-specific. Still, if a simple service element typology could be developed, it would be helpful in assigning production elements to service elements. The following typology uses the nature of the service elements to determine the type of 'satisfiers' required. Table 11.4 depicts the service element typology and the accompanying type of production element.

Table 11.4   Allocation typology

Type of service element	Type of production element	Example
What	General specifications	Colour, size, accessories, etc.
How	Method of . . .	. . . delivery, production, etc.
Who	Organization specific	Dedicated supplier
When	Time specific	Delivery time
Where	Location specific	Production areas

Five generic types of service element are distinguished: 'what', 'how', 'who', 'when' and 'where'. The first type concerns specifying the general product or service: 'what product or service do I want?' The other four mainly concern additional (value-adding) requirements that require additional activities. The 'who' type, for instance, allows the customer to specify which organizations, units or people should co-operate in the virtual organization. The co-ordinator, in turn, is then limited in its choice of subcontractors. Combinations of types are also possible. Express-delivery is an example of a 'how' and a 'when' type of service element. Overall, a straightforward typology like this could be a first step to formalization of the allocation procedures.

Looking ahead, KLM Distribution is now considering integrating MND into other planning and scheduling systems. In addition, other research currently underway aims to test and extend the concepts of MND in other organizations.

Note

We would like to thank KLM's John van Kesteren, Roland Spijker, Herman van de Vijver and Fred Westdijk for their time, effort and moral and financial support during the execution of this study.

References

Alexander, M. (1997). Getting to grips with the virtual organization. *Long Range Planning*, **30**, 122–24.

Anderson, J. C. and Narus, J. A. (1995). Capturing the value of supplementary services. *Harvard Business Review*, January–February, 75–83.

Ashkenas, R., Ulrich, D., Jick, T. and Kerr, S. (1996). *The Boundaryless Organization: breaking the chains of organizational structure*. Jossey-Bass Publishers.

Baldwin, C. Y. and Clark, K. B. (1997). Managing in an age of modularity. *Harvard Business Review*, September–October, 84–93.

Benjamin, R. and Wigand, R. (1995). Electronic markets and virtual value chains on the information superhighway. *Sloan Management Review*, Winter, 62–72.

Byrne, J. A., Brandt, R. and Port, O. (1993). The virtual corporation: the company of the future will be the ultimate in adaptability. *Business Week*, 8 February, pp. 36–40.

Checkland, P. and Scholes, J. (1990). *Soft Systems Methodology in Action*. Wiley.

Chesbrough, H. W. and Teece, D. J. (1996). When is virtual virtuous? Organizing for innovation. *Harvard Business Review*, January–February, 65–71.

Ciborra, C. U. (1996). The platform organization: recombining strategies, structures and surprises. *Organization Science*, **7**, 103–18.

Clemons, E. K., Row, M. C. and Millar, D. B. (1992). Rosenbluth International Alliance: information technology and the global virtual corporation. *Proceedings of the 25th Hawaii International Conference on System Sciences*, Maui, Hawaii.

Davidow, W. H. and Malone, M. S. (1992). *The Virtual Corporation: structuring and revitalizing the corporation for the 21st century*. Harper Business.

Davis, S. M. (1987). *Future Perfect*. Addison-Wesley.

Davis, T. R. V. and Darling, B. L. (1995). How virtual corporations manage the performance of contractors: the super bakery case. *Organizational Dynamics*, **24**, 70–75.

DeSanctis, G. and Monge, P. (1998). Communication processes for virtual organizations. *Journal of Computer Mediated Communication*, **3**, 1–21.

Eicher, J. P. (1997). Post-heroic leadership: managing the virtual organization. *Performance Improvement*, **36**, 5–10.

Englman, S. (1993). Securing the virtual corporation. *Security Management*, **37**, 28–30.

Hardwick, M. and Bolton, R. (1997). The industrial virtual enterprise. *Communications of the ACM*, **40**, 59–60.

Hoogeweegen, M. R. (1997). *Modular Network Design: assessing the impact of EDI*. Ph.D. Thesis. Erasmus University Rotterdam.

Ives, B. and Mason, R. O. (1990). Can information technology revitalize your customer service? *Academy of Management Executive*, **4**, 52–69.

Jarvenpaa, S. L. and Ives, B. (1994). The global network organization of the future: information management opportunities and challenges. *Journal of Management Information Systems*, **10**, 25–57.

Katzy, B. R. (1998). Design and implementation of virtual organizations. *Proceedings of the 31st Hawaii International Conference on System Sciences*, Maui, Hawaii.

Lovelock, C. H. (1992). *Managing Services: marketing, operations, and human resources*. Prentice Hall.

Loebbecke, C. and Jelassi, T. (1997). Concepts and technologies for virtual organizing: the Gerling journey. *European Management Journal*, **15**, 138–46.

Lucas, H. C. and Baroudi, J. (1994). The role of information technology in organization design. *Journal of Management Information Systems*, **10**, 9–23.

Malone, T. and Rockart, J. (1993). How will information technology reshape organizations? In S. Bradley, J. Hausmann and R. Nolan, eds, *Globalization, Technology and Competition: the fusion of computers and telecommunications in the 1990s*. Harvard Business School Press, pp. 37–56.

Miles, R. E. and Snow, C. C. (1986). Organizations: new concepts for new forms. *California Management Review*, **28**, 62–73.

Morris, B. and Johnston, R. (1987). Dealing with inherent variability: the difference between manufacturing and service? *International Journal of Production Management*, **7**, 13–22.

Mowshowitz, A. (1997a). On the theory of virtual organization. *Systems Research and Behavioral Science*, **14**, 373–84.

Mowshowitz, A. (1997b). Virtual organization. *Communications of the ACM*, **40**, 30–37.

Normann, R. and Ramirez, R. (1993). From value chain to value constellation: designing interactive strategy. *Harvard Business Review*, July–August, 65–77.

Ogilvie, H. (1994). At the core, it's the virtual organization. *Journal of Business Strategy*, **15**, 29.

O'Leary, D. E., Kuokka, D. and Plant, R. (1997). Artificial intelligence and virtual organizations. *Communications of the ACM*, **40**, 52–59.

Orton, J. D. and Weick, K. E. (1990). Loosely coupled systems: a reconceptualization. *Academy of Management Review*, **15**, 203–23.

Pine, B .J. (1993). *Mass Customization: the new frontier in business competition*. Harvard Business School Press.

Rayport, J. F. and Sviokla, J. J. (1995). Exploiting the virtual value chain. *Harvard Business Review*, November–December, 75–85.

Sanchez, R. and Mahoney, J. T. (1996). Modularity, flexibility and knowledge management in product and organization design. *Strategic Management Journal*, **17**, 63–76.

Shostack, G. L. (1982). How to design a service. *European Journal of Marketing*, **16**, 49–63.

Ulrich, K. T. and Eppinger, S. D. (1995). *Product Design and Development*. McGraw-Hill.

Venkatraman, N. and Henderson, J. C. (1998). Real strategies for virtual organizing. *Sloan Management Review*, Fall, 33–48.

Voss, H. (1996). Virtual organizations: the future is now. *Strategy and Leadership*, **24**, 12–17.

Wexler, J. M. (1993). Ties that bind. *Computerworld*, **27**, 97–98.

12

Knowledge and teamwork in the virtual organization

John Gammack and Simpson Poon

Introduction: current trends in organizational forms

In recent years, new forms of organization have begun to emerge from the synergies between technological developments and changing paradigms of corporate culture. The resulting uncertainties and imponderables have led to a need for newer organizational forms to be structured dynamically for responsiveness to change and to provide effective ways to achieve competitive advantage. The evolution from hierarchical to network and now to virtual organizational forms suggests increased demands for flexibility and coordination. Although no single organizational form can serve all purposes (Miles and Snow, 1992), the drive to globalize and the demand for high volumes of information exchange means organizations – both traditional or emerging – need to re-think their organizational strategies.

In addition, today's workforce is well educated, independent, and often required to be responsive to changes within career structures, skill sets and work environments. Organizations in the hyper-competitive industries (e.g. software and Internet commerce sectors) are dealing with changes and expectations that were unthought-of only a decade ago (Munk, 1998). This calls for a workforce with high degrees of innovation, creativity and specialization. The increased mobility of such workers, however, implies that the organizational knowledge and normative standards embodied in stable organizations becomes vulnerable to dissipation. Knowledge is a major asset of an organization. Thus, it becomes crucial effectively to manage the knowledge embodied in the workforce and organizational experience with business practices.

Advances in IT have also transformed the meaning of being competitive. A company can no longer boast the size of its workforce, the amount of physical assets or the layers of management as a measure of dominance. In fact, all these can become a burden to the ability to change – particularly in industries where smaller firms are carving-up 'high profit' niche markets. Successful companies are often found to have ways to exploit information effectively; such firms use information to satisfy customer needs beyond expectation and provide high quality products or services that are second to none (Farkas-Conn, 1999). Therefore, the ability to capture and process relevant and critical information for organizational decision-making may be the key to future dominance.

The Internet, together with software systems such as Enterprise Resource Planning, Groupware and Concurrent Engineering Support, provide the information infrastructure for an organization that may be distributed geographically and/or functionally. Coupled with ongoing organizational transformation schemes such as Business Process Reengineering (BPR) and delayering, the middle management 'channel' which mediates knowledge between strategy and operations is often compromised. Instead, the new breed of organization is often a hybrid of forms connected together based on needs, tasks and projects. To be competitive, firms with such new organizational forms need to be able to aggregate and integrate business partners' competencies effectively (Eversheim *et al.*, 1998). Steps need to be taken to ensure that the virtual competence chain (VCC) is optimally configured and managed; the VCC should consist of an integrated set of core products, core processes and core technologies.

One notable current trend is that the size of an organizational unit is decreasing – even sometimes down to singularity. The outsourcing process often sees small firms being set up by ex-employees who possess the necessary expertise to be re-employed by their former company for similar purposes (Occhiogrosso, 1998). The trend of earlier retirement – either voluntarily or involuntarily – plus the increasing longevity of the population means there is a growing group of experienced professionals who are likely to be self-employed (Minerd, 1999). This new 'grey wave' of entrepreneurs is likely to be a new economic force; such individuals possess both the wealth and expertise to become future small business employers. The 'receding' organizational boundary calls for effective inter-organizational communication, and a comprehension of the expertise and knowledge involved in successful coordination and co-operation.

A *virtual team* is 'a group of people who interact through interdependent tasks guided by common purpose' that 'works across space, time, and organizational boundaries with links strengthened by webs of communication technologies' (Lipnack and Stamps, 1997: 7). Following this definition, Ahuja and Carley (1998) define the *virtual organization* as: 'a geographically distributed organization whose members are bound by a long-term common interest or goal, and who communicate and coordinate their work through information technology'. Managing virtual teams effectively often needs an integrated strategy for people management, relationship management, work management, knowledge management and technology management (Fritz and Manheim, 1998). Alongside, there must be ways objectively to measure the performance of virtual work, including productivity and cost-based measurements.

Beyond technology and management frameworks, virtual organizations are often sustained through trust. The importance of trust in distributed organizational forms has been mentioned in numerous studies (e.g. Jarvenpaa and Shaw, 1998; Holland, 1998). Since virtual organizations are formed with groups that may not have the same strategic objectives and may even have competing interests, it is important to ensure the over-arching purpose for such formation is respected and given priority. There can be many ways to effect such 'trust' – from legally binding policies to friendship. Mutual agreements – in contractual, understood or emotionally trusting arrangements – will also vary with the cultural context. However, trust is an essential substrate of social activity, and where trust does not exist, explicit attention to building it becomes a prerequisite. When co-operation and mutual reliance in online communities is a necessary business practice, its nature must be understood (Goulding and Rooksby, 1998). With globalization of the workforce, such communities are likely to become increasingly prevalent.

The manufacturing and engineering sectors are prime examples showing the impact of globalization. Many firms now have manufacturing plants in countries where labour and material costs are low, but produce supreme quality goods rivalling those previously made in first world countries. Labels such as 'Designed in the USA – Made in China' are increasingly common. Virtual organizational forms are the most effective (if not the only) way to maintain the viability of such a set-up. The sporting company Nike provides a good illustration. For Nike, relocating manufacturing operations is no longer just about moving production facilities, but involves forming an 'emotional partnership' with its Asian factories and workforce (Knight, 1998). In this case, the concept of virtual organization goes well beyond management and operations, towards linkage at the human relationship level.

Manufacturing is not the only sector that can take best advantage of this trend. Firms in the software sector are now employing developers of equal or better calibre from countries of lower labour costs (e.g. India). These firms are outsourcing the labour intensive programming processes either physically to such countries or through employment immigrants (Wheatley, 1997). Given that, in this industry, intellectual processing capacity is the only limitation to producing a good product, it is entirely feasible to outsource software development to the most cost-effective countries. Using global networks, software code can be transferred to the other side of the world and sent back within a matter of minutes, costing no more than a local call and Internet access charge. The 'Designed in the USA – Made in India' approach has allowed smaller sized software firms to remain competitive and allowed large software companies to reduce product prices. Without the use of IT, such organizational forms could never be viable. These examples show that the fluidity of an organization is critical to obtaining the best result; this involves targeting the best resources around the world and using global group-support technologies to coordinate the processes.

Although technology makes it possible to embrace these opportunities, it comes at the cost of radical changes in business practices. Change must also recognize levels of stability and continuity (Hall, 1999). When a business practice is essentially knowledge based, the nature of the work and the elements that can be redesigned for virtual operation must be considered in detail. The four levels of a virtual organization infrastructure (in descending order of hierarchy) are:

1 Collaboration.
2 Conversation.
3 Communication.
4 Connection.

Each of these levels must be coherently addressed so that the impact of change can be contained and stabilized. Without addressing these issues, the new organizational form will not be sustainable due to weak linkages. Although enabled by technologies, each of these levels is essentially embodied in people, and will succeed or fail to the extent that human collaboration is cohesive. In the next section, we consider several of these human factors that determine the success of virtual organizations.

Human nature and the virtual organization

Through the lens of a human-centred theory of organization, we now consider some inescapable characteristics affecting the virtual organization, particularly those applicable in effecting an organizational transition to virtual team working. Although organizations may be viewed in various ways, teams and organizations – virtual or not – are essentially composed of individuals. Computer based agents, though they may be increasingly considered 'intelligent' and 'autonomous', play a symbiotic role in organized teams, primarily providing complementary expert assistance or information during relevant processes. People are central to the dynamics of organizations; a shift from traditional organizational forms to networked and virtual forms requires recognition of the nature of this human contribution. Human factors such as motivation, creativity, resistance to change, communication styles, commitment, loyalty, trust and many other facets of the human psyche, distinctly affect the success (or otherwise) of an enterprise. Effective knowledge management requires an understanding of the nature of human knowledge and its construction, and the creation and maintenance of an organization's intellectual capital.

Key elements in our earlier definitions of virtual teams and organizations include 'goal' and 'bound together'. Purposes tend to be broader than goals, embodying powerful motivations that individuals bring to their work. Although arguments about procedural means, tactics and operations properly occur within self-organizing teams, it is essential to identify common purpose at a high level. This ensures commitment and unity of direction – particularly in product-oriented sectors. Many individuals gain an important motivation from belonging to, and serving, a greater cause. In such instances, an organization and its direction is an actual or surrogate host. Conflicts and competitions at lower levels may even be productive if the larger design is right, as demonstrated by hierarchical sports federation programmes or economically aligned blocs.

Some definitions of virtual organization embrace organizational forms in which non-core competencies are outsourced (on such grounds as expertise value added, promised cost savings, and a need to focus on internal core competencies) (Straub and Ang, 1998). Core competencies – which are those central skills that create unique value for an organization – depend on in-depth knowledge bases and management systems that convert expertise into reputation (Quinn and Hilmer, 1994). Familiar arguments against outsourcing include a decline in morale, and losses in corporate memory, loyalty and personal sense of mission. Notwithstanding, these are necessary preconditions for organizations that require creative thinking and knowledge generation. Shaping virtual organizations requires particular attention to this aspect; the loss of experiences that can critique new ideas is as essential as the generation of fresh ones.

Established organizations adapting to forms of virtual functioning necessarily engage in a significant change exercise. Change initiatives inevitably bring their measure of operational trauma, confusion, redistribution of power, devaluation or possible redundancy of previous functioning, and understandably, all the associated discontent, anxiety and resistance that goes with reformation of a past order. That said, many people actively embrace and champion change. Such change enthusiasts tend to be powerful forces within future-oriented organizations. Entrepreneurship is vital, complementing the slower changing – but substantial – backup and service delivery work that needs to be done. Managing and sustaining both kinds of activity is essential psychology in successful change management.

In particular, communication practices are being transformed and mediated by the technological potentials now available. Postman (1986) describes how introducing an alphabet or movable type printing press into a culture profoundly changes the society's cognitive habits, social relations, and even its deep-seated notions of community, history and religion. Introducing the forms of computer-mediated communication which exist today and are projected to exist tomorrow are nothing less than revolutionary. These communication technologies herald new forms of business practice, and permit new forms of networking that open up previously undreamt of possibilities for organizations.

The intellectual capital or knowledge within an organization – and its ability to 'create' knowledge – is central to a sustained ability to provide products or services. An organization's knowledge resides primarily in its networks of people, procedures and data resources, and in being able to use these assets effectively. More so than traditional organizations, virtual organizations require their knowledge assets to be understood, accessible, useable, and stored and managed competently.

It is necessary to understand that data, information and knowledge have disparate qualities, and designing systems in networked organizations requires a comprehension of each. In essence, *data* are literally 'things given', the isolated facts or traces of activity; *information* is a state of data contextually interpreted as meaningful and, typically, communicated for a purpose; *knowledge*, in its ideal form, is certain, timeless, stable and true. Each of these three currencies is at work in the virtual organization. They each have their own proper technologies and limitations, operating against a background of cultural understandings, at mythological, regional, educational, industry sectoral, organizational, and workplace levels. In shaping the virtual organization – where such shared concepts may not always be simply assumed – accommodating the creation of the knowledge, information and data that operate in effecting business processes and relationship networks must be explicitly considered. What is increasingly clear is that the communities themselves participatively construct their own systems of information, and procedures by which the work takes shape (Crowe *et al.*, 1996). The design challenge for effective information systems organizations is in providing organizational environments in which this can take place, and yet be managed by those who resource, interact with, audit or monitor the activities.

The assets of the virtual organization are not traditional 'bricks and mortar,' but the ability of human networks to leverage relationships and to reinvent themselves by drawing on rich memory banks and flexible workspace identifications. The potential for sustained diversification and new products or services is enhanced by the relationships structure of the organization. In the Japanese tradition, the creation of new 'knowledge' emerges from interactions amongst diverse parties. Patterns evident from mining data can only suggest innovations to human intelligence; it is the human mind that has the contextual awareness and spark of creativity to produce something truly inventive. The organizational products, tangible or otherwise, will emerge from the creativity of the participants. The role of management – be it hierarchical or participative – is to provide the virtual *environments* that encourage this creativity. In the next section we illustrate several of the above themes with respect to particular organizational examples. This is followed by a description of a specific environment for virtual working that was designed for one of these organizations.

Motivations for the shift to virtual work: some case studies

In this section we analyse three different UK organizations, focusing on the business processes that motivated a shift to virtual working solutions. The first two examples are indicative and are described briefly to show generic possibilities. The third example is detailed in considerably more depth. This last case study shows many of the requirements and issues faced by numerous large and distributed organizations.

Process control in steel manufacturing

The client organization was a large producer and distributor of strip steel. The steel output from the plant was intended for the manufacture of cars, ships and so on. This plant produced different qualities or grades of steel by design depending on what was required by the target market. Sometimes, a fault or variation in the process would mean the plant produced a batch of steel unacceptable for its intended purpose. To avoid this, vision inspectors observed the process through a remote video link, checking for signs of defects, and advising the process controller accordingly. Inspection is a tedious vigilance task, and operators naturally become fatigued. The signs of a defect require accurate identification, since they are diagnostic of specific process faults. However, the typically fast speed of the rolling mill makes it hard to distinguish defects from interference or normal markings. Teams of inspectors, with differing experience levels, worked at a video screen in two to three hour shifts. The decision to shut down production is costly and not taken lightly, so a system that could automatically detect and classify defects – and advise operators accordingly – would be very useful. The organization also wished to extend this inspection process to one of its other plants. Quality control like this is typical in many production organizations. The full study is reported in Stephens and Gammack (1994), but for our present purposes some relevant details are summarized.

First, the task was subtler than simply assigning visual stimuli into an established set of defect categories. Instead, inspectors formed their own quite differentiated vocabulary for making distinctions. This language was only understandable to those who were familiar with the material and work context – and had little consensus between inspectors. Any knowledge or recorded data from this work would have to be referenced to the workplace vocabulary used. Although a naturally remote task, the teams are linked to the rest of the physical workplace, and would generally be aware of issues with the materials and processes originating the images.

Second, quality inspection was intimately bound-up with the larger issue of process control. The defects identified fell into distinct categories: (1) those identifying the progression of a defect in a process; (2) those identifying the origin of a defect; and, (3) simple appearance defects. For example, a black patch on the steel might indicate a cosmetic blemish or an overheating furnace. This means that isolating a process for automation (as in the study's initial conception) is inappropriate, and that other knowledge must be brought to bear from elsewhere in the organization. In a virtual organization, some processes are intended to be isolated, but this experience cautions against simple disembodiment of a task.

Third, the decision-making involved is naturally distributed, and potentially globally so. In an extension to this work, an analysis showed the emergence of a decision across a distributed organization (Gammack and Stephens, 1994). In this case, the empowered decision to shut down production had to be made at the front line, or periphery of the organization, but the consideration of the decision required a lot more input than directly available to the process manager. The decision to stop production ultimately depended on a cost-benefit analysis of a distributed process.

Let us consider this decision in an idealized form. Initially, the vision inspector provides (knowledge-based) data input that the product is becoming substandard at a certain point in the process. The process controller can triangulate this with other process knowledge to decide whether an adjustment will retrieve the run quality, or if the entire remaining batch will be affected. The remaining production run can be quickly costed, and this information may then be relayed to an expert who has knowledge of the market for a product of the identified quality (e.g, the underneath of a car does not need to be of the same standard as the body). There may also be a requirement to store the product until a market can be guaranteed, which brings additional costs. Another expert may have knowledge of what is involved here. If this latter knowledge can be brought through a cost-benefit analysis to the process controller, an informed decision can be made to stop or continue the process. In addition to the original vision inspector, this decision-making is likely to involve communication between a factory workplace and head office. These intermediary experts could, in principle, be software agents – with detailed databases of markets, storage costs and the like. Such processes exemplify the definition of the virtual organization given by Ahuja and Carley (1998).

Workflow management in a construction services department

This example describes a study undertaken in the construction services department of a geographically large district council in the UK. This area of local government is responsible for architecture, housing developments, building planning, site surveying, building codes, public works, and administering the whole lifecycle of jobs involving design tenders or associated bids. Issues of regulation, audit, and quality standards accreditation apply to many of these functions. In particular, at the time of the study, the council was standardizing and documenting procedures to obtain and sustain the BS5750 (ISO 9000) quality standard. The immediate interest of the department was to become involved in a research project using an innovative groupware package to facilitate workflow for some specific functions. They also had the further view of developing their staff's skills in such technology, for future general use of the package in any of the council's design processes.

A researcher was based in the department during the project. This allowed an ethnographic description of processes to be obtained as part of the project scoping activity. This was supplemented by subsequent semi-structured interviews. The practice manager identified relevant business sections on the organization chart, including architects/

engineers, quantity surveying, and the clerks of works. Furthermore, in addition to the workflow processes identified by the researcher, the practice manager also suggested some immediate areas that were suitable for application. These included: assisting architects based in different offices to collaborate on drawings (particularly via conferencing software which could update screens in several locations) and remote viewing of faults on sites (via images transmitted directly to office computers). These latter applications translated directly into identification of – and cost benefit analyses relating to – hardware, software and network infrastructure. The workflow applications are described below.

Building projects commissioned by area committees

These projects (whether large or small) involved time-consuming paper-based systems, thus reducing profit for small assignments. Improving the efficiency of this process would increase profitability, but unfortunately this is not possible in the paper-based system. The process involved an architect producing a drawing, a surveyor producing a bill of quantities, and then forwarding this to the contractor. Once returned from the contractor, the surveyor checks the quote, and the winning contract is sent to management for approval. The contractor is then informed and work can begin.

Providing a secure virtual environment for this would ensure the project went on site more quickly, had a recorded audit trail, and could be monitored throughout its lifecycle. The council would also be seen as responsive. Such an environment could, for the most, be provided using existing technologies.

Project initiation and tracking

When any commission is received, a form is produced which initiates a well-defined paper-based process. However, with large numbers of projects it can be difficult to track any given one (e.g., bottlenecks may not be obvious and can be hard to detect). The process identified by the researcher involved a physical meeting each morning to produce a commission confirmation document (white) based on re-entered data from user-supplied documentation on upcoming projects (pink). After this, relevant data is re-entered into a blue form, which allows departments to begin their work. Shifting this workflow into a networked and mediated environment allowed: effective tracking with a clear audit trail; identification of bottlenecks and inefficient or ineffective processes; and avoided the double handling and transcription of data. Again the technologies for this could be readily identified.

Site visits

During a project, various staff must visit sites to check work against standards and specifications. Problems noticed at site visits by unqualified personnel necessitate subsequent visits from experts, who may identify further problems. For sites that are remote, there is a time and travel cost, possibly entailing delays to the project. The suggested solution involved an audiovisual link from a site to head office, enabling drawing and document transfer.

The sets of application areas identified above were each considered in the light of the organizational change required. This issue is considered generally after the next case study, where it also applied. However, several other features impacting the move to virtual work are relevant from this particular study.

Although the above application areas are sector specific, many organizations have tasks characterized by paper-based workflow, distributed decision-making, occasional consultancy inputs, and monitoring and tracking of projects. Many organizational tasks are functionally or geographically dispersed. A project provides a common goal, requiring input from various experts. Such expertise may be rare, remote, or not available in-house. Audit trails are generally required, and clients prefer assurance that their quality needs can be met across the project lifecycle. Business processes can be made more efficient and effective by a networked solution: paper-based processing is slower, error prone, and subject to other physical limitations. Using a network, accountabilities are clearer and expert services may be provided in previously unavailable ways. Naturally, the organizational change involved is a major consideration. In the next section we consider in detail the development of an online environment facilitating virtual work practice.

An environment for collaborative design work

Our detailed case study concerns the requirements of a large, geographically distributed organization concerned with contract design of sensitive marine engineering projects. In particular, we focus on the development of a virtual environment to facilitate these requirements. This organization has many sites, covering various specialist functions and involving coordinated overlap. The need for coordination among sites and design synchronization has motivated a move towards electronic ways of working. An initial investigation with senior managers indicated high level organizational needs related to the following:

- Organizational change (e.g., the ethos of virtual working).
- Technical requirements (e.g., security, platform, or application area).
- Problems associated with physical travel and coordination of workforce.

Requirements analysis

A detailed and prioritized requirements analysis highlighted the relative importance of communication needs, organizational directions, and extant technologies (e.g., pen computing, 'universal' e-mail and Internet access). To collect this data, traditional interviewing and questionnaire techniques were used in favour of ethnographic methods. This was partly because security issues precluded an ethnographic approach, which would involve possible exposure to confidential information. In addition, the existing technology baseline was highlighted, indicating areas where audio-and video-conferencing were sufficient for particular aspects, and showing which new technologies would require integration. Consistent with findings in the literature (e.g., Herring, 1996), senior management viewed critical decision-making meetings as more effectively handled in face-to-face mode, whilst electronic meetings were considered sufficient for technical discussions. Dubrovsky *et al.* (1991) show how higher status participants can dominate face-to-face discussion, and perhaps this was seen as important for meeting control as well as for confirming intuitions gained via non-verbal cues. To this end, desktop conferencing was identified and its utility considered in the user context.

Shared extended desktops and electronic whiteboards or clearboards (Ishii *et al.*, 1994) were seen as likely to find a place within the new modes of operation. Although at the time a PC was not on every desk, this was rapidly changing, and is obviously essential for virtual organizations or virtual team functions. The change in culture implies that initial use within specific individual sites is critical to uptake. However, as Bødker and Pedersen (1991) note, within a relatively small workplace environment there may exist subcultures with values distinguished from those of the overall organization. In dispersed organizations with semi-autonomous organizational units, local and workplace culture factors are assumed to be more applicable than a homogeneous corporate culture for many activities. Unilever, for example, although retaining control of their central IT functions, followed a progressive strategy in their early 1990s move towards distributed computing, effecting the change as people became ready, and leaving the culture change of subsidiary companies to their own pace (Horten, 1993). Small user groups on an intranet, through organizational diffusion processes, may establish collaborative design practice within a larger context. In any case, such teams will establish their own working norms, and change through infection and critical mass development.

It is worth noting that the main difficulties anticipated by senior management were largely concerned with integrating technologies within working practices, and issues of organizational culture and change. The choice of technology did not create significant problems. The above-outlined ways of virtual working were viewed from the outset as 'inevitable', whilst successful implementation within certain workplace sites was seen as likely to lead to more general change in the organization. Our analysis also showed that senior staff viewed groupware technologies as addressing coordination and monitoring, whilst juniors viewed them as helping with specific tasks, suggesting an impact on introduction strategies. Such an application plays a double role: at the operational level it can help designers with their everyday work, and be taken up on that basis; at a strategic level the practices can be reflected upon and learning may take place. As awareness of the need to learn in organizations increases, the importance of shared memory in industrial firms and design teams is beginning to grow (Konda *et al.*, 1992). The Online Design Journal and the related Design History Editor (described later) fulfil this requirement, and have the potential to facilitate group design whilst also supporting detailed audit. The Journal exemplifies an intranet-based development integrating enterprise-wide activity at operational and strategic levels.

Having identified the high level requirements early on, a detailed pilot study was conducted within the user organization. This study concerned a large team (peaking at 240 personnel) across three sites over fourteen months, drafting and then expanding a reference design in a marine engineering project to a level of detail allowing confident decisions regarding build and cost. As a project naturally distributed geographically and functionally, the previous practice had been to 'take a floppy disk in the car and drive several hours on the motorway', with little satisfactory alternative.

One of the areas targeted by our study was the design of propulsion machinery, which involved twenty people across two sites. Here, specialized groupware was installed and evaluated. The initial study concerned transmission of design information and mediation of design conferences through two PCs, one at each site, as connected by a dedicated ISDN line. For security reasons, the PCs could not be networked more widely, and the dedicated line was not part of a public utility. Leading groupware and desktop conferencing packages, which allowed both synchronous and asynchronous working, were the chosen application technologies to be tailored in line with user requirements. During this phase, the need for a shared record of online design journal pages was identified.

In addition to the intranet infrastructure being installed, specialist software was to be developed for the application domain, and the requirements for this were established through ethnographic studies of designers. One of our colleagues had observed the practices of designers and other creative individuals during a secondment to the Engineering Design Research Centre, and especially, had noticed the flexibility afforded by daybooks as compared with prescriptive packages (Bebbington and Jenkins, 1992). Before any software was designed, further 'confirmatory' ethnographic studies took place in other design organizations, particularly the Construction Services Department described earlier. These informal studies of the practices of software and civil engineers suggested that this way of working applied across various branches of design work, and that early design decisions were influential. Just as bad drawing cannot be fully compensated by good painting, it is recognized in design work that, by the time that detailed design is firming up, the crucial decisions have been made. These undocumented processes have the highest cost impact if incorrect.

At the start of the project, detailed issues of setting up and maintaining the equipment and attracting designers to using it took more effort than anticipated. Moreover, before reaching the users, the groupware applications had to be written, tested and pre-evaluated for usability and utility. Problems identified included the typical engineering company culture of less than one computer per desk – making assumptions such as universal e-mail unrealistic. In addition, lack of overall industry technical standards created issues of incompatibility (e.g., among network cards and operating systems).

Another issue involved finding locations for the pilot machines, with the implication that potential users on a site may have to walk for some time to use these PCs. To encourage use, training was linked to staff development, and task-related procedure sequences were written. Without prescribing how to carry out a project task, these sequences indicated how the shared database could be relevantly used. A member of the user organization reviewed these procedures prior to the issue of user manuals to the team. The training materials created were *minimal manuals*: a proven way of providing simple instructions for the acquisition of computer skills (Carroll, 1990). The associated software was introduced to the group during a dedicated training day, followed subsequently by ad hoc training and user support.

The specialist software consisted primarily of an online design journal (ODJ), which was implemented on top of a groupware standard. This recognized the strong need for electronic alternatives to design notebooks (Brown and Bansal, 1991). As such, ODJs allowed design protocols to be captured, automatically time and author stamped, and distributed in various ways – whether the designers are on site or not. The ODJ visually emulated a physical (A4) journal, allowing designers to paste in spreadsheets, sketches, CAD diagrams, annotations, models, previous designs and numerous other everyday applications in their work. These were invisibly logged, stored, hyper-linked and made sharable to named journal co-owners on the team. Other features seen as desirable – including basic meeting support – could also be included. Ideologically, the research team was committed to the human-centred approach (Gill, 1991). As such, it did not prescribe alien ways of working, and the ODJ design was informed by the need to retain as much of existing practice as possible. A sample open page from one design journal is shown in Figure 12.1; this was available to the team allocated to a shared piece of work. The example pages demonstrate the articulation work required in organizing a face-to-face meeting, involving the import of maps, sticky notes, documents confirming an agenda, and so on. All this is mediated via standard groupware products and an intra-or Internet substrate, maintaining chronology and decision-making accountabilities. In the actual design work, the pages might include spreadsheets and draft design documents; these would be archived centrally in some form for audit, design reuse and organizational learning, usually as an indexed, summarized and edited history.

Evaluation of the initial system

Evaluation studies of collaborative virtual systems concern the relationship between the social organization and the technical system being implemented in that organization. To this end, Lester (1997) has provided a guidebook for evaluation in the virtual context. If systems are to be

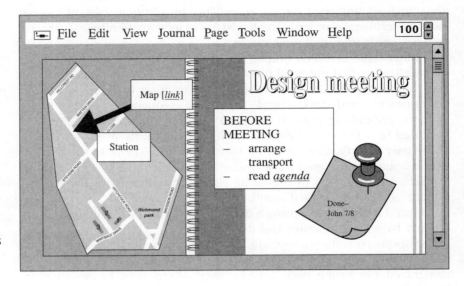

Figure 12.1
An emulated
screenshot showing
opened online
design journal pages

designed and implemented effectively, it is important that the interdependence of work practice and technology is remembered (Plowman *et al.*, 1995). Evaluation of collaborative technologies is difficult for several reasons (Turner, 1996):

- Individual uptake and opinion is not indicative of the success at group level (Orlikowski, 1992).
- The intimate link with work practice and change caused by new technologies implies that disentanglement of effects is difficult.
- Rigorous methods require laboratory type conditions incompatible with real situations.
- Many techniques do not address relevant organizational effectiveness measures. Even when a system is considered successful on the basis of user-oriented factors (e.g., acceptance, ease of use, and amount of use), it may not be a success at the organizational level.

The initial evaluation exercise embraced several measures, involving logging various activities, interviews, observational techniques and questionnaire assessments (Turner, 1996). Results indicate an increase in the number of users from those originally trained, despite time pressure constraints, with e-mail and file transfer the preferred applications among a generally slower than anticipated take-up. Desktop conferencing – used on a few occasions – helped to save time in fixing bugs on remote machines, and the pilot network was used to capacity on several occasions, indicating its usefulness. The provision of an online design journal allowed geographically dispersed designers to co-operate and share ideas, diagrams, spreadsheets, models and sketches in seamless ways hitherto unavailable. The access privileges to the journal provided for closed teams to share specific information in manageable ways.

Acceptance of the system

Later interview and questionnaire data showed that as virtual working began to take hold, the designers were delighted with the opportunities it brought them. The perceived usefulness of – and enthusiasm for – the pilot network increased considerably since the start. Reports in the trade press indicate that several companies have reported similar requirements for early effort and the need for applications that show obvious benefit.

Collaborative work systems are particularly susceptible to acceptance problems, due to the required levels of technological sophistication and the critical mass of their users. In addition, any new system introduces changes which potentially impact on preferred ways of working. Therefore, the uptake strategy adopted was bottom-up and evolutionary; as design decisions sped up and enthusiastic responses were publicized, this was seen to 'infect' others within the company who began to see possible applications in their own work life. Particular workgroups who were offered access to dedicated machines and communication lines could enhance their own operation and be seen to do so. Training days linked to career development were built into the delivery of the tools, and the provision of an online journal did not constrain, but rather enhanced, existing ways of working. This strategy met Beer *et al.*'s (1990) requirements for changing culture: supporting junior staff and their lower level concerns is a key to ensuring the commitment and ownership required for change. It is at this point that structural decisions about which groups become networked and a detailed configuration of 'backbone and membranes' are best determined. Linking the strategic vision to the technical and organizational process changes is important in any organization, but for effecting the transition to the virtual organization in which organizational knowledge is the core asset, managing the changing systems of knowledge is critical. This is summarized in Figure 12.2.

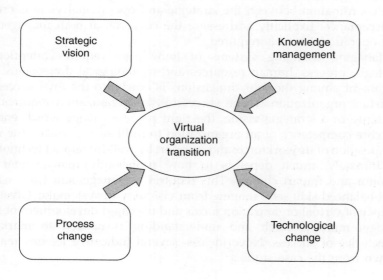

Figure 12.2
Four success factors in the transition to a virtual organizational structure

Conclusions

Transformation of organizational forms involves more than just techno-logical change. Many factors drive such occurrences including new competitive forces, change of demands from customers and the compet-itive position of nations. New industries, particularly those which rely heavily on the use of knowledge and those which generate knowledge, will find that traditional organizational models no longer provide the necessary support. Coupled with the change in workforce composition, all these factors push for new ways of organizing and coordination.

Based on a number of case studies, it was shown that organizations in the manufacturing and engineering sectors could benefit from virtual organizational forms. Although the success which emerged from such transformation was context-based and involved the concurrent adjust-ment of process, attitude and technology, the common message is that this will be the future for many organizations with a similar profile of distributed locations and shared design or decision making activity. The case studies also highlighted that attaining further benefit from new organizational forms is a gradual and sometimes complex process, with identification of business processes, human factors and the diffusion of 'acceptance' being more important than the technology itself. Although we have not disclosed financial details, the cases show that even if imple-mentation of new organizational forms or work practices is costly in the beginning when major infrastructure changes are taking place, this is more than offset by the savings in coordination costs and increase in efficiency. Naturally, detailed and quantitative cost-benefit analyses would need to be carried out for particular ventures.

Facilitating meta-information exchange is also likely to be necessary. Here, not only is information on the business processes communicated, but also expectation of the new working environment and its tools. This need is highlighted in the marine engineering firm studied where different groups perceived the role of such changes quite differently. The coordination between the strategic and operational view is crucial to acceptance. Explicitly addressing the concerns of both management and operational staff is required.

Managing changing systems of knowledge requires attention to strategic, process, human resources and technological dimensions. The alignment among the four dimensions is crucial to the final success of a virtual organization. To be successful, an organization requires: the existence of a strategic vision; the right process change which enables the core competence of an organization to fulfil such a vision; the right composition of its workforce; and, support by well-integrated technology.

Ultimately, much depends to how proficiently management can monitor and impart change. This requires a management team with a well-balanced skill set – ranging from visionary to systematic. Given the infancy of virtual organization forms and the rapid development of tech-nology, more research and understanding is needed to mark the trajectories of success. Nevertheless, several indicative lessons may be drawn from the case studies.

Important considerations include: recognizing the innate conservatism in human nature (some of which is necessary), the advantage of building on successful work practices, and retaining within the organization the core specialized knowledge used in such practices. All these should be explicitly considered and designed into the change exercise. The strategic interests of organizational memory monitoring and managing, and the operational interests of more convenient work practices, were both served by the transition to virtual working. Finally, although roles, communicative possibilities and mediating forms may change, it is important to recognize that knowledge remains the essential asset underlying effective service and productive work.

Note

Much of the work reported in this paper was supported by the DTI/EPSRC's Computer Supported Co-operative Work (CSCW) programme grant. We also acknowledge the PhD work of Robert Stephens and Shicheng Tian.

References

Ahuja, M. K. and Carley, K. M. (1998). Network structure in virtual organizations. *Journal of Computer Mediated Communication*, **3**. Available online. http://jcmc.huji.ac.il/vol3/issue4/ahuja.html

Bebbington, J. and Jenkins, D. G. (1992). *Research Directions for the Design History Editor*. KIREDE Project Paper. Engineering Design Research Centre, Glasgow.

Beer, M., Eisenstat, R. and Spector, B. (1990). Why change programs don't produce change. *Harvard Business Review*, November-December, 158-166.

Bødker, K. and Pedersen, J. S. (1991). Workplace cultures: looking at artefacts, symbols and practices. In J. Greenbaum and M. Kyng, eds, *Design at Work*, Lawrence Erlbaum Associates, pp. 121–136.

Brown, D. and Bansal, R. (1991). Using design history systems for technology transfer. In D. Sriram, R. Logcher and S. Fukuda, eds, *Computer Aided Co-operative Product Development*. Springer-Verlag.

Carroll, J. M. (1990). *The Nurnberg Funnel*. MIT Press.

Crowe, M., Beeby, R. and Gammack J. (1996). *Constructing Systems and Information: a process view*. McGraw-Hill.

Dubrovsky, V. J., Kiesler, S. and Sethna, B. N. (1991). The equalization phenomenon: status effects in computer-mediated and face-to-face decision making groups. *Human Computer Interaction*, **6**, 119–146.

Eversheim, W., Bauernhansl, T., Bremer, C., Molina, A., Schuth, S. and Walz, M. (1998). Configuration of virtual enterprises based on a framework for global virtual business. In P. Sieber and J. Griese, eds, *Organizational Virtualness*. Stampfli AG, pp. 77–83.

Farkas-Conn, I. (1999). Globalization and information technologies: new emerging partnerships. *Bulletin of the American Society for Information Science*, **25**, 4–6.

Fritz, M. B. and Manheim, M. L. (1998). Managing virtual work: a framework for managerial action. In P. Sieber and J. Griese, eds, *Organizational Virtualness*. Stampfli AG, pp. 123–135.

Gammack, J. G. and Stephens, R. A. (1994). A model for supporting interacting knowledge sources. In J. H. Connolly and E. A. Edmonds, eds, *CSCW and Artificial Intelligence*. Springer-Verlag.

Gill, K. S. (1991). Summary of human centred systems research. *Systemist*, **13**, 1–2.

Goulding, P. R. and Rooksby, E. (1998). Trust and online teaching: some reflections. *Proceedings of the Australian Institute of Computer Ethics Conference*, Lilydale, Victoria.

Hall, J. (1999). Six principles for successful business change management. *Management Services*, **43**, p. 16.

Herring, S. (1996). *Computer-Mediated Communication: linguistic, social and cross-cultural perspectives*. John Benjamins Publishing Company.

Holland, C. P. (1998). The importance of trust and business relationships in the formation of virtual organizations. In P. Sieber and J. Griese, eds, *Organizational Virtualness*. Stampfli AG, pp. 53–64.

Horten, M. (1993). Working order. *Computing*, 28 January, 11–15.

Ishii, H., Kobayashi, M. and Arita, K. (1994). Iterative design of seamless collaboration media. *Communications of the ACM*, **37**, 83–97.

Jarvenpaa, S. L. and Shaw, T. R. (1998). Global virtual teams: integrating models of trust. In P. Sieber and J. Griese, eds, *Organizational Virtualness*. Stampfli AG, pp. 35–51.

Knight, P. (1998). Global manufacturing: the Nike story is just good business. *Vital Speeches of the Day*, **64**, 637–640.

Konda, S., Monarch, I., Sargent, P. and Subrahmanian, E. (1992). Shared memory in design: a unifying theme for research and practice. *Journal of Engineering Research*, **4**, 23–42.

Lester, M. (1997). *Introduction to the Evaluation of Computer Supported Co-operative Work and Groupware: a guidebook*. Available online.
http://tortie.me.uiuc.edu/~m-lester/Evaluation/Introduction.html

Lipnack, J. and Stamps, J. (1997). *Virtual Teams: researching across space, time, and organizations with technology*. John Wiley and Sons.

Munk, N. (1998). The new organization man. *Fortune*, **137**, 62–74.

Miles, R. E. and Snow, C. C. (1992). Causes of failure in network organizations. *California Management Review*, Summer, 53–72.

Minerd, J. (1999). A 'gray wave' of entrepreneurs. *The Futurist*, **33**, 10.

Occhiogrosso, J. J. (1998). Professional employers for small companies. *Management Accounting*, **80**, 38–42.

Orlikowski, W. J. (1992). Learning from Notes: organizational issues in groupware implementation. *Proceedings of the ACM Conference on Computer Supported Co-operative Work*, New York.

Plowman, L., Rogers, Y. and Ramage, M. (1995). What are workplace studies for? *Proceedings of the Fourth European Conference on Computer-Supported Co-operative Work (ECSCW)*, Stockholm.

Postman, N. (1986). *Amusing Ourselves to Death*. Heinemann.

Quinn, J. B. and Hilmer, F. G. (1994). Strategic outsourcing. *Sloan Management Review*, Summer, 43–55.

Straub, D. and Ang, S. (1998). Production and transaction economies and IS outsourcing: a study of the US banking industry. *MIS Quarterly*, **22**, 535–552.

Stephens, R. A. and Gammack, J. G. (1994). Knowledge elicitation for systems practitioners: the constructivist use of the repertory grid. *Systems Practice*, **7**, 161–182.

Turner, S. (1996). *DUCK: the early years*. MARI Computer Systems.

Wheatley, M. (1997). IT's passage to India. *Management Today*, April, 56-58.

13

The contribution of Internet electronic commerce to advanced supply chain reform – a case study

Robert B. Johnston, Horace Cheok Mak and Sherah Kurnia

Introduction

The use of electronic commerce technologies to improve the efficiency of supply chains has been widely promoted in the retail and general merchandizing industry. This business-to-business EC makes use of standardized product numbering, bar coding and EDI as its essential core technologies (Johnston, 1998, 1999; Mak, 1998). Many large retail chains now make use of EC with their larger, technologically sophisticated suppliers to control a significant proportion of their replenishment transaction value. To that extent, EC can be thought to have reached significant adoption levels in the industry. Direct operational savings accrue from the elimination of data re-keying through the speed and accuracy of application-to-application transfer of machine-readable data and the automatic identification of products and shipments. However, in keeping with the Pareto principle, the remaining transaction value is spread over a large proportion of non-EC-compliant suppliers, usually SMEs who are technologically unsophisticated.

Furthermore, it is being realized increasingly that the greatest benefits of supply chain EC are to be derived through its role in enabling advanced replenishment and distribution techniques that require strong co-ordination between the operational activities of various supply chain parties. To be practical, such tight co-ordination of activities demands 100 per cent compliance to EC. Thus, despite their small contribution to transaction value, the existence of a large proportion (by number) of non-EC-enabled suppliers creates a barrier for large retailers and distributors in implementing supply chain reforms. Unwillingness on the part of SMEs to adopt EDI in particular, has proved to be a problem for large retailers. These SMEs typically have little to gain from the application–application functionality and global connectivity offered by the traditional approach to EDI, to justify its high cost (Scala and McGrath, 1993; Ritchie, 1994; Iacovou *et al.*, 1995; Mak and Johnston, 1998). In comprising the most transient and least strategic-thinking sector of the economy they have also proved difficult to coerce.

Increasing interest is being shown by large retail players in the Internet – a potential new medium for the exchange of electronic trading documents with unsophisticated small suppliers (Mak, 1998; Mak and Johnston, 1999). Not only is the Internet a global network of networks with high throughput and low cost, but it brings, especially through the Web, new open and highly standardized data exchange protocols that are ideally suited to transfer and presentation of digital business documents (Mak, 1998). A large number of products and services have recently appeared purporting to support Internet-based EDI and a significant target for these products has been the particular requirements of small trading partners (Mak and Johnston, 1997, 1998).

The aim of this chapter is to elaborate the way in which these new Internet-based EC products and services are transforming the prospects for universal supply chain EC compliance in the retail industry. We illustrate this analysis using a case study of the new EC infrastructure under development by Australia's leading supermarket chain, Coles Myer Limited (CML), which makes use of these new Internet-based EC products. CML's aim is to leverage their considerable existing EC investment by the achievement of 100 per cent supplier compliance to EC and its enabling role for advanced supply chain reforms.

We begin by describing in detail a new distribution technique known as cross-docking. Cross-docking is currently being widely advocated in the grocery industry, for instance as part of the influential Efficient Customer Response concept (Kurt Salmon Associates, 1993). Improving existing cross-docking operations and extending the concept to wider product ranges forms one of CML's main motivations for 100 per cent EC-compliance by suppliers. Additionally, cross-docking affords an excellent example of the basic paradigm shift of advanced supply chain reforms in general, away from islands of automation and towards the use of a high-quality data communication channel between trading parties to deal with operational complexity. This shift brings high operational efficiencies, but virtually demands EC compliance in the construction of such a channel for co-ordinated activity. This analysis of cross-docking also sets the scene to discuss the contribution that Internet EC can make to enable these reforms.

We then analyse in detail why the traditional approach to EDI was unable to deliver 100 per cent EC compliance. We also analyse two key ideas that the new Internet-based EC products and services have contributed that seem set to overcome these difficulties. We then present the case study of CML's new EC infrastructure that strongly incorporates these ideas. Finally, we conclude by describing what appears to be the emerging new conception of supply chain EC that features a richer choice of network topology, delivery media and message types commensurate with the variety of participating trading-partner capabilities.

Cross-docking as an example of EC-enabled supply chain reform

Cross-docking (Andel, 1994; Kurnia and Johnston, 1999) is a new method, currently being advocated in the grocery and general merchandise retailing industry, of distributing goods from a large number of manufacturers to a large number of retail outlets via a centralized distribution centre (DC). As an innovation it typifies new approaches to supply chain acceleration and buffer stock reduction, which employ greater co-ordination of the activities of participating parties by means of EC.

The traditional approach to distribution of high variety products via a distribution centre, the so-called 'pick-and-pack' approach, relies on a buffer stock of each product at the DC. (In the following discussion we use CML's terminology for various distribution techniques since across the industry there is some variation in the use of various terms.) Goods are generally ordered from the DC frequently and in small quantities by the retail store in order to minimize its stock levels. However, replenishments of stocks from the manufacturers are triggered by re-order point methods. In the interests of economies of scale these orders are generally large and infrequent. There is thus little co-ordination between the replenishment by the retailers of goods *from* the DC and the replenishment of goods from the manufacturers *by* the DC. This lack of co-ordination of activities has several consequences. Firstly, it results in large stocks of products at the distribution centre. This problem becomes worse as a retail chain tries to distribute a greater variety of products. Managing this stock requires both a large area for storage and also sophisticated systems. Managing stocks within a finite warehouse capacity under variable demand also requires sophisticated computerized warehouse management systems, forecasting systems and inventory management systems. To some extent it also requires double handling of goods since these are put away in store and then picked at a later time. Finally, since replenishment orders are consolidated at the distribution centre, the manufacturer is ostensibly denied sight of events at any individual store. The manufacturer, therefore, cannot gauge consumer buying patterns. The advantage of the method is in its ability to provide rapid replenishment to stores, at low risk.

Cross-docking seeks to eliminate all DC buffer stocks by converting the distribution problem into one of sortation. Retailers place frequent small replenishment orders directly with manufacturers, preferably using EDI. Manufacturers deliver goods, generally for several stores, to the distribution centre for immediate distribution. Shipments are broken down to individual store level and sorted by destination, preferably using bar-coded destination information and electromechanical means, and then repacked by store for dispatch. Such an approach has a much more efficient use of space, requires no double handling of goods and sortation can be accomplished with relatively low technology. However, it requires strong co-ordination between the activities of the retail stores and the manufacturers. Such co-ordination can generally only be achieved through speed-of-light electronic communication. This is accomplished firstly by using EDI purchase orders between the retailers and manufacturers. It is also necessary to simplify, as much as possible, the processing of goods at the distribution centre. The minimum technical requirement to automate sorting is the use of manufacturers' bar coding on cartons from which the destination store can then be machine-read. However, the additional requirement to check actual articles against orders can be reduced by the use of other electronic commerce technologies such as the International Article Numbering Association standardized product numbering scheme (European Article Numbering (EAN) International, 1997) and bar coding, to increase data accuracy through procedures at the manufacturer's dispatch site. For example if, as goods are packed, an EDI advanced shipping notice (ASN) message is created by scanning product bar codes (so called 'scan-packing') and this is sent to the DC ahead of the shipment and a unique shipment number for the ASN is bar coded on the cartons, the contents of the cartons can be retrieved at the DC by scanning the shipment number. Individual item checking can be automated or eliminated.

Thus, while cross-docking promises operational and infrastructure cost savings it presents a new range of system implementation issues that require co-operation across the boundaries between retailers, distributors and manufactures (Kurnia and Johnston, 1999). The pick-and-pack approach uses sophisticated physical and computer systems to deal with the complexity of distributing a large variety of products between multiple manufacturers and retail stores, essentially by predicting and planning the future. By contrast, cross-docking relies heavily upon electronic commerce technologies for the establishment of a high-quality communication channel between participating parties to achieve co-ordinated action, since the use of paper-based control documents provides insufficient processing speed, accuracy and data integrity. The level of technology involved in establishing such a communication channel is fairly low. The key challenge is not the technology itself but achieving 100 per cent participant compliance to the technology. Thus, advanced supply chain reforms, which incorporate electronic commerce, can be seen as part of a general paradigm shift. This fundamental shift is in the perception of the role of IT in business performance improvement. It is a shift from the earlier vision of computers as intelligent logic engines (to be applied to problem solving and planning), to a view of computers as a medium for communication and co-ordination between parties and business transactions.

The failure of traditional EDI in advanced supply chain management

Prior to the commercial use of the Internet, the standard method for implementing electronic business information exchange in a large supply chain was with EDI. This used a Value Added Network service (VAN) that provided store and forward facilities for messages transmitted over private wide area networks (WANs), which they frequently owned (Emmelhainz, 1990; Kalakota and Whinston, 1996; Johnston, 1998). Outputs from diverse business applications operating on diverse platforms were translated into standard EDI transaction sets using mapping software – again often provided by the VAN. This use of industry-wide, national or international EDI message standards ensured that the EDI network was open, since it allowed potential participants to choose mapping software and VAN services independently. It was assumed that these EDI messages would be transmitted from computer application to computer application, in order that the maximum operational benefits of labour reduction, increased accuracy and greater speed would be realized through the elimination of unnecessary data re-entry.

In the grocery and general merchandise retailing industry, this traditional approach to EDI has been widely adopted by the larger, more technically sophisticated retailers and manufacturers. Since interactions between these sophisticated players represent perhaps 80 per cent of all transactions in the supply chain, from the point of view of the value of transactions controlled, traditional EDI can be thought of as having achieved considerable penetration in the industry. This translates to considerable direct cost saving in the replenishment cycle. However, a large number (perhaps 80 per cent) of all suppliers, who are technically unsophisticated and generally small, fail to use EDI. Their non-compliance is not a significant barrier to achieving the direct benefits of EDI, since their transaction value is small. But it does nevertheless present an obstacle to achieving the more significant benefits obtainable from EC as an enabling technology for supply chain reform initiatives such as cross-docking, which do not run smoothly with less than 100 per cent EDI compliance. The size of this obstacle is measured in terms of the number of firms that have to be persuaded to come on board, rather than their transaction value.

It is now clear to many large retail chains, who have the most to gain from advanced supply chain management, that 100 per cent EC compliance cannot be achieved using the traditional approach. A decade ago, it was generally believed that small suppliers could be brought into the EC network through mutual benefit, coercion or critical mass effects (Zinn and Tahac, 1988; Sarich, 1989; Emmelhainz, 1990). However, as a result of the persistence of the non-compliance problem, it must now be recognized that these ideas are flawed and new solutions must be sought. The problem is that these traditional approaches to achieving compliance are not compatible with the profile of the typical SME (Scala and McGrath, 1993; Ritchie, 1994; Iacovou *et al.*, 1995; Mak, 1998). Small to medium-sized enterprises typically interact with a small number of trading partners (Johns *et al.*, 1989), and often have only one large customer. They therefore have little to gain from the global connectivity offered by the traditional EDI open network. The system purchase, installation and running costs of the traditional approach were high, largely because of the oligopolistic position afforded to SMEs by their ownership of wide area networks. Such firms typically have simple (often manual) operational and financial systems (Iacovou *et al.*, 1995; Rodwell and Shadur, 1997) and therefore have little to gain from the application-to-application connectivity offered by the traditional approach (Scala and McGrath, 1993). Thus, both the initial set-up costs and on-going operating costs of the traditional approach cannot generally be justified by any operational benefit to SMEs. These businesses would need to bear these costs simply to protect themselves against the threat of 'desourcing' (Zinn and Tahac, 1988). Moreover, small enterprises form the most transient and least strategically oriented segment of the economy, which makes them difficult to influence on this basis. Finally, because the VAN offerings were designed to interact with existing applications on diverse platforms they were usually general-purpose rather than turnkey in nature, and to install and operate generally required higher levels of technical sophistication than is typically present in SME organizations.

The role of Internet EDI in enabling supply chain reform

The large EDI players with the most to gain from supply chain reforms are increasingly looking to the Internet as a means of resolving the problem of EDI non-compliance of small unsophisticated trading partners. The Internet is a worldwide network of networks with excellent throughput capabilities. Compared with those of VANs, Internet transmission charges are low and do not depend on the amount of data transferred. More importantly, the Internet is provided with highly standardized and widely understood new information exchange and presentation methods (Hruska, 1995; Kalakota and Whinston, 1996), which, particularly with the advent of the Web, are ideally suited to the exchange of business documents. To comply with their EDI-enabled trading partner's information requirements, non-EDI-enabled trading partners can use a Web browser to fill in a form-based Web page representing a business document. To access the Internet they need only a personal computer, a modem and an Internet Service Provider (ISP). They require little more computer expertise than is now fast becoming common knowledge.

The last few years have seen a large number of new software products and services that purport to enable Internet-based EDI. These products have been conceived in response to this new cost structure of the Internet, the access to a global market it creates and the reduction of the stranglehold of the traditional VANs upon EDI software and services that this new global public network has afforded. Mak and Johnston (1997, 1998), who have made a classification of fifty specific products, have reviewed these new products and strategies. Some of these products merely translate the traditional approach to the new Internet transport medium. For instance, message-mapping software is available to translate application output to traditional standardized EDI messages. These EDI massages are then sent between parties using Internet protocols such as Internet Simple Mail Transport Protocol (SMTP), Multipurpose Internet Mail Extensions (MIME), File Transfer Protocol (FTP) or/and Secure/HyperText Transfer Protocol (HTTPS/ HTTP). ISPs then provide the store-and-forward facilities formerly provided by VANs. The traditional VANs are responding by establishing Internet-based third-party services, variously called Internet Value Added Networks, Integrated Value Added Networks (IVANs) or Internet Value Added Services (IVAS), which add new forms of value to EDI transfers.

However a significant proportion of the new products differ markedly in their approach from traditional EDI. Two important new concepts are being increasingly embodied in this group of Internet EDI products that are crucial to a new match between EDI requirements and SME capabilities. These are:

1 The provision of a *new* mode of distribution and collection of electronic business documents between large players and their small unsophisticated trading partners that is more appropriate to the capabilities and requirements of the small players. These products (for examples see Mak and Johnston, 1998) generally provide the tools to build a hub-and-spoke network between the large player and its small suppliers using Web-based client-server technology. Since these products generally require that the client and server programs be built with the proprietary tools provided, these sub-networks are not open in the traditional EDI sense, and often use proprietary or Web messaging standards rather than traditional EDI standards. These products feature the capability to tailor business documents and document handling processes to the needs of the large player while providing a cheap, easy-to-use and turnkey client package to the small trader. These products recognize the inadequacy of the one-size-fits-

all approach of traditional EDI, which was only appropriate for inter-actions between sophisticated trading partners.

2 The recognition of the need for large players to support and efficiently manage *multiple* modes of delivery and receipt of electronic business documents appropriate to the existence of multiple kinds of trading partners. This requirement is addressed in 'intelligent gateway' products (Mak and Johnston, 1998) that are capable of receiving either application flat-file or EDI message inputs, and routing the data to trading partners using various formats and media based on a profile of the trading partner. The reverse process is also supported. The media supported include private VAN networks, the Internet, public telephone lines and dedicated connections. The formats supported include traditional standards-based EDI messages intended for sophisticated trading partners, proprietary or Web-form messages of the type described above intended for unsophisticated partners, proprietary formats specific to use in high-volume exchanges between co-operating trading partners and fax for non-EDI-enabled trading partners.

Intelligent gateways provide a link between the traditional open EDI network of sophisticated trading partners, who value global connectivity and application-to-application functionality, and the hub-and-spoke networks specifically catering to large players' needs and small players' capabilities. Thus, what is emerging is a new vision of universal business-to-business EC based on a richer network that explicitly recognizes the existence of multiple kinds of trading partners and trading relationships and a fairer distribution of costs, benefits and risks between participating parties. From the large traders' point of view these new products allow them to leverage their considerable investment in traditional EDI by achieving the benefits of 100 per cent EDI compliance at relatively small extra cost. We would argue that the emergence of these new EDI concepts is the greatest contribution that the Internet is making to advanced supply chain management.

Case study – Coles Myer Limited

Coles Myer Limited is Australia's largest retail store chain and its largest non-government employer, with more than 148 000 staff and annual sales of over A\$19 billion. CML operates eleven retail brands through 1800 stores in Australia and New Zealand including Coles, Bi-Lo, Myer Grace Bros, Myer Direct, Kmart, Target, Fosseys, Liquorland, Red Rooster, Katies and Officeworks. CML spends over A\$15 billion each year on buying merchandise and services (Coles Myer Limited, 1997). It has more than 15 000 suppliers (including grocery, general merchandise and service suppliers): 1800 suppliers use the traditional EDI approach, while the remainder use conventional paper-based document processes via regular mail, phone calls or fax, to exchange business data with CML.

This case study describes how CML is making use of the new Internet-based EDI products to enable them to handle all their grocery and general merchandise replenishments (approximately 10 000 suppliers) through a single centralized EC system. CML is aiming for 100 per cent compliance to electronic purchase orders and ASNs by using the system that includes an Internet-based component tailored to the needs of small suppliers. The following account of the proposed new EC infrastructure at CML and its significance in enabling cross-docking is based on a number of data sources. These sources include semi-structured interviews and follow-up communications with the Electronic Trading Co-ordinator; study of company documents; and participation in CML's 'Proof of Concept' project as an observer, and in the product and Internet EDI strategy evaluation for CML's front-end Internet EDI system as an independent evaluator.

This in-depth case study and participatory research method was chosen to gain deep access to the practices of a significant industrial player. In keeping with the limitations of this research method (Yin, 1989; Galliers, 1992) it has been used mainly to generate novel propositions concerning the role of the Internet in advanced supply chain management that will be tested empirically in future research.

Currently, CML has various business applications for different retail brands, running on different system platforms. There are a number of translators mapping flat-file outputs from these applications into traditional EDI messages that are sent via the store-and-forward facilities of a VAN to EDI-enabled trading partners using the VAN's private network. In addition, there are multiple manual systems to send and receive trading documents to and from non-EDI-enabled suppliers via regular mail, phone calls or fax. The current EDI infrastructure is shown in Figure 13.1.

This EDI infrastructure presents a number of problems to CML, both in achieving direct operational cost saving through EDI, and in implementing EC-enabled supply chain reforms such as cross-docking. Firstly, there is the basic undesirability of maintaining multiple document distribution systems, including manual ones. Secondly, manual systems offer little opportunity to control the integrity of delivery data received from

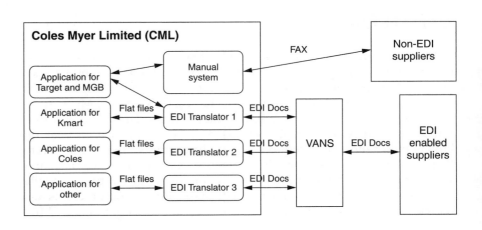

Figure 13.1
The current EDI infrastructure at CML

non-EDI-enabled suppliers. When preparing a manual delivery docket from a CML purchase order (PO) suppliers can easily alter the quantity, price or the ordered item itself, either intentionally or by error. Ideally, CML would like suppliers to base an electronic ASN upon data received in the electronic PO in order to improve data integrity. The principle at work here is the data turnaround principle (Johnston, 1999), which states that data received by a trading partner is likely to be more accurate if it is derived from data sent earlier by that trading partner. Accuracy would further increase by providing some intelligent data checking to the supplier's interface and using bar-code scanning to acquire product numbers direct from the packed items.

Owing to reliance on the traditional VAN-based approach, CML has experienced difficulty over many years of EDI operation in bringing small suppliers into the network. Small suppliers lack the technical, financial and human resources to develop a traditional EDI system to handle all the functionality required by CML. According to the Electronic Trading Co-ordinator at CML, the conventional VAN-based EDI development cost for small suppliers, including the costs for purchasing an EDI translator and communication software, is in the range of A$5000 to A$20 000. Transferring 10 kilobytes of data via a VAN might cost a SME, at list price, A$4 per document, plus a monthly VAN subscription fee of A$100. While these costs may be justifiable for a larger supplier who can gain mutual benefit from the investment, small suppliers generally have primitive in-house business systems (often manual) and cannot use the potential benefits of application-to-application transfer of data of VAN-based EDI approach, to justify the decision. With very few customers, they also gain little from the global connectivity of traditional EDI.

Finally, two further issues have prevented CML from reaping the full benefits of existing cross-docking operations and extending them to further product ranges: lack of data accuracy resulting from the use of paper-based trading documents and operational complications resulting from the existence of non-EC-compliant suppliers. While it is possible to use cross-docking without EC-compliance, this necessitates distribution-centre activities which are labour-intensive, such as manual bar coding of cartons and manual inspection and verification of carton contents. Such activities can be substantially reduced when all suppliers are compliant to standardized product and shipment numbering schemes, such as the EAN numbering system, bar coding and electronic ASNs.

Based on a need to overcome these problems and extensive experience with the capabilities of small suppliers, CML determined the following requirements for the new system:

1 The systems need to support existing VAN-based EDI. Both CML and its larger suppliers have a considerable investment in the existing VAN-based infrastructure and it was decided that investment in the new Internet system should leverage this existing investment rather than replace it.
2 There should be a single centralized system to handle business documents from all retail brands.

3 Use of the Internet should be part of the system because of its ability to deliver documents to small suppliers at low cost and in user-friendly form. According to the Electronic Trading Co-ordinator at CML, the incremental cost of transferring a 10 kilobyte message over the Internet is about A$0.50 (mainly associated with telecommunication costs, such as telephone call charges) plus, typically, a A$25 monthly subscription fee for an ISP. Small suppliers could use a CML-provided Web-form Internet application as a data entry system, not necessarily using the traditional EDI standard format needed for application-to-application data transfer. However, this use of the Internet requires consideration of issues of security and reliability. It was decided that mission-critical transfers should continue to be made via the VAN network. Thus the transfers to be made via the Internet component were not subject to high security and reliability requirements. Nevertheless, the security of HTTPS using Secure Socket Layer (SSL) – which enables point-to-point data transmission without storage at the ISP site – together with the password protection and document control facilities provided routinely by third-party Internet EDI development software, will provide a secure and reliable transport mechanism for these Web forms and other file types. Eventually, this may provide a low-cost alternative transport system even for standard EDI files.

4 A limit was placed on the system so that the cost to small suppliers of participation should be no more than A$500 for a basic system and A$1000 with extra bar-code scanning and label-printing facilities. The monthly running cost should not be greater than A$25 for an ISP subscription plus phone calls. Suppliers must also provide a PC, modem and printer.

5 The requirement to keep operating costs down to these low levels has led to an additional requirement that the front-end used by the small suppliers must be capable of running offline from the central CML system while shipments are packed. Otherwise ISP charges might become prohibitive.

6 In order to facilitate cross-docking distribution the system should provide for the highest quality data about impending shipments. This led to the requirement that the system should make use of the electronic turnaround document concept and scan packing. A paper-based turnaround document is one that is expected to be returned by the receiver to the sender with certain data added. From the viewpoint of data integrity, this approach is superior to receiving a separate manual response, since it does not require transcription of data on the original document. In electronic form this means that a document message sent by a small supplier to CML can only be constructed based on the contents of the original document source from CML to which it is a response. Initially, the turnaround concept will be applied to the construction of ASNs from CML purchase orders, but other trading document pairs may be included later. Scan packing means that any data used to construct the ASN should be entered by directly scanning the EAN product number bar codes on the products as they are packed.

To satisfy these requirements, CML's proposed new EC infrastructure makes use of both the intelligent gateway concept and an Internet-based hub-and-spoke network for use by small unsophisticated suppliers. The intelligent gateway replaces the multiple translators of the current system and transfers flat-file outputs to and from the various brands' application programs. It translates these flat files to various formats, determined from a trading-partner-profile database, including fax, traditional EDI and Web-forms, which are also routed via various communications media including the private network of their VAN, the Internet, telephone lines and point-to-point fixed connections. The new EC infrastructure at CML is shown in Figure 13.2.

An important component of the new infrastructure is the Internet EDI hub, shown shaded in Figure 13.2. There are many products now available for exchange of business documents over the Internet using a wide range of approaches (Mak and Johnston, 1997, 1998). These differ mainly in their use, or non-use, of traditional EDI standards; whether they involve third-party Internet sites; and whether they force the use of software from the same provider at both sender and receiver sites. The choice between these various options should be made on the basis of the degree of system integration (application-to-application or application-to-person) and the degree of connectivity (global or hub-and-spoke) required of the Internet EDI system (Mak, 1998). On the basis of their evaluation process and 'Proof of Concept' project, CML has chosen an approach which uses software from a single provider to create both the CML hub and the small supplier front-end data-entry application. This allows for document exchanges not structured using traditional EDI standards and facilitates the participation of SMEs in the EC network, without needing full EDI translation facilities.

For this Internet EDI subsystem CML chose to use client server technology. The server interfaces with business applications via the intelligent gateway and distributes business documents as Web-forms that can be displayed by the small suppliers using a client program incorporating a Web browser. CML will produce customized form-based document templates using tools provided by the software vendor, and these will be distributed with the suppliers' front-end program.

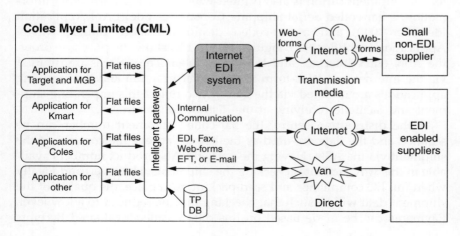

Figure 13.2
The proposed new EC infrastructure at CML

Next CML had to choose between so-called 'thick client' and 'thin client' approaches. In the thin client approach, nearly all the data processing operations are performed by the server (hub) program and the client software may consist of little more than a Web browser. In the thick client approach, the client program has some capability of processing the exchanged data, independently of the hub. A typical example is where the client program performs data editing without needing to refer back to data stored at the hub. This would generally result in duplicate storage of data at the hub and client. It can therefore be argued (Mak, 1998), that a thick client approach is more suitable when the business running the client program wishes to use the exchanged data in their own applications because, in this instance, the well-known problems that attend data duplication might be justified. Hence, we would normally associate the choice of thick client approaches with a desire for application-to-application system integration.

CML had an additional requirement that the small suppliers should be able to perform much of their data entry offline, that is, while not connected to their ISP. Consequently, motivated by the desire for a high standard of data integrity, CML has chosen to adopt a thick client approach in order to enable extensive data editing to be performed while processing offline. While not a primary requirement, this choice also reserves the opportunity for suppliers to integrate their in-house applications with the front-end data-entry system by re-using the local database or exporting the data from the front-end system.

The Internet EDI subsystem incorporates the 'data turnaround' principle. Purchase orders are received by the hub program from the application programs via the gateway and are converted to Web-forms. These can be retrieved by the client front-end program over the Internet using HTTPS and can be displayed or printed. Upon despatch of goods these purchase orders form the basis for the creation of an ASN and a bar-coded carton label. The original purchase order is stored temporarily at the client site and is used as a basis for edit checks upon packed quantities and product numbers. In the scan-packing process, the product numbers and quantities for the ASN are entered by actually scanning the EAN product number bar codes onto the items being packed. A label for the shipment carton is also printed which shows, among other information, a bar-coded Serial Shipping Container Code (EAN Application Identifier '00'), and a bar-coded destination store number (EAN Application Identifier '90'). Figures 13.3 to 13.5 show the purchase order, the ASN entry interface and the carton label. The ASN is transmitted via the Internet as a Web-form to the server program and the receiving applications are updated via the gateway to reflect this impending shipment and facilitate receiving at the distribution centre.

At the distribution centre, the bar-coded shipment number can be scanned and the data are used as the key to retrieve the contents of the shipment via the ASN. Having the packed EAN product numbers available in this way facilitates checking the shipments. However, and ideally when full EC compliance and scan-packing is in place, the quality of the shipment data will be such that checking may be reduced to a low level. Payments can be made based on this data – called Evaluated Receipts

Purchase Order

Order from:	**BI-LO**		Order #:	123/26A
Deliver:	601 via Pt.Melb		Date needed:	15–5–97

Product	TUN/APN	$ Price	Q-Ord
Light	9312345123450	8.50	20
Switch	9312345543210	9.35	10
Bulbs	19312345987651	64.60	2

Figure 13.3
Sample Purchase Order displayed or printed from the Web browser

Advance Shipment Notice

Order from:	**BI-LO**		Order #:	123/26A
Deliver:	601 via Pt.Melb		Date needed:	15–5–97

Product	TUN/APN	$ Price	Q-Ord	Q-SoFar	Q-This-Ctn
Light	9312345123450	8.50	20	0	8
Switch	9312345543210	9.35	10	0	4
Bulbs	19312345987651	64.60	2	0	2

Supplier X-ref	361–May 97
This Carton SSCC#	0039312345 1234567894

Figure 13.4
Sample form for turnaround ASN data entry (entry-enabled fields are boxed)

Settlement (Johnston, 1998, 1999) – leading to further process simplification. The bar-coded store number is used to control the electromechanical automatic carton sorting facility. With full ASN, bar code and scan-packing compliance, there is the potential to approximately halve the all-up distribution cost per carton using cross-docking compared with the pick-and-pack method (Kurnia and Johnston, 1999). The main savings are through reduced warehouse and computer system infrastructure and reduced double handling of cartons.

FROM Horace Pty Ltd Tooronga VIC 3146	To: **9293** BI-LO Altona DC 3311
Carrier: DHL Con #: 8012345675 B/L #: XYZ1234567	FOR: **0601** Pt Melb City St. 3004

PO: 123/26A
SSCC (00) 393151680000000260

(421) 0363911 (90 : 0601

(00) 9931516800000000860

Figure 13.5
Sample shipping
container label

Discussion and conclusions

This chapter has analysed the role that Internet-based EC is playing in making advanced supply chain management initiatives, such as cross-docking, achievable in the grocery and general merchandise retailing industry. We have described the problems that the traditional approach to EDI poses to large retailers in achieving 100 per cent EC-compliance from small, unsophisticated suppliers. We have also indicated two contributions that the new Internet-based EDI products are making towards a viable solution to this problem that recognizes the limited capabilities and requirements of small suppliers. In a case study we have illustrated how these new ideas are being used in a large retail chain in Australia.

The proposed infrastructure at CML is one company's approach to achieving a richer connection to a variety of trading partners through Internet-based electronic commerce. CML chose to purchase and install a gateway product provided by a third-party software provider and also to use third-party software to build their Internet-EDI sub-network. CML is a sufficiently large player in the industry to justify these outlays in terms of operational benefits and the flexibility that a tailored solution offers them in designing new business processes. However, these same Internet EDI connectivity concepts are also available to sophisticated EDI players in other ways. The new breed of third-party Internet-based EDI service providers, IVANs, also offer services based on these same concepts to allow traditional EDI-enabled players to reach both other EDI-enabled trading partners and small unsophisticated trading partners. Typically, IVANs will receive traditionally structured EDI messages and route them on via private networks or the Internet, or convert them to Web-forms or fax for small trading partners. They also support the reverse translation processes. The Perth, Australia, based company Atkins Carlyle (Anonymous, 1998) has recently chosen this approach to EC with small trading partners. Other examples of this third-party gateway approach are 'AT&T InterCommerce' (AT&T, 1999): an IVAN service that enables SMEs to reach their EDI-enabled trading partners using Web-based solutions. In Australia, the Pharmaceutical Electronic Commerce and Communication (PECC) project, which is mainly funded by government agencies, industry participants and associations, has set up the Pharmaceutical Extranet Gateway (PEG) to provide Internet EC services for the pharmaceutical supply chain (PECC, 1999).

Thus, through an analysis of the new connectivity concepts reflected in the new Internet-based EDI software products, the new services offered by Internet-based third parties, and the initiatives of large retail supply chain players such as CML, the outlines of a new vision for universal supply chain EC can be discerned. There will be a backbone open network based on traditional standardized EDI message exchanges between technologically sophisticated trading partners requiring application-to-application functionality and wide connectivity. Given investment levels in traditional VAN products and store-and-forward services, and concerns about Internet reliability and security, this backbone may remain on VAN private networks for some time, but it seems likely to gradually migrate to the Internet. An interesting and as yet open question is the likely role of third-party services for this Internet-based but traditional EDI. However, attached to this backbone we will increasingly see the appearance of relatively closed Internet-based hub–spoke networks using proprietary or Web-form messages, catering to the particular needs and capabilities of small players. The hubs will be centred on large players or Internet third-party sites.

In this new vision the relaxation of a number of rigid and utopian ideas of the traditional, one-size-fits-all approach can be seen. In the traditional approach, the universal adoption of internationally regulated message-formatting standards was supposed to provide unlimited connectivity between trading partners and to facilitate application–application data transfer between diverse application platforms. Although using the Internet as a transport medium does not preclude this traditional standards-based EDI approach, the proliferation of Internet EDI software (Mak and Johnston, 1997, 1998), which does not use traditional standards, appears to pose a challenge to these original aims. When used in hub-and-spoke sub-networks, the relaxation of traditional standards requirements by these products may not be a backward step. It provides greater flexibility to the large players to develop systems quickly that meet their particular needs. Because application-to-application and global business connectivity are not particularly important to small trading partners, Web-form formats can be used by them in a hub-and-spoke configuration, without compromising the global nature of the back-bone network. The platform independence of the network that was traditionally supposed to require universal compliance to standards, is now achieved in additional ways through intelligent gateways at large player or Internet third-party sites, and also through the platform independence that the Internet brings via Web client-server technology using HTTP/HTTPS.

Additionally, the new vision embodies more realistic ideas about the nature and relations between trading partners within and along retail supply chains. It recognizes the existence of a variety of levels of technical sophistication and capability amongst trading partners, but also an uneven distribution of potential benefits from EC amongst them, particularly from the most advanced supply chain management initiatives. The new range of connectivity options made available by Internet-based EC allows for a more equitable distribution of the costs and risks commensurate with benefits, which, being more in keeping with the political realities of the industry, should enhance the chances of wide adoption of EC over traditional enforcement approaches.

The benefits of this new richer network for large players have already been stated. For the small players this new form of Internet EDI may prove to be a palatable point of entry into electronic commerce with subsequent benefits. With a working familiarity of electronic exchange of data, initially through an application-to-person approach, the benefits of transferring data directly to a simple accounting package may become apparent. Knowledge gained through the use of a single customer EDI system might be leveraged by a small supplier to provide a first-mover advantage over their peers with other customers. Internet EDI may play the role for electronic commerce that graphical user interfaces played for end-user computing. An important issue will be the provision of migration paths for small trading partners between these alternative modes of connection, moving to the greater EC network as the sophistication of small players increases.

References

Andel, T. (1994). Define cross-docking before you do it. *Distribution*, **35**, 93–98.

Anonymous (1998). Technologies to grow electronic trading communities for Atkins Carlyle. *EC Edge: Newsletter of Tradegate ECA*, **3**, 13.

AT&T (1999). *AT&T InterCommerce*. October.
http://www.att.net.au/products/interc.html

Coles Myer Limited (1997). *Company facts*. December.
http://www.colesmyer.com.au/shared/company_facts.htm

European Article Numbering (EAN) International (1997). *EAN Numbering and Barcoding of Non-Retail Items: including an introduction to EAN application identifiers and EAN-128 barcodes*. EAN International.

Emmelhainz, M. A. (1990). *Electronic Data Interchange: a total management view*. Van Nostrand.

Galliers, R. D. (1992). Choosing information systems research approaches. In R. D. Galliers, ed., *Information Systems Research: issues, methods and practical guidelines*. Blackwell Scientific, pp. 144–62.

Hruska, V. (1995). The Internet: a strategic backbone for EDI. *EDI Forum: The Journal of Electronic Commerce*, **8**, 83–85.

Iacovou, C. L., Benbaset, I. and Dexter, A. S. (1995). Electronic data interchange and small organizations: adoption and impact of technology. *MIS Quarterly*, **19**, 465–85.

Johns, B. L., Dunlop, W. C. and Sheehan, W. J. (1989). *Small Business in Australia*. George Allen & Unwin.

Johnston, R. B. (1998). *Trading Systems and Electronic Commerce*. Eruditions Publishing.

Johnston, R. B. (1999). Principles of digitally mediated replenishment of goods: electronic commerce and supply chain reform. In S. M. Rahman and M. Raisinghani, eds, *Electronic Commerce: opportunities and challenges*. Idea Group Publishing.

Kalakota, R. and Whinston, A. (1996). *Frontiers of Electronic Commerce*. Addison-Wesley.

Kurnia, S. and Johnston, R. B. (1999). The mutuality of ECR benefits, costs and risks in supply chain reform. *Proceedings of The 3rd Annual Collecter Electronic Commerce Conference*, Auckland, New Zealand.

Kurt Salmon Associates (1993). *Efficient Consumer Response: enhancing consumer value in the grocery industry*. Food Marketing Institute.

Mak, H. C. (1998). Use of the Internet to Facilitate Electronic Data Interchange between Small and Large Enterprises. Unpublished Masters Thesis. Monash University.

Mak, H. C. and Johnston, R. B. (1997). A survey of Internet strategies for EDI. *Proceedings of 1st Annual Collecter Workshop on Electronic Commerce*, Adelaide, Australia.

Mak, H. C. and Johnston, R. B. (1998). Tools for implementing EDI over the Internet. *EDI Forum: The Journal of Electronic Commerce*, **11**, 44–56.

Mak, H. C. and Johnston, R. B. (1999). Leveraging traditional EDI investment using the Internet: a case study. *Proceedings of The 32nd Hawaii International Conference on Systems Sciences*, Maui, Hawaii.

Pharmaceutical Electronic Commerce and Communication (1999). 'PECC' Project. October.
http://www.pecc.org.au/

Ritchie, S. K. (1994). A 'Road Map' to EDI. Unpublished Honors Thesis. Curtin University of Technology.

Rodwell, J. and Shadur, M. (1997). What's size got to do with it? Implications for contemporary management practices in IT companies. *International Journal of Small Business Management*, **15**, 51–62.

Sarich, A. (1989). The outlook for pan-European EDI. *Proceedings of Electronic Messaging and Communications Systems*, London, UK.

Scala, S. and McGrath, R. (1993). Advantages and disadvantages of electronic data interchange. *Information and Management*, **25**, 85–91.

Yin, R. K. (1989). *Case Study Research: design and methods*. Sage Publications.

Zinn, D. K. and Tahac, P. F. (1988). *Electronic Data Interchange in Australia: markets, opportunities and developments*. Royal Melbourne Institute of Technology Press.

14

Virtuality in the IT industry

Pascal Sieber

Introduction

The concept of virtuality is based in general accounts of a new corporate world in which companies co-operate spontaneously in order to exploit temporary market opportunities (see Davidow and Malone, 1992; Malone and Rockart, 1993; Rodal and Mulder, 1993; Scotton, 1993; Sheridan, 1993; Goldman *et al.*, 1994; Hamel and Prahalad, 1994; Birchall and Lyons, 1995; Sydow, 1996). Virtual organizing leads to greater flexibility in forming alliances and ultimately to the removal of geographic ties. In achieving this objective, the use of open, freely accessible and flexible information and communication systems (ICS) is often a prerequisite.

In sectors with a tradition of collaborative arrangements between companies – such as the automobile industry – proprietary platforms and systems have emerged to meet the need for inter-company information processing. By contrast, similar changes in other sectors – such as the IT industry – are taking place at a time when worldwide, open platforms are becoming available for the first time. The precursor of these is the Internet (see Sieber, 1996a). Two import effects – the strategic need for virtualization and the technical capability to achieve it – are beginning to become inextricably linked. Many entrepreneurs no longer know whether their choice of strategy was driven by 'competitive pull' or 'technology push' (see Venkatraman, 1991).

To elucidate developments in this area, this chapter focuses on a sector that is undergoing considerable change – the IT industry. After a brief discussion of relevant theory, this chapter selects three examples and uses them to show how the principles of virtual organization are being applied. The chapter ends with a discussion of the issues involved in the design of ICS for virtual organizations and some pertinent conclusions.

Theoretical background to the research

Beyond the institutional view of the virtual corporation, the functional approach is now increasingly gaining acceptance (Venkatraman and Henderson, 1994). According to this latter approach, the 'virtual corporation' is not a distinct, clearly defined concept; instead, it describes a property exhibited by many companies – 'virtuality' (see Figure 14.1). In this study, the accepted definition of 'virtuality' is as follows:

> ... the ability of the organization to consistently obtain and coordinate critical competencies through its design of value-adding business processes and governance mechanisms involving external and internal constituency to deliver differential, superior value in the marketplace. (Venkatraman and Henderson, 1994)

According to Venkatraman (1995), a company goes through three stages of virtuality as it attempts to achieve the three main efficiency objectives – resource efficiency, market efficiency and process efficiency. In each case, virtual organization activities are used as a means to advance on these goals. However, as yet, there are few empirically supported studies into how companies implement the three strategic objectives of virtual organizing, so the activities involved are only partially known (e.g., see Lucas, 1996). The following two are considered important:

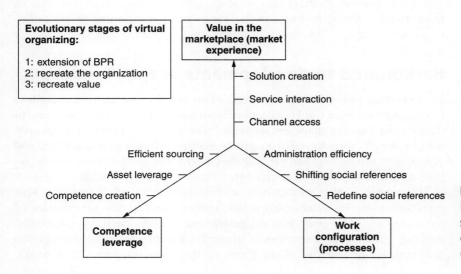

Figure 14.1 Dimensions and stages of virtual organizing (Venkatraman, 1995)

1 Processes are distributed over different geographic locations. Consequently, experts, systems and business partners cease to be location-dependent.
2 The efficiency and effectiveness of all processes are reviewed, taking account of resources that are externally available.

The descriptive model represents the partly prescriptive image of what is understood by virtual organizing. Although intuitively appealing, the practical applicability of this tool has not been tested. Therefore, it seems useful to describe the possible options for virtual organizing via some examples. This is the primary purpose of the next section. More detailed theoretical considerations can be found in Sieber (1996c).

Virtuality in the IT industry

This study of the IT industry follows on from two exploratory case studies of virtual organization – a systems house in Germany (Sieber, 1996b) and one of the 'big six' auditing companies (Sieber and Griese, 1997). The main aim was to fit the companies studied into Venkatraman's (1995) descriptive model; this framework had, as yet, not been operationalized. Importantly, this framework provides an analytical tool for comparing companies in the specified categories. In addition, the research provides the model with some hitherto unavailable empirical evidence.

The research design was based on the case study approach (Yin, 1994). As a first step, a written questionnaire was sent to all IT companies based in Germany and Switzerland (see Bohr and Sieber, 1996). From the responses, three individual cases were selected for intensive exploration. Further data collection was based around unstructured, personal interviews with the three companies, in the working environment of the interviewees. This was supplemented by secondary information provided by the companies, particularly annual reports, Web pages and memos. Thus, the following short case studies are the result of an analysis of the content of the interviews, annual reports and companies' own profiles of themselves.

Background to developments in the IT industry

As a starting point for the analysis, let us consider some of the context to recent changes in the IT industry. Steffens (1994) provides some useful observations on the changing strategic behaviour of multinational companies in the PC industry. For example, Steffens shows that multinational companies are opting for vertical de-integration, outsourcing sub-activities and making their organizational structure more flexible.

The result is that companies increasingly rely on suppliers. This produces complex relationships that extend beyond the boundaries of the company. The only way to guarantee quality, delivery times and costs of products and services is through intensive negotiation between the companies and the many firms in the value system. As a result, networks emerge, in which the output of several companies is jointly co-ordinated. The decision by companies to concentrate on some of their activities and outsource others is motivated by the synergy effects that can be achieved internally (concentration) and externally (outsourcing; Rockart and Short, 1991). This is often achieved by pooling resources in networks of companies. Reconfiguring activities in this way also means that co-ordination has to be reshaped (Porter, 1986). Using ICS for co-ordination creates the potential for more efficient networks. Evidence suggests that the purely hierarchical form of co-ordination is increasingly being superseded (see Malone *et al.*, 1987; Gurbaxani and Whang, 1991; Siebert, 1991; Venkatraman and Kambil, 1991).

Where companies in the IT sector enter into alliances and support these by means of the Internet, they become potential partners in virtual corporations. These two characteristics enable them to deploy their resources beyond the organization and give them greater freedom to shape their own organization (structure and conduct). This increases the potential for adding value and thus for safeguarding their competitive position.

Taken to a higher level, we can perceive several patterns in the development of virtuality in the IT industry. In particular, two main trends can be discerned:

1 *Quasi externalization*. Seemingly, pushing operations 'outside' the business
2 *Quasi internalization* (Sydow, 1992). Seemingly, bringing operations 'inside' the business.

The following examples describe the second process.

Case study 1: Beaugrand Systems

Beaugrand Systems GmbH is a family company, founded in 1927. It deals in hardware and software for office automation applications. From the outset, the company built its competitive advantage on relationships with vendors of 'interesting products and problem solutions'.

Alliances with Polaroid and Laserex Technologies make Beaugrand a very successful value-added reseller of presentation products. The aim of the company is to support users with hardware, software and designs for putting together presentations. The company offers the full range of modern technologies, including input devices (slide projectors, digital cameras, scanners), processing equipment (special notebooks) and output devices (dye sublimation printers, LCD projectors).

Located near Frankfurt, Beaugrand currently has seven staff and a turnover of around DM3 million. Consultancy and design services account for 7.6 per cent of the turnover, complex hardware solutions for 80 per cent, while 12.4 per cent comes from sales of components for which Beaugrand acts simply as the distributor. The company's customers include major industrial concerns, service companies and, to a significant extent, universities and schools. In the past five to ten years the market situation has undergone considerable change. In particular, we note the following:

- users have a better understanding of technology. Thus, there is not the same need for consultancy services as there was ten years ago
- partly in response to this trend, manufacturers now sell their products direct (and at lower prices). Wholesalers have also appeared – with considerable advantages of scale
- the resulting pressure on prices has had the effect of eliminating intermediaries.

In this situation, the only option for the value-added reseller is to concentrate on products that generate a need for consultancy. However, the problem is that such products are undergoing radical changes. In the past, the focus was on packages for word processing, databases and spreadsheets. Today, there are complex issues surrounding, for example, operating systems compatibility, network technologies and communication systems. The technology cycle is becoming much faster. So much so that an SME – even a player in a niche market – is no longer able to keep its staff abreast of new developments. It is clear that simplified global communication and logistics mean the ability to select the right imported product no longer produces a competitive advantage. Globalization – and in this case the standardization of products for markets all around the world – represents a major threat for Beaugrand Systems.

In response to the inevitable intensification of competition, Beaugrand has developed a four-point plan:

1 better purchase prices by centralized purchasing
2 reducing costs by cost sharing wherever possible
3 joint, national advertising activities

4 improved know-how through the mutual exchange of information.

To achieve the objectives associated with these points, Beaugrand set up an association called Pro Image. The aim of this association is to deliver products, expert consultancy and support to customers in Germany, Austria and Switzerland.

Virtuality in general

As indicated by Beaugrand's four-point plan, in setting up an association it is attempting to achieve the virtual size necessary to be able to negotiate better conditions with suppliers. At the same time, the association aims to promote expertise and to achieve cost savings in advertising and administration by centralizing as many activities as possible (see Figure 14.2).

Market experience

Pro Image – a horizontal collaboration of legally and, at present, financially independent companies – has ten members that serve the German-speaking countries on the basis of regional agreements. The aim

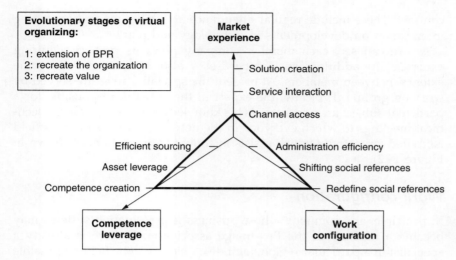

Evolutionary stages of virtual organizing:

1: extension of BPR
2: recreate the organization
3: recreate value

Figure 14.2
Virtuality in
Beaugrand Systems

is to extend the network to fifteen or sixteen partners. Beaugrand's management regard this as the 'critical size'. At the moment, goods and services offered by all the companies in the network are presented in a jointly produced brochure. This tells customers the locations of dealers with particular product expertise and how to obtain services that go beyond the scope of their local dealer. All the companies in the network are potential contacts. If a member company is unable to deal with a particular inquiry on its own, it will seek assistance from the relevant specialist. In addition to their joint advertising brochure, the companies also exhibit together at trade fairs and can be reached via a shared home page on the Internet. In all these areas, networking means that costs can be reduced by a factor of ten. Furthermore, major customers have more confidence in the pooled competence of what would otherwise be small, local companies (i.e., virtuality provides important channel access, as shown in Figure 14.2).

Looking ahead, future plans include joint product development. For example, a successful start was recently made when a specialized solution was developed in conjunction with a hardware vendor. The product bears the Pro Image label – even though the association had it developed by a third party.

Competence leverage

One of the main motivations for the ten companies coming together is to present a joint front to manufacturers. So far, two companies have agreements with vendors granting exclusive distribution rights to the network. In each case, the company which signs the agreement is responsible for purchasing for the entire network, selling the products on to member companies at a fixed margin of 10 per cent. This margin recompenses the company for its services in selecting and evaluating the manufacturer. In addition, rules are being drafted which define more precisely the services provided by any company entering into such a contract. These include regular attendance at exhibitions and providing information on developments in technology and markets.

As we can see, each member company plays its part in acquiring expertise. In addition, such expertise is also transferred – to some extent – between members. At present the specialist areas are served by working groups. Typically, the expert in the network responsible for a particular subject area documents his knowledge and then arranges technical meetings to which everyone in the network interested in that field is invited (an activity which assists in competence creation, as shown in Figure 14.2).

Work configuration

In principle, any company whose business is presentation systems may become a member of the Pro Image association. If there is already a specialist in a particular region, joint discussions will be held on possible admission into the association. However, some important rules have been formulated; contravention of these rules can lead to other companies in the association calling for exclusion of the offending member:

- the members must opt exclusively for at least one product of the association
- in each region, the companies have exclusive distribution rights
- the conditions do not discriminate against any member
- co-operation in marketing, training and purchasing is a binding requirement for all members
- a company may leave the association at any time provided it has fulfilled any obligations that it has undertaken
- the association elects a representative who arranges and chairs the joint meetings for a twelve-month period. Any entrepreneur in the network can be elected on a simple majority.

These rules show that legal and economic ties are emerging between the companies although, at present, each company is still responsible for its own operating accounts. Overall, the trend is towards shifting and redefining social references (as shown in Figure 14.2).

Comments

It is still rather early to say which type of network this collaborative arrangement will evolve into. The Managing Director of Beaugrand expressed the view that they may wish to create a separate legal entity for Pro Image – a holding company. However, it is not yet possible to assess the advantages and disadvantages of varying degrees of legal association, as it is not yet clear how financially interdependent the companies may become.

Beaugrand Systems GmbH is seen as the 'mastermind' behind the network. Without the drive and commitment of Michael and Wolfgang Beaugrand – the owners and directors of Beaugrand Systems – the network would no longer exist.

Case study 2: The Seitz Group

The Seitz Group sees its role as an IT service specialist for the manufacturing and retail sectors. With a staff of approximately 250 and
activities throughout the German-speaking countries, Seitz is one of the
longest-standing and largest German systems houses. It serves over 650
customers, of all sizes and from every sector, with software solutions
developed by Seitz itself. Group sales were around DM60 million in 1997.
It is estimated that employee numbers double every five to six years.
The company is headed by two of the original four founders.

Since 1994, Seitz has been the first R/3 systems house providing
medium-sized users with products and services in the SAP environment.
Twenty-four R/3 projects are currently underway. The extensive range
of products and services on offer includes: R/3 software, add-on and
value-added solutions, outsourcing (facilities management), hardware,
training/project management and general contractor services in R/3
projects.

Growth in turnover is estimated to be 15 per cent per annum, putting
it above the average for systems houses in Germany. In-house products
account for some 20 per cent of turnover, hardware sales make up 30
per cent, other-vendor software products account for 15 per cent, whilst
services making up the remaining 35 per cent. Indeed, Seitz GmbH
provides a number of services including consultancy, outsourcing of
computer centre services and training. Its main rivals in the service sector
include EDS and DEBIS, plus a few smaller companies. Competition
from other IT and business consultants is regarded as less important,
since consultancy is seen as an auxiliary service.

In the field of total solutions for production, planning and control,
and accounting, only SAP has a significant market share in Germany.
The remaining providers, numbering around 200, share the remaining
market volume, each having a very small market share. Seitz ranks as
approximately the sixth largest provider and, as such, it does not directly
rival SAP. Of the systems houses offering introduction and customization of SAP solutions for SMEs, the Seitz Group ranks as the market
leader in Germany, Switzerland and Austria.

Virtuality in general

Seitz is located predominantly in German-speaking countries. The relo-
cation of certain activities to newly industrialized countries (NICs) –
where lower software development costs in particular could be enjoyed
– is not seen as an option by the company. Reasons for this decision
include the personal attachment of company management to central
Europe, and the desire to safeguard the company's know-how. However,
the fall in communication costs in recent years has allowed some activities to be concentrated. For example, there are now only three computing
centres covering fifteen separate sales and marketing locations.

Basically, Seitz is structured as a simple linear organization divided
according to function. In almost every area, work is carried out exclusively in the form of projects. Project teams are chiefly made up of

employees who belong to the same organizational units, plus others drawn from partners, customers and suppliers. The established organizational structure has only temporary forms superimposed on it for the development of new products and for opening up new markets.

At present, the company generates approximately 20 per cent of its turnover through its partners. The intention is to increase this figure to 40 per cent in the medium term. 'Temporary outsourcing' is most widely applied in the area of R/3 implementation, with an average 40 per cent of tasks being outsourced. The network of partners is essentially open and geared to the long term. Project managers maintain their own personal networks, and these often make it easier to form project teams.

Some of the partners generate almost 90 per cent of their turnover in projects with Seitz. Legal autonomy, combined with the high financial dependence, leads to a de facto integration. However, this is not what the Seitz management intends – it results in autonomy losing its effect as an incentive. At present, Seitz is trying to tie its partners as closely as possible to the quality standards of the company while, at the same time, encouraging them to be independent. What binds partners to Seitz therefore is a combination of financial dependence, economic advantages, quality control as regards contracts and, ultimately, mutual trust.

Seitz addresses the issue of mutual trust through its open information policy. Partners have the same access rights in the network as Seitz employees. Some suppliers have their own workplace at Seitz. They can all consult each other's electronic diaries. Training and marketing documents are freely available. Some key data, personnel information and the order book are, of course, protected. The open exchange of information on spheres of interest also serves to build trust. Achieving a convergence of objectives is seen as a factor for success in joint projects, and brings an economic benefit.

Figure 14.3 gives an overall assessment of virtuality as demonstrated by Seitz.

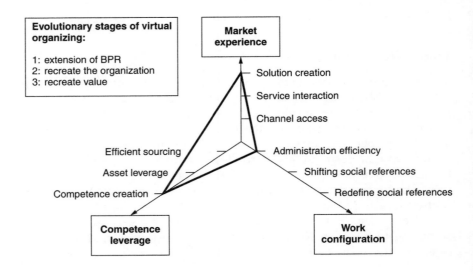

Figure 14.3
Virtuality in the Seitz Group

Market experience

Seitz is able to achieve a high level of customer satisfaction by combining its own products with standard solutions such as SAP R/3. In most projects, other commercially available products supplement those of Seitz. Each project delivers a customized solution, even though the component products are (in many cases) highly standardized. The same applies to the outsourcing service. Under the banner of 'selective outsourcing', Seitz offers around fifteen individual services which can be put together in any combination. Here too, collaboration with the customer's IT department and with other solution providers (particularly SAP, Hewlett Packard and Microsoft) is the norm. Collaboration with the customer in a familiar environment is essential in order to be able to adapt the solution to the particular enterprise. Importantly, the customer usually provides knowledge of the particular sector in which it operates – which the consultant can only do to a limited extent.

To summarize, Seitz gains access to the marketplace chiefly via partners (channel access). By combining its own products with those of expert partners such as SAP and other anonymous suppliers, the overall service can be enhanced (service interaction). Finally, close collaboration with the customer delivers customized solutions (solution creation).

Competence leverage

As part of its strategy of forming partnerships with R/3 consulting companies, Seitz has formed a network of thirty partners to focus on IT projects with medium-sized companies. Generally in such projects, Seitz products complement the service provided by the R/3 consulting company. Seitz can also take on the role of prime contractor, if necessary. In addition, once the solution has been installed, Seitz can provide a maintenance service. Overall, the primary reasons for working with partners include:

- more cost-effective and easier access to projects
- the opportunity to reduce in-house capacity
- the resulting flexible access to (what then become) external resources
- access to local knowledge of markets and customers.

By co-operating with independent sales partners, five countries are now served. However, set against the cost savings and greater flexibility in utilization of personnel, there are costs involved in finding and maintaining partners. In particular, senior management see problems mainly in:

- the sometimes divergent aims of partners
- partner loyalty
- quality assurance.

One reason for working mainly with small, independent consultants is that of maintaining quality. When working with large consultancy companies, the same people cannot always be used on joint projects. By opting for small consultants, Seitz may not benefit from their image, but it does have greater control over the quality of the people used and – equally important – over the quality of the co-operation. According to senior management, long-term partnerships with large companies are only possible to a limited extent, largely because the contact people change too frequently. Such partnerships tend to be characterized more by the exchange of products (e.g., SAP R/3) than by joint problem-solving. For this reason, Seitz wants to intensify its collaboration with small partners.

Working with suppliers from a variety of specialist areas results in a higher quality of service and lower costs. Via its relationships with suppliers – such as SAP, HP, Microsoft and similar companies – Seitz is able offer a service requiring a level of expertise which it could not develop alone (asset leverage). Naturally, joint projects also generate expertise, and each partner can then reuse this expertise in subsequent projects. The only partnerships designed explicitly for the joint acquisition of new knowledge, e.g., about individual sectors, are those with sales partners (competence creation).

Work configuration

Approximately 10 per cent of employees no longer have a permanent workplace. They are free to use the company infrastructure, but use different sites, facilities and tools, depending on the particular task. Their own personal materials are stored in a trolley. Great emphasis is also put on creating more flexible work models. In principle, each employee is free to set up a tele-working base at home, and is therefore not obliged to turn up at the office. To equip a tele-worker's office requires only a PC linked to the network, support software from DIAPRO or SAP, an answering machine and a facility for rerouting telephone calls.

The strategic intent of the Seitz group does not encompass making employees shareholders in the company or forcing workers to leave and become self-employed. However, the heads of the regional companies and individual managers do have shares in the company.

Comments

Seitz has put the principles of the virtual corporation into practice by setting up a strategic network. In partnerships designed for the long term, there is always going to be a turnover of management personnel. However, the company retains a high degree of autonomy in the strategic management of the network of companies.

Case study 3: Conceptware Consult

Conceptware Consult GmbH was established in 1992. The aim was to develop tailored software solutions for large companies in the chemical and waste disposal industries, both in domestic and international markets. However, it soon became evident that multinational customers could not be served solely from Germany. Knowledge of local conditions was essential, not only for systems analysis but also for support, training and numerous other activities. To meet this need, two important developments occurred: a new company, Atlantic Conceptware, was set up in London, and a strategic alliance was formed with Leading Edge Systems (LES). LES is a medium-sized firm with operations in the USA and India. It employs around 78 people in New Jersey and 110 in Bombay. Thus, there is a collaborative arrangement between four sites – Germany, UK, USA and India – and these are currently being turned into autonomous companies. There are four directors, each with a majority holding in their own particular company, but with the other three holding a small share. At present, Conceptware employs eighteen people, while Atlantic Conceptware has a staff of five. With employee numbers and turnover growing at over 50 per cent per annum, turnover for the Conceptware group was more than DM20 million in 1997. The activities of Conceptware can be broken down into four business sectors:

1 general management consultancy
2 design consultancy for closed material cycles
3 design and development of client/server systems
4 Internet access and service providing.

Conceptware's core competence is in project management and systems analysis. The activities connected with this core competence are not outsourced or temporarily contracted out to third parties. In contrast, the partners in India handle all detail planning, prototype development and programming. In Germany, Conceptware's main rivals are Softlab, Arthur Andersen Consulting and Plönzke. Siemens is both a partner and a competitor.

Virtuality in general

Conceptware has systematically extended its sphere of influence in recent years by forming strategic alliances. It is now in a position to serve the multinational corporate segment with tailored software. Alongside this, initial standard software solutions were also provided. In addition, less intense partnerships in sales and support provide access to the market in all geographic areas. Each of the four corporate units is organized in a functional structure and their size dictates that they have flat hierarchies. Hierarchies are only created for development projects (see Figure 14.4).

Market experience

The potential for acquiring new business – built up via intermediaries in Germany – allows Conceptware to offer its services in any geographic area it wishes. The orders can only be fulfilled because LES – with its expertise in software development – is active in the background (channel access).

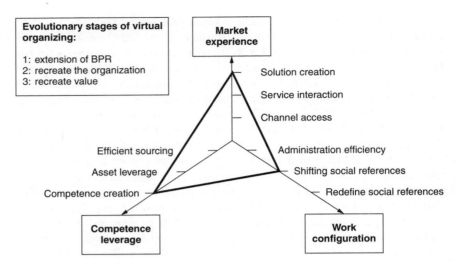

Figure 14.4
Virtuality in
Conceptware Consult

The products are designed and transformed into individual solutions by local representatives. The projects do, however, involve working with other parties such as management consultants, systems houses and software companies. In these situations, whole ranges of separate products are often incorporated into the customized solution (service interaction).

In each project, the customer is always very closely involved. Conceptware may lack the specialized knowledge of the particular sector or organization for which needs to analyse processes. In proactive development projects, industry specialists are called in temporarily to provide such knowledge (solution creation).

Competence leverage

Via collaboration with LES in India, Conceptware can take full advantage of flexibility in recruiting and shedding staff. A viable project never has to be turned down or delayed because of capacity problems (efficient sourcing). Conceptware also benefits from the systems in India. Simulation calculations, for example, are often done on the partner's computer systems (asset leverage).

Top management at Conceptware refer to the partnership with LES as a 'learning community'. It is easier for the European company to become familiar with its suppliers' products (standard software, hardware, operating systems) on home soil, than is the case in India. Therefore, a great many training courses are offered in Germany every year. Some of the technical staff from India are employed temporarily in Germany so that this knowledge can be transferred. In turn, the Indian partners often learn about the new development tools and methods very much earlier. In the USA, one tends to find first movers and early adopters of new technologies. Consequently, Europe can often build on experience gained when the first customers in the USA decide to move onto new technologies. Overall, top management sees the exchange of staff between sites as an important tool, both for improving knowledge transfer and for cultivating relationships between employees (competence creation).

One of the most important features of the network is the separation of target markets. Since the partner SMEs are so geographically remote from one another, they are not in competition with one another. This is critical given the significant overlap of competencies between Conceptware and LES in the USA.

Work configuration

One of the main reasons for collaborating with software developers in India is the flexibility in the availability of staff. LES currently employs 110 developers, but this number can be increased greatly at short notice by taking on freelance staff, currently running at 10 to 15 per cent. The other partner companies have more conventional structures. They are sufficiently small for it to be possible to have an overview of all processes without the need for formalization. The exception is the production process, which is very highly formalized and defined in binding directives and guidelines. The collaboration is based on defining quality standards. As mentioned above, all parts of the virtual organization (USA, India, UK and Germany) are being converted into autonomous companies. Consolidation of the balance sheets is only done for internal purposes (shifting social references).

Discussion and conclusions

The literature recognizes two main types of collaboration:

1 temporary, project-type co-operation
2 ongoing co-operation with a medium- to long-term perspective.

In the IT environment, the first type is encountered primarily, particularly with software developers and systems houses. In the retail sector, the second type is more widespread. However, both types are found in all the companies studied here, depending on the particular task.

If the two types of collaboration are defined, not in terms of the duration of the co-operation, but in terms of the time available for integrating the value chains, then the demands made on ICS are different. The following discussion concentrates on the first type of collaboration, for two main reasons:

1 the literature contains little about supporting temporary, project-type collaboration by ICS
2 available information on the functions typical of a virtual corporation – i.e., co-ordination and configuration beyond the boundaries of the enterprise – tends to favour type-two collaborations.

The requirements for ICS in virtual corporations can be defined more precisely by taking a 'differential perspective'. This could be obtained by asking, 'What do virtual corporations do which conventional corporations do not do?'. The answer could be based on life cycle models and on the roles in the virtual corporation. Unfortunately, it has not yet been possible to build taxonomy of these two phenomena; by its reliance on company function, the sample is obviously too small for this. Subsequently, Venkatraman's (1995) model – the relevance of which is underlined by the empirical findings – will be used for further analysis (see Table 14.1).

Two types of information exchange can be found in Table 14.1: monologue and dialogue. These two types are characterized by greater uncertainty than in the conventional enterprise. This is because – in arrangements extending beyond the bounds of the corporation – the communication paths are not regulated to the same extent and do not have a structure with which everyone is familiar. As uncertainty increases, processes that cannot be formalized become more significant. Consequently, a great many unstructured communication networks and large amounts of unstructured communication content are to be found in virtual corporations. This calls for a higher degree of ad hoc co-ordination in the form of dialogues.

Table 14.1 ICS in virtual corporations

Work configuration	
Administration efficiency	Internal and external integration of known information systems: EDI, WMS, DMS, teleworking.
Shifting social references and Redefining social references	Coordination processes are not based on the hierarchical principle of command. Decision-making powers are increasingly decentralized. A need emerges for systems such as groupware which support discourse.
Competence leverage	
Efficient sourcing and Asset leverage	Suppliers are integrated into the network, processes are rationalized and automated: EDI, WMS.
Competence leverage	Knowledge can only be transmitted in part by monologue methods. Dialogue methods actually encourage the creation of new knowledge: groupware.
Market experience	
Channel access	Open WANs play a role primarily in relation to the consumer. Electronic markets can also increase access to customer segments.
Service interaction	Providers are linked by communication networks: proprietary IS specific to one sector or open WANs.
Solution creation	The product evolves through dialogue with the customer and in service. Again dialogue processes are important: groupware.

Again, taking the 'differential' perspective, attention needs to be focused on the decisions that are difficult to structure. Conversely, once the problem has been structured, the integration of geographically remote value chains can be given less prominence. What is needed therefore – from the second but particularly in the third stage of virtualization – is to provide ICS support for management tasks with temporary, ad hoc hierarchies (or hierarchies which evolve through group dynamics).

The co-ordination processes do not obey principles that are exclusively hierarchical and/or always stated in advance. For this reason, the ICS must accommodate as many forms of external communication as possible. Communication needs can be subdivided analytically into at least two components: transmission of content and transmission of relational aspects (Watzlawick *et al.*, 1990). All those interviewed consider the second of these to play a decisive role. How the transfer of relational aspects can be adequately 'machine mediated' is explained in part by media richness theory (Dennis and Valacich, 1994). According to this theory, videoconferences are the best available alternative to face-to-face communication (see Zerbe *et al.*, 1995). Of the companies interviewed, Seitz is the only one to use such systems. However, they do not use the technology to maintain relationships but primarily to transmit content. From this finding, we might assume that electronic communication – even when applied by pioneers in the use of such technology – is conducted predominantly on the basis of existing relationships.

Further examining the use of ICS software in the case organizations unravels some interesting issues. Unfortunately, there is insufficient fundamental material for us to be able to comment on improvements to available standard software. Nevertheless, we can draw a number of relevant points. As a starting point, consider the proposal by Zerbe *et al.* (1995) to stress the *shared virtual desktop* – and to provide various types. There is evidence of the type of shared material (*'gemeinsames material'*) described by Zerbe *et al.* (1995) in all the companies interviewed. At Beaugrand, this takes the form of documents made available – offline and online – to all partners. At Seitz, there are four people dedicated to adapting virtual desktops to the changing composition of teams. At Conceptware, the project management tools used are available to all partners via the Internet. Seitz and Conceptware are using standard components to support this 'shared material', suggesting that simple technical solutions are perhaps more likely to be adopted than systems developed specifically for virtual corporations (see also Upton and McAfee, 1996).

In conclusion, analysis of the cases shows that management tasks in the virtual structures are being undertaken with little technical support. Therefore, we can assume that companies are only using electronic communication for microco-ordination of work processes (at a low level). Metaco-ordination – in the form of resource allocation and general regulation – is either done face-to-face or hierarchically. In the latter, where possible, electronic support is used. The additional ICS for virtual corporations must therefore support dialogue processes.

References

Birchall, D. and Lyons, L. (1995). *Creating Tomorrow's Organization: unlocking the benefits of future work*. Pitman.

Bohr, D. and Sieber, P. (1996). IT companies on the Internet: an empirical study in Switzerland and Germany. *Proceedings of the SISnet Research Workshop 'Internet and Business'*, Lisbon.

Davidow, W. H. and Malone, M. S. (1992). *The Virtual Corporation: structuring and revitalizing the corporation for the 21st century*. Harper Business.

Dennis, A. R. and Valacich, J. S. (1994). Rethinking media richness: towards a theory of media synchronicity. *Proceedings of the 27th Hawaii International Conference on System Sciences*, Maui, Hawaii.

Goldman, S. L., Nagel, R. N. and Preiss, K. (1994). *Agile Competitors and Virtual Organizations. Strategies for enriching the customer*. Van Nostrand Reinhold.

Gurbaxani, V. and Whang, S. (1991). The impact of information systems on organizations and markets. *Communications of the ACM*, **34**, 59–73.

Hamel, G. and Prahalad, C. K. (1994). *Competing for the Future*. Harvard Business School Press.

Lucas, H. C. (1996). *The T-Form Organization: using technology to design organizations for the 21st century*. Jossey-Bass.

Malone, T. W. and Rockart, J. F. (1993). How will information technology reshape organizations? Computers as coordination technology. In S. P. Bradley, J. A. Hausman and R. L. Nolan, eds, *Globalization, Technology and Competition: the fusion of computers and telecommunications in the 1990s*. Harvard Business School Press, pp. 37–55.

Malone, T. W., Yates, J. and Benjamin, R. I. (1987). Electronic markets and electronic hierarchies. *Communications of the ACM*, **30**, 484–97.

Porter, M. E. (1986). *Competition in Global Industries*. Harvard Business School Press.

Rockart, J. F. and Short, J. E. (1991). The networked organization and the management of interdependence. In M. Scott Morton, ed., *The Corporation of the 1990s: information technology and organizational transformation*. Oxford University Press, pp. 189–219.

Rodal, A. and Mulder, N. (1993). Partnerships, devolution and power-sharing: issues and implications for management. *Optimum*, **25**, 27–48.

Scotton, G. (1993). First virtual reality; now there's the virtual corporation. *Financial Post*, 4 September, 1–13.

Sheridan, J. S. (1993). Agile manufacturing: stepping beyond lean production. *Industry Week*, 19 April, 3–46.

Sieber, P. (1996a). *Die Internet-Unterstützung Virtueller Unternehmen*. Working Paper No. 81. Institute of Information Systems, University of Bern.

Sieber, P. (1996b). The Dr. Materna GmbH on its way to be a virtual corporation? *Proceedings of the 4th European Conference on Information Systems*, Lisbon.

Sieber, P. (1996c). *Virtuelle Unternehmen in der Wirtschaftsprüfungs-und informationstechnologiebranche*. Working Paper No. 89. Institute of Information Systems, University of Bern.

Sieber, P. and Griese, J. (1997). Virtual organizing as a strategy for the 'big six' to stay competitive in a global market. *Proceedings of the 30th Hawaii International Conference on System Sciences*, Maui, Hawaii.

Siebert, H (1991). Ökonomische analyse von unternehmensnetzwerken. In W. H. Staehle and P. Conrad, eds, *Managementforschung 2*. De Gruyter, pp. 291–311.

Steffens, J. (1994). *New Games: strategic competition in the PC revolution*. Pergamon Press.

Sydow, J. (1992). *Strategische Netzwerke. Evolution und organization*. Wiesbaden.

Sydow, J. (1996). Virtuelle unternehmung: erfolg als vertrauensorganization. *Office Management*, **7**, 10–13.

Upton, D. M. and McAfee, A. (1996). The real virtual factory. *Harvard Business Review*, **74**, 123–33.

Venkatraman, N. (1991). IT-induced business reconfiguration. In M. Scott Morton, ed., *The Corporation of the 1990s: information technology and organizational transformation*. Oxford University Press, pp. 122–58.

Venkatraman, N. (1995). The IS function in the virtual organization: who's wagging whom? *Proceedings of the Sixteenth International Conference on Information Systems*, Amsterdam.

Venkatraman, N. and Henderson, C. (1994). *'Avoiding the Hollow': virtual organizing and the role of information technology*. Unpublished. http://web.bu.edu/SMG-SRC/projects/virtual.html

Venkatraman, N. and Kambil, A. (1991). *Strategies for electronic integration: lessons from electronic filing of tax-returns*. Working Paper 3127-90-BPS. Sloan School of Management, MIT.

Watzlawick, P., Beavin, J. H. and Jackson, D. D. (1990). *Menschliche Kommunikation*. R. Piper and Co.

Yin, R. K. (1994). *Case Study Research: design and methods*. Sage.

Zerbe, S., Schwarzer, B. and Krcmar, H. (1995). *Kooperation, Koordination und IT in neuen organizationsformen*. Working Paper No. 93. Institute for Information Systems, University of Hohenheim.

15

Recognizing the limitations of virtual organizations

Lucas Introna

Introduction

The preceding chapters in this section have examined the notion of virtual organization in a number of respects. However, the predominant view is that of support for this concept. It therefore also seems appropriate to step back and take a critical perspective. Is the virtual organization the model for future corporate life or is it merely another management fad? This must be a substantive question in need of articulation and debate; there is so much at stake for those firms that choose to embark on this road. Hence, the purpose of this chapter is to develop a critique of the virtual organization. It is then up to the reader to draw from both the thesis and the antithesis a set of ideas that will develop into a sensible judgement about the validity – or not – of the now all too pregnant concept of a virtual organization. The critique will draw mainly on the phenomenological and critical schools of thought.

From a phenomenological viewpoint the critique will take the reader back to the implicit and tacit background practices that organize our everyday experience even before conscious awareness – the world of the preconsciousness. This is intended to show that our preconscious root-edness in the world acts in a very fundamental way; providing the context that gives meaning to all conscious social activity – such as communication, learning and so forth. One could almost say they are the 'spaces' in the social sentences that allow us to parse and make sense of the words/acts. Although they are essentially empty of meaning (as blanks or spaces), and we cannot say much about them as such, we depend – in a very subtle way – on their important contribution to our day-to-day sense making. To neglect these preconscious spaces of our everyday world would be to reduce experience to that which can be represented – that which can be explicitly thought. Such a view would imply a type of reductionism that impoverishes our understanding of the social. Ultimately this path would lead us to embrace contradictory positions when attempting to transform social practices – as seems to be the case with the current thinking about virtual organizations.

From a critical perspective we want to highlight the inherent – always already there – political forces that convert every attempt at transformation into resources for power. If we deny power an adequate role in our discussion of virtual organization, then we overlook some very important issues; in particular, there will be a tendency to end up with idealistic concepts that ignore the messy realities of everyday practice. Clearly such a procedure is perilous. It is believed that the phenomenological and critical perspective will provide a more balanced view of the issues we are facing when trying to establish the new forms of organization and work demanded by the emerging socio-economic context.

Trust and conflict

Almost without exception, the proponents of the virtual organization operate with the assumptions of a sociology of regulation (Burrell and Morgan, 1979). Essentially, they are concerned with describing a social reality characterized by social order, social integration, consensus, solidarity, need satisfaction and actuality. In contrast to this seemingly coherent social world there is another, more radical view of the social. This radical view sees the social world as characterized by modes of domination, emancipation, deprivation and potentiality – known as the sociology of radical change. Somehow, proponents of the virtual organization see the chaos, conflict and fluctuation in the environment, but then assume a social reality (such as in the virtual organization) in which individuals will tend to trust each other and co-operate in a cohesive and seamless manner. This paints a picture of society as inhabited only by winners and not losers. This does not quite square with reality. In addition, it seems naive to think that in a post-modern society, where the enlightenment idea of institutionalized trust (as embodied in the institutions of the State and the Church, for example) has been deconstructed, that all participants would suddenly embrace the notion of trust on face value. In an age of deep mistrust, to call on this idea as key to the success of the virtual organization seems counterintuitive. However, if trust is indeed an essential element of the virtual organization then we need to understand the ways in which it emerges in the social context.

Although we do not have consensus on the particular ways in which trust emerges and dissipates in social relationships, there is sufficient reason – and intuitive empirical evidence – to believe that trust and mistrust operate within the Kuhnian notion of a gestalt switch and resulting paradigm shifts (Kuhn, 1977). Trust is not merely the exchange of objects. Rather, it emerges as a result of sustained interaction in which the parties continually take note of the coherence between their held paradigm (of trust or mistrust) and the actual behaviour of the partner in the interaction. When two parties engage in co-operative activity in which they are mutually interdependent they tend to start with a particular paradigmatic view of the trustworthiness of the partner. This may be a position of relative trust or mistrust depending on a number of factors including their individual propensity for risk, the cost of failure and past experience. As they interact they observe the other's behaviour and tend to maintain the prevailing paradigm even in the face of a number of anomalies that may suggest their prevailing paradigm is incorrect. However, if the anomalies (evidence of trustworthiness or untrustworthiness) accumulate to a point where the prevailing paradigm can no longer be sustained, a gestalt switch occurs. In a gestalt switch, the prevailing paradigm will be completely aborted for a new paradigm (of trustworthiness or untrustworthiness). This means that if the prevailing view is one of mistrust then it will take *a large number of anomalies* to achieve a gestalt switch. Thus, trust is a social capital that may need a significant reciprocal social investment from the partners. If this is the case then it seems that the virtual organization lacks some of the important requirements for trust to emerge.

In the virtual organization interactions will be short-lived and will tend not to provide the shared social space to generate the anomalies required for trust to emerge. Most significant in generating evidence of anomalies is an assessment of the validity claims raised in the exchange of communication (Whitley and Introna, 1996). We tend to believe the claims (truth, sincerity, normative claims) people make in their communication to the degree that we can validate them. For example, we judge the sincerity of a request by eliciting cues from the context (place, situation, facial expression, bodily movements and so on). If there are limited institutional obligations (such as participants work for the same organization) then generating anomalies (as evidence for a prevailing paradigm) becomes all the more important. Yet, these rely on a shared history and context – exactly that which is lacking in the virtual organization. This is the first paradox in the virtual organization argument; trust is central to the functioning of the virtual organization but the virtual organization does not have the resources to generate this trust. This may mean that such organizations would need to set up elaborate structures of guarantees and guarantors – compliance through contracts and agreements (such as trade agreements between nation states). This would again limit the supposed flexibility and fluidity implied by the proponents of the virtual organization.

Wholes and parts

It is well known in systems theory that combining a number of very efficient and effective parts does not necessarily produce an efficient and effective whole (Ackoff, 1971; Beer, 1966; von Bertalanffy, 1968; Churchman, 1968). This may only be the case when all constituent parts act as 'black boxes' (i.e., all behaviour is completely localized) and are linked together in a mechanistic manner in the pursuit of explicit and unambiguous (uncontested) global goals. This is the situation in a typical engineering design context. However, in the case of the virtual organization neither of these requirements is present.

Logically, each partner brings into the whole that which they do best (their core competencies). These constituents are then combined into the virtual operation through a set of processes (as outlined above) with the understanding that synergistic combination of core competencies will render the whole more successful than any of the parts. This may happen, but it also may not. The core competence may not be 'relocateable', for the simple reason that many firms do not necessarily know what it is that they do well. Most of this knowledge may be tacit and distributed. Once a successful unit is dislocated from its context it may cease to be successful. The success of an employee, unit or organization is not only located 'in' them, but in the whole that they draw upon 'in doing' what they do well. This causes a problem in locating the 'competence' (as such). For example, the success of a world-class athlete is not solely 'in' the athlete, or solely 'in' the technology, or solely 'in' the coach, or solely 'in' the facilities and so forth. It is simultaneously in each and all of these. To locate a core competence could be extremely difficult – hence the problem of black boxes.

A further difficulty is in assuming an explicit unambiguous and uncontested goal. There is no reason to believe that the partners automatically accept and commit themselves to the goals of the virtual organization. It may be that extensive renegotiation and realignment of the goals in the process of integrating partners' core competencies reveals the loss of the very focus that constituted the core competencies in the first place. The whole logic of combining the 'best of everybody' is rather naive and based on a very mechanistic black box perspective.

Knowledge and language

Organizational knowledge is the most important asset of an organization (Argyris, 1993; Nonaka, 1994; Pentland and Reuter, 1994). However, it is no simple matter to discover where in the organization this knowledge is embedded. It may reside in the technology, in the heads of people, in the information systems, in the organizational structures and so on. The best answer to this question is to say that it is in each of them and in all of them together. Nevertheless, most authors on organizational knowledge – such as Nonaka (1994), Pentland and Reuter (1994) and Von Krogh and Roos (1995) – agree that the most important source of organizational knowledge is tacit knowledge (Polanyi, 1973). Tacit knowledge is that we can apply *in doing* but which, when asked, we may not be able to articulate. It is a truism to say we do not know what we know, we only know in the sense that we can apply knowledge or demonstrate how to apply it (riding a bicycle being an often cited example). The tacit basis of organizational knowledge has many implications for the virtual organization concept. We will limit ourselves to two aspects.

If tacit knowledge is the most important source of organizational knowledge, how is this to be 'located' in a way to make it available to partners in the virtual organization? This problem was touched upon above. Even if we assume we can locate it, how do we make it accessible to our virtual partners? It is well known that tacit skills can only be trans-ferred through a process of socialization, i.e., working together (such as in the master–apprentice relationship). If virtual partners need to draw on this source of tacit knowledge, as one would expect, where and when will this socialization be realized – unless we see partners as black boxes (an option ruled out above). We would therefore argue that unless the partners really do things together for a reasonable period of time (in some time/space dimension) the exchange of expertise in the partnership would tend to be limited to concrete explicit knowledge (such as tech-nology artefacts). In such a case one might ask whether this could instead be bought in the 'market'? Why, indeed, enter into a partnership at all? Without sharing this significant organizational knowledge resource the partnership merely becomes a legal or financial entity and not an *organi-zational* entity. Let us remember the notion of an organization requires that the elements 'work' together – i.e., they engage in co-operative activities. Without significant sharing and co-creation of organizational knowledge the idea of a virtual organization is simply a meta-entity. Moreover, this is nothing new, as the financial markets indicate.

To share a world is to share a language (Maturana and Varela, 1987). Wittgenstein (1956) argues that language is invariably already situated. We understand each other because we *already share a world*, a form of life. The language of doing in everyday work is 'constructed' intrinsi-cally as part of *what we do*; the 'language and the actions into which it is woven' are fused together (Wittgenstein, 1956). To speak a language is not solely to construct and utter grammatically good sentences. We always speak *in a situation* as part of doing something. Speaking, like doing, always assumes a shared world, a form of life. We have 'lawyer-speak', 'nurse-speak', 'shopping-speak', 'fishing-speak' and so forth. These are all 'forms of life', each with its own language-game – here understood as a collection of words and associated ways of using these words that make sense to those that participate in that form of life. For example, there is a language-game – a particular way of speaking – which a theatre nurse may use to instruct a ward nurse to 'prepare this patient for the operating theatre' in the form of life called 'nursing'; this could be something such as 'do a prep on her!' The 'rules' – or way of talking about the world – in each language-game evolve in and through situated action and interaction. The way we speak about the world is the way we think about the world, and thus is the way we do things in the world. Speaking, thinking and doing are fused together in and through action and interaction – separating these facets for technical design may be analytically valid but does not ring true in day-to-day organizational practice.

Moreover, each language-game is, by its nature and in some absolute sense, incommensurate with the others. Obviously, in a practical sense one would tend to try to 'work it out' utilizing all sorts of heuristics – but this working out takes time and involvement. To become a 'native speaker' of a form of life is not merely a matter of constructing a dictionary. If this were the case then we could learn a language through studying a dictionary, and creating ordinary language translation software would be a simple affair. Nevertheless, it is only when one becomes a 'native speaker' in a form of life that subtle and important tacit knowledge can be shared; one can only fully participate in a culture once 'native speaker' status is reached. In addition, it is this very cultural background that provides the subtle meanings, which gives a language its expressive power. This means that the notions, terms and ideas that really matter do not just move from one form of life to another without losing the meaning (sense) that is local to that form of life. Therefore, if each partner has a locally situated language that captures what and how they do things, and if these languages are incommensurable, then the only option available is to develop a new language-game that situates the discourse of the different partners into a new combined context. This implies that they have to share a form of life, i.e., they have to do things together for a reasonably extended period of time in a shared space. Hence, it seems that notions such as the quick 'in and out', flexibility and adaptability and high degree of electronic mediation – as put forward by the proponents of the virtual organization – do not seem to take note of the complexity of everyday practices.

Being-in-the-world and understanding

We understand the world because we are 'in' the world (Heidegger, 1962). This does not imply the idea of inclusion in the sense of the chair being 'in' the room. Being 'in' the world implies that we are involved in the world; we are 'in' the world because we do things in it. In our involvement, our actions make sense because they refer to other actions (in the past, present and future). Our projects, actions and equipment weave together in a seamless world available for our use – merely there: like the chair, door and table. They are merely there in our preconscious as possibilities for sitting or for entering or as a surface for placing things. We use them as part of what we do. In using them they slip into the background of our focal attention. As available, our bodies deal with them in the way they deal with a step that is suddenly there, or not there. Further, in a similar manner to everyday objects, so too with language, supposition, categories and the like. As we engage them in our world they slip into the background as possibilities for doing, saying and thinking.

This tacit, preconscious world is the whole that situates and renders individual actions meaningful – for those involved in that world. It provides the rationale and intention that ground our action. Similarly, an involved actor 'knows' what to do without necessarily being able to make it explicit why. The logic for action is not only a matter of cognition, but emerges as coherence between conscious thought and involved action in an already-there world in which we find ourselves already immersed. We dwell in this world and find ourselves entangled – always already entangled. As such, it provides both our possibilities and our limits.

Thus, to be-in-the-world, according to Heidegger (1962), means that we always already understand – or have a sense of that world – even before thinking about it. We understand it because we are immersed 'in' it through our everyday doing. Any explicit understanding (knowledge) always assumes this already present familiarity with the world – our being-in. In this understanding of the world we do not normally *make* decisions or explicitly think about what we are doing, we simply do what is available for doing. This is the tacit and available pool of understanding that makes up our common sense of how to do things, in doing what we do well. To share this understanding is to share this world – a referential whole. This is why it is possible to tell someone who shares your world, 'I understand', without needing to make the 'what' of that understanding explicit.

As was the case with the tacit knowledge concept of Polanyi (1973), the question now becomes: 'how will this shared understanding evolve when the virtual partners do not share a world?'. These partners may think they understand, but since this understanding is always only implicit, how will this be validated? (Normally this will be done in shared action at moments of breakdown.) One may find that the initial saving realized by pooling core competencies will be neutralized by a whole series of efforts to try to render coherent worlds that do not intersect. The foundation of all organizational interactions is this *always already shared* world that is sustained through shared action. There is no quick 'cut and paste' solution for this shared understanding. The organizational discourse makes sense (i.e., is deeply meaningful) to its participants because they share a referential whole (i.e., a world) that makes it sensible (Introna, 1997). Without this referential whole the dialogue can only be superficial; it must, by necessity, refer to very general, widely understood, notions. We would argue, therefore, that there is a large underestimation of the effort needed to share knowledge in the world. Furthermore, there seems to be no short cut. It also seems problematic to think that we can mediate content-rich communication without some fairly significant level of shared action in a shared world. The split between cognition and action may hold on a superficial level, but will not hold when it comes to sharing the extremely subtle understanding that is the very source of our expertise. The current thinking – as espoused by proponents of the virtual organization – is simply too naive about the complexity of cognition and action in the world.

Synthesis and conclusions

In the first chapter of this section, the main proponents of the virtual organization concept made the claim that it could become the predominant organizational metaphor for the next century. The arguments being put forward are that socio-economic forces are pushing all organizations into this almost inevitable position of having to become fast, flexible and fluid – and therefore virtual. There is no doubt that the pressures articulated are substantive and real. There are many dynamic forces at play, and these have long since been recognized by many commentators, both academic and populist (Drucker, 1978). It is also easy to see why the idea of a virtual organization seems to be the 'right' answer for the issues at hand; on an obvious level it makes a lot of sense. However, we believe the concept of the virtual organization is a little naive and somewhat mechanistic. Our antithesis suggests that there is much more to 'organizations' than meets the eye; organizations are not black boxes that one could simply tie together in an obvious and non-problematic way. Many questions have been raised that create doubt over the legitimacy that the idea seems to have in academic and popular circles.

The Ameritech case study is frequently cited (Graves, 1994; Kupfer, 1994; Grenier and Metes, 1995) as a model of the virtual corporation. Seemingly, the essence of the partnership is built around organizational knowledge in the form of explicit technological artefacts. Co-operation of this sort is not new. In such instances the core competence can, to a large extent, be located and made explicitly available (through disciplines such as configuration management). Here, the issues of virtual organization become a technology-transfer issue, for which there exist many examples of success and failure (such as the transfer of technology to developing countries).

Without wishing to unduly simplify an obviously complex issue, and by way of an example only, we want to propose a situation where the virtual organization may be feasible (see Figure 15.1). For instance, this could occur where the core competency consists of explicit technological artefacts; and the level of integration between the core competencies (in the virtual operation and product) is fairly low or unproblematic owing to, e.g., existing industry standards. This is demonstrated by area A in Figure 15.1. Also, there may be some feasibility in the idea of a virtual organization where the core competency is tacit but where very limited integration is required in the virtual product (as indicated by area B in Figure 15.1). In such a case the virtual organization may merely become an entity that is meta-legal or financial. An example of this could be a firm of consultants (each with their own expertise) that serve a common customer-base but function relatively independently from each other. However, from our discussion above, it seems that where the core competence of the partners is tacit and the level of integration in the virtual process and product is high (as shown in area C in Figure 15.1), the barriers to virtualization are immense and perhaps impossible to overcome. Further, in the situations indicated by areas B and D in Figure 15.1, we would expect a large amount of effort to make virtualization

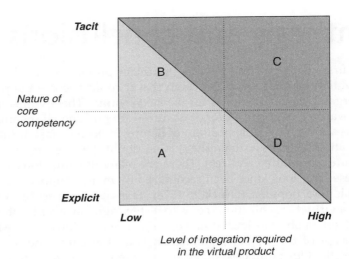

Figure 15.1
The space of
possibilities for the
virtual organization

possible, if at all. We would suggest – based on the above discussion rather than from empirical work – that some of the following conditions would tend to improve the probability of success:

- *A limited number of participants.* The greater the number of participants the greater the effort needed to create a common language-game (native tongue) to express and share knowledge.
- *Strong and shared values.* The presence of strong and shared values would increase the probability that the tacit dispositions of participants coincide. In other words, there would be an 'already there' common sense to work from.
- *A strong incentive to share expertise.* Even if there are shared values there must also be significant incentive for participants to make the sharing of knowledge a priority. This may imply incentives for collaborative efforts – even if they are not strictly functionally needed.
- *A limited presence of strategic action.* The greater the level of strategic action – that is, action directed at self-interest – the lower the levels of trust and the incentive for sharing knowledge.
- *A strong culture of experimentation and reflection.* Since most of the important knowledge would be tacit, it would be necessary for the participants to engage in experimentation and reflection. Thus, through processes of experimentation and subsequent reflection, taken-for-granted practices can be accessed and articulated.

Obviously there are many other aspects that may, or may not, influence the success of a virtual venture. The point is simply this: conditions for virtual organization success may be so varied and contingent, and the space of possibilities so limited, that there is no reason whatsoever to think of the virtual organization as *the* organizational metaphor for the future. This is not to say that it has no possibilities at all, merely that these possibilities are far more limited than the proponents would like to suggest. Furthermore, the idea is so complex that it may represent a very high-risk organizational strategy for those who enter it without a full understanding of the issues involved.

References

Ackoff, R. L. (1971). Towards a system of systems concepts. *Management Science*, **17**, 83–90.

Argyris, C. (1993). *Knowledge for Action*. Jossey-Bass.

Beer, S. (1966). *Decision and Control*. John Wiley and Sons.

Burrell, G. and Morgan, G. (1979). *Sociological Paradigms and Organizational Analysis*. Heinemann.

Churchman, C. W. (1968). *The Systems Approach*. Delacorte Press.

Drucker, P. F. (1978). *The Age of Discontinuity: guidelines to our changing society*. Harper and Row.

Graves, J. M. (1994). Bye-bye, smarties. *Fortune*, **130**, 12–13.

Grenier, R. and Metes, G. (1995). *Going Virtual: moving your organization into the 21st century*. Prentice Hall.

Heidegger, M. (1962). *Being and Time*. Translated by J. Macquarrie and E. Robinson. Basil Blackwell.

Introna, L. D. (1997). *Management, Information and Power: a narrative of the involved manager*. Macmillan.

Kuhn, T. S. (1977). *The Essential Tension: selected studies in scientific tradition and change*. University of Chicago Press.

Kupfer, A. (1994). New bedfellows on the Infobahn. *Fortune*, **129**, 9–10.

Maturana, H. and Varela, F. (1987). *The Tree of Knowledge: the biological roots of human understanding*. Shambhala.

Nonaka, I. (1994). A dynamic theory of organizational knowledge creation. *Organization Science*, **5**, 14–37.

Pentland, B. T. and Reuter, H. (1994). Organizational routines as grammars of action. *Administrative Science Quarterly*, **39**, 484–510.

Polanyi, M. (1973). *Personal Knowledge: towards a post-critical philosophy*. Routledge and Kegan Paul.

von Bertalanffy, L. (1968). *General Systems Theory*. Braziller.

Von Krogh, G. and Roos, J. (1995). *Organizational Epistemology*. Macmillan.

Whitley, E. A. and Introna, L. D. (1996). How do you make a deal when you can't shake hands? *Telecom Brief*, June, 32–34.

Wittgenstein, L. (1956). *Philosophical investigations*. Translated by G. E. M. Anscombe. Basil Blackwell.

Citation index

Subject index